Raising Student Achievement Through Rapid Assessment and Test Reform

Raising Student Achievement Through Rapid Assessment and Test Reform

STUART S. YEH

Teachers College
Columbia University
New York and London

Published by Teachers College Press, 1234 Amsterdam Avenue, New York, NY 10027

The author acknowledges permission to reprint adaptations of the following:

Yeh, S. S. (2006). High stakes testing: Can rapid assessment reduce the pressure? *Teachers College Record, 108*(4), 621–661. Adapted as Chapter 1.

Yeh, S. S. (2006). Can rapid assessment moderate the consequences of high-stakes testing? *Education and Urban Society, 39*(1). Adapted as Chapter 2.

Yeh, S. S. (2006). Reforming federal testing policy to support teaching and learning. *Educational Policy, 20*(3), 495–524. Adapted as Chapter 3.

Yeh, S. S. (2005). Limiting the unintended consequences of high-stakes testing. *Education Policy Analysis Archives, 13*(43). Adapted as Chapter 4.

Figures 1.1 and 1.2 are adapted from *Journal of Experimental Child Psychology, (8)*1, Smith, D. E. P., Brethower, D., & Cabot, R., Increasing Task Behavior in a Language Arts Program by Providing Reinforcement, pp. 48 and 58, Copyright 1969, with permission from Elsevier.

Figures 6.1 through 6.7 are computer screen shots reprinted from the Nutrition Clinician software program with permission from Christopher Riesbeck.

Library of Congress Cataloging-in-Publication Data

Yeh, Stuart S.
 Raising student achievement through rapid assessment and test reform / Stuart S. Yeh.
  p. cm.
 Includes bibliographical references (p.) and index.
 ISBN-13: 978-0-8077-4723-0 (pbk. : alk. paper)
 ISBN-13: 978-0-8077-4724-7 (cloth : alk. paper)
 ISBN-10: 0-8077-4723-8 (pbk. : alk. paper)
 ISBN-10: 0-8077-4724-6 (cloth : alk. paper)
  1. Achievement tests—United States. 2. Academic achievement—United States—Testing.
 3. Motivation in education—United States. I. Title.
  LB3060.3.Y44 2006
  371.26′2—dc22

                                                                    2006020810

ISBN-13:   ISBN-10:
978-0-8077-4723-0 (paper)   0-8077-4723-8 (paper)
978-0-8077-4724-7 (cloth)   0-8077-4724-6 (cloth)

Printed on acid-free paper

Manufactured in the United States of America

13 12 11 10 09 08 07 06   8 7 6 5 4 3 2 1

For Alys, Gregory, and Jackie

Contents

Acknowledgments

The author gratefully acknowledges the assistance of numerous individuals, including the teachers, principals, superintendents, and directors of testing in Kansas, Massachusetts, Michigan, Minnesota, and Texas who shared their views with the author, as well as the school staff who made those interviews possible. Drafts of various chapters or the manuscripts on which some chapters were based were read by Cryss Brunner, Lyn Corno, Sherman Dorn, Richard Elmore, Jon Engelhardt, Edward Haertel, Darwin Hendel, Deanne Magnussen, Ana Martinez Aleman, Christopher Riesbeck, Charles Russo, Lynn Scearcy, Karen Seashore, David Weiss, Adriane Williams, Jim Ysseldyke, and anonymous reviewers. Brian Ellerbeck, Shannon Waite, and Aureliano Vázquez supervised the editing and production of the book at Teachers College Press. Research assistance and transcription were provided by Henry Brennan, Sarah McDonald-Arends, Emily Thompson, Gwen Willems, and Karen Wrobbel. Support was provided through grants by the University of Minnesota.

Introduction

Raising Student Achievement Through Rapid Assessment and Test Reform is based on peer-reviewed research studies recently conducted in Texas and Minnesota. This research suggests that there are specific changes in test design, implementation, and policy that can greatly improve the benefits and reduce the educational costs of high-stakes accountability policies. Of these changes, the most significant is the implementation of testing systems that are complementary to state-mandated tests, and provide feedback to students and teachers regarding performance in math and reading several times per week. The implementation of these rapid assessment systems could have extremely positive effects on student engagement and learning, and could reduce pressure on teachers by making it easier to address learning difficulties and improve student achievement without teaching to the test.

Raising Student Achievement Through Rapid Assessment and Test Reform draws upon interviews with teachers and school administrators, as well as reviews of quantitative research studies, to present a compelling argument that improved feedback can have broad, powerful effects on teaching, learning, and student achievement. The interviews provide insight into how rapid assessment works and how teaching and learning are affected. These insights are then analyzed and supported through focused reviews of the research evidence.

My interest in feedback systems originated in a conversation in 1983 with Donald E. P. Smith, professor of education at the University of Michigan, regarding his work in developing an instructional program for teaching children to read. After struggling with the difficulty of engaging low-achieving children, he found an effective solution. Children who previously seemed unmotivated became extremely motivated and eager if they could see their progress on individual charts. Feedback regarding progress motivated children.

Eventually, my research centered on the McKinney Independent School District in McKinney, Texas. McKinney has adopted computer technology that permits instruction to be individualized for each student and tests students after each book that they read and after each set of completed math problems. Since the books are graded according to reading level, students know exactly when they are advancing to the next level—they can see themselves making progress. In math, students can see when they have successfully learned, for example, 2-digit multiplication, because the computer provides a report that tells students the percentage of problems that were correctly completed for that objective. As a result, students know when they are making progress. According to McKinney's teachers, this ability to see progress helped students who previously disliked reading and math to enjoy those subjects.

Why is the ability to see progress so important? In McKinney, teachers reported that students were motivated because individualized curricula and feedback on progress gave students the feeling that they were in control of their achievement—that their efforts paid off. Numerous research studies support the idea that when math problems and books are geared to each student's individual ability level and feedback is provided regarding progress, students tend to be successful and feel successful, and these feelings of success are rapidly translated into excitement and engagement.

Not only did rapid assessment have positive effects on student engagement but, according to administrators, it had positive effects on the degree to which teachers worked together to improve instruction. Teachers believed that the assessments provided a common framework to discuss and address instructional problems.

Teachers believed that rapid assessment contributed to a much faster cycle of learning: quick identification of instructional problems led to quick responses, and the ability to quickly judge the effectiveness of those responses led to subsequent rounds of rapid adjustments. Thus, rapid assessment potentially may help to change the culture of slow-moving schools into learning organizations that are able to quickly solve problems and improve learning and achievement.

Rapid assessment is especially significant given the current context of American education. The federal No Child Left Behind (NCLB) Act, enacted in 2002, imposes sanctions on public schools that fail to demonstrate "adequate yearly progress" in improving student achievement, especially for poor and minority students. As a result, teachers nationwide are under severe pressure to raise test scores. Existing research shows that this type of pressure can lead to unintended negative consequences: teaching to the test, stress for students and teachers, and increased dropout rates. Schools where most students demonstrate high achievement risk sanction under the new law if minority students do not perform well.

Ultimately, the entire staff can be fired and the school can be taken over by the state.

Rapid assessment offers a potential solution to this dilemma of improving student achievement while avoiding teaching to the test, excessive stress, and increased dropout rates. According to teachers in McKinney, the use of rapid assessment reduces the number of students who fall behind, increases their preparation for critical thinking activities, and allows teachers to spend more time on critical thinking because fewer students need remediation on basic skills. As a result, teachers can prepare students for the state test without having to give up critical thinking activities.

Raising Student Achievement Through Rapid Assessment and Test Reform presents research suggesting that three additional changes in test design and testing policy can greatly improve the benefits and reduce the educational costs of high-stakes testing. First, the use of computer-adaptive tests that change the difficulty of test items to match the ability level of each student would allow low-achieving students to avoid the frustrating experience of taking a test that is too difficult. Interviews with teachers and administrators, reported in chapter 3, graphically describe the reduced level of frustration that is felt by low-achieving students when taking the computer-adaptive test. Inexplicably, the U.S. Department of Education has banned the use of this type of test for NCLB purposes. Second, the implementation of testing systems modeled after Minnesota's approach, described in chapter 4, could reduce unintended narrowing of the curriculum. Third, the adoption of minimum competency exit exams (rather than high standards exams) could avoid high failure rates, while the implementation of a system where students are given multiple options for obtaining a diploma, ranging from the minimum competency level to more prestigious diplomas signifying higher levels of achievement, would provide incentives for all students to achieve at high levels and reduce pressure to dumb down the curriculum, without denying diplomas to large numbers of students. Chapter 5 reviews research by John Bishop suggesting that this type of system improves student achievement.

What about the future of testing? Chapter 6 describes the author's collaboration with Chris Riesbeck, professor of Computer Science at Northwestern University, and an innovative not-for-profit testing company to develop a new type of test involving computer simulations of real-world experiences. Instead of simply choosing "correct" and "incorrect" answers, students use computers to explore a simulated world but, unlike video games, students will have to gather evidence and reason from this evidence to formulate conclusions. The computer will provide feedback to help students diagnose errors in reasoning. This type of test will assess critical reasoning, rather than the recall knowledge that is common on many multiple-choice tests. The use of computer technology will make it practical to assess students in a way that is better aligned with the reasoning skills that educators wish to instill, and to provide rapid feedback regarding performance.

The potential result of the proposed changes in testing described in *Raising Student Achievement Through Rapid Assessment and Test Reform* is dramatic improvement in the ability of schools to engage students, improve student achievement, and avoid the stress and frustration that are usually associated with testing. *Raising Student Achievement Through Rapid Assessment and Test Reform* concludes by placing the rapid assessment proposal in the context of current policy proposals. Chapter 7 presents results suggesting that rapid assessment is 8 times as effective as a 10% increase in per pupil expenditure, at least 7 times as effective as charter schools or vouchers, and 14 times as effective as accountability alone.

This book is especially timely because the passage of the federal No Child Left Behind Act provides strong sanctions for schools that are classified as "in need of improvement." Teachers and school administrators are desperately struggling to find ways to improve student achievement without resorting to drill and practice. Parents fear that the quality of their children's education will suffer and teachers will resort to endless test preparation. Legislators are hearing from principals and superintendents that the federal law is causing great harm. Policymakers want to know how to maintain the high standards set by the law while addressing the concerns of teachers, administrators, and parents. This book suggests that the implementation of rapid assessment systems could dramatically improve student achievement and thereby assist schools in avoiding the sanctions required by federal law when schools are classified as "in need of improvement."

Regarding the research methods for the book, readers will note—and some will question—the extensive use of interview methods to derive the conclusions in chapters 1 through 5. While each chapter also draws upon reviews of relevant research literature, including many quantitative studies, there is an urgent need for research using interview methods. The case for interview methods has been made for research regarding standards-based reform and applies broadly to research regarding educational testing:

> The problem with analyses [by] economists is that the question of whether and how standards-based reform is working is probably not easily answerable without companion information on how the reform is affecting the behavior of students, parents, educators and employers. . . . Ques-

tions about the relative effectiveness of any type or set of standards-based reforms cannot be answered without more fine-grained analyses of how the attitudes, values, and beliefs of students, parents, educators, and employers change in response to different sorts of interventions. . . . This sort of analysis, whether through survey data, interview, or ethnography, is needed to describe the mediating mechanisms that link changes in educational policy to changes in student outcomes. (Steinberg, 2001, pp. 338–339)

1

Motivating Students Through
Rapid Feedback

Is there really a "crisis" in American education? The best evidence comes from the National Assessment of Educational Progress (NAEP), which is a federally mandated series of tests administered regularly to nationally representative samples of American students in the 4th, 8th, and 12th grades. The results show that many students perform poorly, with an unacceptable percentage falling into the lowest category, labeled "Below Basic," at the time they leave high school. Students in this category are unable to display even "partial mastery of prerequisite knowledge and skills that are fundamental for proficient work" at their grade level. In reading and writing, more than one-quarter of all American students are Below Basic (U.S. Department of Education, 2002a, 2002b).[1] In math, a third of all students are Below Basic (U.S. Department of Education, 2000a). In science, almost half of all students are Below Basic, and in history, the figure is over half (U.S. Department of Education, 2000b, 2001).

These figures are alarming, yet the performance of minority students is even worse. Four of every ten African-American students fall Below Basic in writing, close to half in reading, nearly seven of every ten in math, almost eight of every ten in science, and eight of every ten in history (U.S. Department of Education, 2000a, 2000b, 2001, 2002a, 2002b). The figures for Hispanic students are somewhat better, but not much. What this means is that the American educational system is failing to provide an adequate education for large numbers of students, especially African-American and Hispanic students. These students simply are not equipped with the reading, writing, and thinking skills that they need.

The scale and persistence of the problem suggests that there is something seriously wrong with our educational system. A common response is that more spending is needed. However, evidence provided in chapter 7 suggests that the most popular policy recommendations—including class size reduction and increased pay for teachers—are unlikely to achieve the desired improvements in student achievement. Instead, the data suggest that researchers have misunderstood the nature of the problem.

History provides a precedent. Lack of medical knowledge about the spread of disease led physicians in the early 19th century to speculate that cholera was spread by "miasma in the atmosphere"—literally, "bad air." Without adequate knowledge, physicians were powerless to contain the disease. Four outbreaks between 1831 and 1854 ravaged England's industrial cities, killing tens of thousands of people.

Although physicians noted that cholera was associated with the presence of poor sewage, the prevailing view was that sewage transmitted the disease through the air, not through contaminated drinking water. Furthermore, outbreaks of cholera seemed to be associated with a number of conditions that ultimately proved to be irrelevant: dampness, the presence of garbage, poor ventilation, crowded living conditions, and immoral behavior. As a result, many policies were advocated, including the construction of housing, parks and playing fields, schools and libraries for the poor, and paved roads—none of which could be effective because they rested on an inadequate understanding of how cholera was actually transmitted.

Eventually the British physician John Snow proved in 1854 that the true source of the problem was contaminated drinking water. During a cholera outbreak near his London home, he identified the cause of the outbreak as the public water pump on Broad Street and disabled it, thus ending the outbreak.[2] He used a spot map to demonstrate that cases of cholera were centered around the pump. The following year, he published a study that included 20 case examples pointing to contaminated drinking water as the main mode of transmission.[3] The study is widely regarded as the founding event of the science of epidemiology. In Snow's own words (in a letter to the editor of the Medical Times and Gazette):

> On proceeding to the spot, I found that nearly all the deaths had taken place within a short distance of the [Broad Street] pump. There were only ten deaths in houses situated decidedly nearer to another street-pump. In five of these cases the families of the deceased persons informed me that they always sent to the pump in Broad Street, as they preferred the water to that of the pumps which were nearer. In three other cases, the deceased were children who went to school near the pump in Broad Street. . . .
>
> With regard to the deaths occurring in the locality belonging to the pump, there were 61 instances in which I was informed that the deceased persons used to drink the pump water from Broad Street, either constantly or occasionally. . . .
>
> The result of the inquiry, then, is that there has been no particular outbreak or prevalence of cholera in this part of London except among the persons who

were in the habit of drinking the water of the above-mentioned pump well.

I had an interview with the Board of Guardians of St James's parish, on the evening of the 7th inst [Sept. 7], and represented the above circumstances to them. In consequence of what I said, the handle of the pump was removed on the following day.

Thus, if history is a guide, seemingly intractable problems can have simple solutions. In retrospect, Snow's insight was simple. But it clearly was not simple to his detractors, including leading physicians of his day. What made the solution simple to Snow was his prior understanding of the concept that germs can be transmitted through contaminated water.

It is instructive to review the salient characteristics of Snow's insight. First, his knowledge of germ theory sensitized him to clues regarding sources of germs, such as contaminated water wells. Second, he interviewed people in the vicinity of the outbreak, focusing his attention on clues related to water wells. He immediately focused his attention on a possible source of germs—the water pump—that was located at the epicenter of the cholera outbreak and was frequented by large numbers of people at the epicenter. Third, he confirmed his hypothesis by removing the handle of the Broad Street pump, preventing people from using the pump and ingesting the germs causing the cholera outbreak. While the outbreak had greatly abated due to residents fleeing the area, the removal of the pump handle essentially ended new cases of cholera in the area.[4]

Snow's methods are instructive for two reasons. First, he achieved his breakthrough by focusing on a precise explanation regarding the transmission of cholera. This precision led directly to a precise, effective policy recommendation—removal of the Broad Street pump handle. In contrast, he rejected the ambiguous, ill-defined, unhelpful notion that transmission involved "miasma." He rejected poorly justified, costly policy recommendations—construction of housing, parks and playing fields, schools and libraries for the poor, and paved roads.

Snow's methods are also instructive for a second reason. His methods demonstrate how scientific research can be conducted and how evidence regarding a causal relationship can be gathered primarily through information from interviews. The Broad Street pump was identified as the source of the problem through the interviews that Snow conducted. Confirmation of Snow's hypothesis required removal of the pump handle and confirmation that no new cases of cholera were reported, but Snow's insight rested primarily on interview data.

Similarly, if the interviewees in McKinney are correct, their transcripts suggest a remarkable insight into how students learn and how schools could be structured in a way that may dramatically improve student achievement. This insight suggests both a precise explanation for the failures of current educational approaches and a precise policy recommendation. This insight is supported by numerous research studies using experimental and quasi-experimental methods, confirming that the presence of rapid feedback regarding student progress can significantly improve student achievement.

Some educational researchers argue that a precise understanding of teaching and learning is unattainable in the field of education and feel that any attempt to achieve it is bound to fail. But the same argument could have been used regarding cholera. It was impossible to conduct a controlled experiment where some communities were deliberately exposed to untreated sewage. However, John Snow was able to conduct scientific research that provided strong evidence and a detailed understanding of the transmission of cholera—without controlled experimentation. How did he achieve this? It is clear that he used qualitative interview methods. However, he also tested his hypothesis by investigating natural variations that created the conditions for a natural experiment.

During 1845–1852, two water companies supplied residents living in the same area with polluted water drawn from the River Thames. However, in 1852, the Lambeth Waterworks Company moved its water intake to a cleaner location upriver, while the Southwark and Vauxhall Water Company left its intake in the same contaminated location. When the next cholera epidemic appeared in 1853–1854, some residents unknowingly received cleaner water from the Lambeth company, while others consumed polluted water from the Southwark and Vauxhall company. Dr. Snow compared mortality patterns by water source and found that they were closely associated. Residents receiving uncontaminated water were far less likely to develop cholera. The evidence from this natural experiment supported his hypothesis that cholera was transmitted by contaminated water.

The comparison of residents who received contaminated water with those who did not is analogous to the type of quasi-experimental evidence that is presented later in this chapter, suggesting that the presence of systems that provide rapid feedback regarding student progress can be effective in improving student engagement and achievement. For many researchers, however, not even this evidence is sufficient. They wish to know the exact details—the mechanism—by which rapid assessment causes improved outcomes. They wish to know the equivalent of what, in contaminated water, causes illness.

Robert Koch (1843–1910) was initially credited with the discovery of the cholera bacillus, *Vibrio cholerae*, in 1884 (later the discovery was credited to Filippo Pacini based on his research 30 years earlier, in 1854).

This bacillus is the cause of cholera. How did Koch discover it? During the 1883 cholera epidemic in Egypt, Koch conducted autopsies and found a bacillus in the intestinal mucosa in persons who died of cholera, but not of other diseases. An autopsy is a detailed examination to determine the cause of death. Thus, Koch's method involved detailed observation. In medicine, this methodology is taken for granted. It is routinely used to gather evidence in support of a causal hypothesis. It should be clear that observational methods can indeed be scientific. Yet in the field of education, the value of observation is questioned and often rejected.

In education, the best-placed observers are teachers and school administrators, who observe the effects of various educational practices on a daily basis. Yet educational researchers tend to discount reports that rely on teacher and administrator observations. As described later in this chapter, those observations provide important clues about how rapid feedback changes teacher decision-making processes and student thinking processes, providing insight into the process by which rapid feedback achieves its effects.

Skeptical researchers require one more link in the chain of evidence before they are prepared to accept the notion that rapid feedback regarding student progress may be a causal factor in improving student engagement and achievement. These researchers wish to know the principles underlying the causal mechanism, and they would like to know if there are empirical studies that support those principles. In the case of rapid feedback, there is an existing set of empirically supported principles that explain and predict the observation that feedback improves learning outcomes. This will be addressed later in the chapter. First, let us turn to the evidence regarding the role of feedback.

Researchers have studied effective schools and have concluded that a variety of factors are associated with effectiveness, although this research has not led to breakthroughs in improving the performance of poor-performing schools. This is consistent with the thesis that educational researchers do not have an adequate understanding of factors influencing learning and achievement. Take, for example, the concept of "leadership," which is generally identified as a key factor in effective schools (Cotton, 2003). Researchers observe that effective schools tend to have effective leaders. But what, exactly, separates effective from ineffective leaders? What, exactly, do effective leaders *do*?

A clue is provided by reviews of research on effective instructional leadership and interviews with teachers and school administrators, which suggest that effective leaders establish a system for monitoring student progress (Edmonds, 1979; Grissmer & Flanagan, 1998; Murphy, 1990). These systems apparently enable teachers and school administrators to be more effective leaders in identifying and responding to weaknesses in curriculum, instruction, teaching, and learning.

In reading this literature, I recalled a conversation twenty years earlier with Donald E. P. Smith, a professor of education at the University of Michigan. Our discussion turned to his work in developing an instructional program for teaching children to read. He had struggled with the difficulty of engaging low-achieving children. However, after a series of experiments, he found an effective solution. Children who previously seemed unmotivated became extremely motivated and eager if they could see their progress on individual charts (Smith, Brethower, & Cabot, 1969). Feedback regarding progress motivated children. The charts showed that student learning accelerated after the introduction of the feedback charts (Figures 1.1 and 1.2).

Reviews of research on feedback support the conclusion that feedback to teachers and students regarding student progress can have significant positive effects on student engagement and achievement. Numerous studies have experimentally compared the achievement of students who were frequently tested with a group of similar students who received the same curriculum but were not frequently tested. In a classic meta-analysis of 21 experimental studies, students who were frequently assessed (2–5 times per week) outperformed students who were not frequently assessed, with an average effect size of 0.7 standard deviations (SD) (Fuchs & Fuchs, 1986). This is equivalent to raising the achievement of an average nation such as the United States to the level of the top five nations (Black & Wiliam, 1998a). A second review found effect sizes ranging from 0.4 to 0.7 SD (Black & Wiliam, 1998b). A meta-analysis of 131 studies found an average effect size of 0.4 SD (Kluger & DeNisi, 1996).

What explains the variability in outcomes? Feedback such as praise or criticism that directs attention to the learner's ego can have negative effects, suggesting that nonjudgmental feedback is more effective (Kluger & DeNisi, 1996). Feedback was more effective when it involved testing (effect size = 0.6 SD) and was presented immediately after a test (effect size = 0.7 SD) (Bangert-Drowns, Kulik, Kulik, & Morgan, 1991). These results suggest the nature of effective feedback systems: nonjudgmental, involving testing, presented immediately after a test. Under these conditions, the effect size for testing feedback is 0.7 SD. Black and Wiliam (1998a) point out that these results suggest that testing can promote learning as well as sampling it, "contradicting the often quoted analogy that 'weighing the pig does not fatten it'" (p. 51). However, Fuchs and Fuchs (1986) point out that the greatest benefits may occur if teachers use the assessment information to individualize instruction for students.

Figure 1.1. Language arts task output without performance feedback.

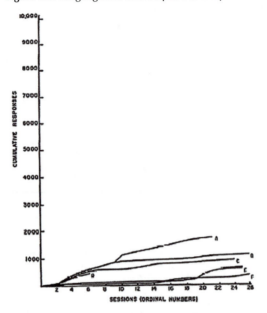

Figure 1.2. Language arts task output with performance feedback.

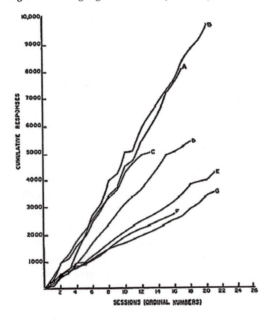

While the research suggesting that feedback can improve student achievement is intriguing, it raises many questions that need to be answered before making a recommendation to implement feedback systems on a broad scale. First, in order to strengthen the conclusion that feedback truly causes improved achievement, research is needed to gain a thorough understanding of the process by which achievement is increased. Second, research is needed to determine if unintended negative consequences might outweigh any benefits of feedback. Do improvements reflect broad gains in learning both basic and critical thinking skills, or do they only reflect more efficient learning of the basic skills that are emphasized on the assessments? What are the effects on student engagement and quality of learning?

RAPID ASSESSMENT PROGRAMS

To investigate these questions, I studied the McKinney Independent School District, which had implemented a system to conduct rapid, frequent assessments of student progress and feed that information back to teachers.[5] Previous research had shown that teachers in the McKinney school district were able to significantly improve student achievement with the help of this system.[6] What was unclear was how, exactly, the process worked.

The rapid feedback programs implemented by McKinney aim to assist teachers in individualizing instruction as well as improve student engagement and achievement. Reading Assessment and Math Assessment are curriculum-embedded assessment programs developed by the Rapid Assessment Corporation.[7] Rapid Assessment Corporation has also developed the District Assessment program based on the same principle of rapid feedback to students and teachers regarding student performance. Approximately 60,000 schools use one or more of the programs with the goal of improving student achievement, suggesting widespread acceptance among educators (Nunnery, Ross, & Goldfeder, 2003).

District Assessment is a system for administering district tests customized by the corporation for client school districts to align with district and state curriculum standards as well as the state-mandated test. The tests are often administered on a quarterly schedule with the goal of informing instruction and allowing teachers to reteach material as needed. Each client selects test items from large item banks and assembles them into appropriate tests. Students take the tests exactly the way they would take the state-mandated test. Tests are machine-scored, with the results available the next day. Reports may be organized by building, classroom, teacher, student, or instructional objective. Two controlled studies of McKinney found that District Assessment has a positive effect on student achievement in reading and math (see note 6 for this chapter).

Reading Assessment

Reading Assessment is a curriculum-embedded assessment program designed to alert teachers to learning difficulties and encourage teachers to provide highly targeted individual tutoring or small group instruction. It is composed of Reading Assessment software and a system for monitoring each student's reading comprehension and book level through points that are awarded based on the level and number of books read by each student. The Reading Assessment software program is designed to encourage students to read books at the appropriate level of difficulty. First, books in the school's existing library are labeled according to reading level. Second, students select books to read based on their interests and their reading level, according to the results of the STAR Reading test, a norm-referenced computer-adaptive test (Renaissance Learning, no date-b). This helps to avoid the frustrating experience of choosing a book that is too difficult. After finishing a book, students take a computer-based quiz, unique to each book, that is intended to monitor basic reading comprehension (Rapid Assessment Corporation has created more than 39,000 quizzes). The Rapid Assessment system for monitoring student progress involves teachers checking the status of each student in the class: book level, number of books read, progress toward reading goal, comprehension scores, and type of book (nonfiction or fiction). All of the information is on computer and is instantly updated as soon as students complete a quiz. Reports may be organized by building, classroom, teacher, or student. After teachers identify areas where students need help, Reading Assessment provides appropriate lesson plans, for example, to teach reading comprehension skills, identify the main idea, or the difference between "fact" and "opinion." Three rigorous research studies have evaluated the effectiveness of Reading Assessment, including two studies of McKinney. The results of all three studies suggest that the implementation of this form of rapid assessment can significantly improve student achievement in reading.[8]

Math Assessment

Similar to Reading Assessment, Math Assessment is a system that assesses student progress, alerts teachers to learning difficulties, and encourages teachers to provide targeted tutoring or small-group instruction. At the beginning of the school year, students take the STAR Math test, a norm-referenced computer-adaptive test (Renaissance Learning, no date-a). Based on the results and the appropriate grade-level curriculum, the teacher selects specific learning objectives for each student. The Math Assessment software prints an individualized set of practice problems for each student. Students complete the problems, bubbling their answers on a machine-scored answer sheet, during a half-hour period each day. Students scan their answer sheets with a small device in the classroom. The computer updates the teacher's database, flags areas where students need help, then prints a report and a new set of practice problems for the student, incorporating new problems and reviewing concepts where performance remains weak. Then it is up to the teacher to provide tutoring or small-group instruction to address those areas. Computerized assessments make it easy for teachers to monitor student progress and intervene when necessary as a coach, tutor, and facilitator. A significant advantage of rapid assessment is that it provides data that can be used by teachers to systematically identify students who are having difficulty and provide individual tutoring regarding specific areas of weakness. The computerized assessments basically automate the process of generating individualized sets of math problems and scoring them, so that students primarily work independently until they need help. The computer does all of the work of flagging students who need help, allowing teachers to focus their energy on tutoring. The Rapid Assessment programs provide instant data on each student's progress, facilitating rapid feedback and intervention by the teacher. Rapid Assessment also prompts teachers regarding lessons for teaching specific math strategies as needed. This type of feedback has been found to help teachers to move beyond standard instructional routines (Fuchs, Fuchs, Hamlett, & Stecker, 1991). Six rigorous quasi-experimental evaluations of Math Assessment have been conducted by independent researchers, including a study of McKinney. The results of all six studies suggest that this form of rapid assessment can significantly improve student achievement in math.[9]

QUESTIONS

Despite the quantitative evidence that the Rapid Assessment Programs can improve student achievement, what was unclear was 1) the *process* by which rapid assessment achieves its effects, 2) the effects that teachers see on the *quality* of the curriculum, and 3) the effects that teachers observe on student *self-esteem* and *engagement*. The first set of questions focused on *instructional* effects: In the judgment of teachers and principals, how does rapid access to diagnostic student assessment data influence teaching? Is the quality of teaching improved? The second set of questions focused on *curricular* effects: To what extent do teachers feel less pressure to dumb down the curriculum and more pressure to teach to high standards when they have rapid access to diagnostic student assessment data? Specifically, do teachers perceive more or less pressure to drill students on basic skills? Do they perceive that opportunities to conduct critical thinking activities have increased or decreased? Do they feel that opportunities to teach a balanced curriculum have increased or decreased? Is the quality of the curriculum better or worse? The third question focused on *student* effects: What, according to teachers, are the effects on student self-esteem and engagement, as well as achievement, particularly of low-achieving students?

A DUAL PROCESS

What is the process by which rapid assessment may achieve its effects? Two themes that dominated interviewee responses will be discussed. First, teachers found that rapid assessment made them more effective by automatically flagging students who needed help and areas where they needed help, promoting immediate instructional adjustments, providing a common benchmark for discussion, thereby encouraging collaboration among teachers to improve instruction. The constant flow of diagnostic information was viewed by teachers as promoting continuous improvement, more reflection about how to improve instruction, less isolation, and more accountability, operating through teachers' sense of professionalism. The teachers reported that improvements in student achievement could be attained with average or novice teachers and were less dependent on having extraordinary teachers.

The second theme is that the type of rapid assessment system implemented in McKinney automatically individualized instruction in reading and math, ensuring that students were exposed to books and math problems that were at appropriate levels of difficulty, and were provided rapid feedback on progress in a way that, according to teacher interviews, motivated their students.

"More Effective" Teaching

The teachers interviewed described several ways they felt their effectiveness was aided by rapid assessment.

Immediate Instructional Adjustments

First, the system allowed them to identify and address areas of student weakness quickly. Unlike the state test results, District Assessment provided immediate feedback and an item analysis. The item analysis helped teachers to pinpoint areas where students needed help. The immediate results and the item analysis helped teachers to reteach areas that were not adequately addressed. Computerized rapid assessment freed teachers to focus on improving the quality of instruction, rather than the mechanics of student assessment. A high school history teacher explained that the advantage of rapid assessment, compared to the state test, is that teachers can use the results to make rapid instructional adjustments:

> What I love with Rapid Assessment is you see results immediately. You know *exactly* how each student is performing and *exactly* what elements of the Texas Essential Knowledge and Skills [curriculum] that they're deficient in. Immediate feedback is huge. If we're able to gather that information in a midterm test, then we can go back, reteach, and cover material that we feel wasn't addressed. That's essential. [*You can't do that with once-a-year, state-mandated, test administration?*] No, all that really does is give you a snapshot of how your year has gone, and it's too late at that point.

If results are not received quickly, they have no impact on instruction. In contrast, a middle school assistant principal explained that the ability to use test results to make rapid instructional adjustments gave teachers ownership of the data and empowered them to address areas of weakness:

> The district where I was before, nothing was really done with the assessment. . . . It had no impact on instruction whatsoever. It was just something that we were doing because central office told us we had to. Here, we are able to get our results immediately. When we download it, the teachers are in charge of it. They have ownership of it, because they're able to immediately score the test and find out where the problems are. And so, they can turn it around right away—we had our staff development the next day. It was that quick. So the strength of District Assessment is that it's more frequent, and we get immediate results. I think it's a fabulous tool for our teachers.

Rapid assessment revealed gaps in learning and helped teachers to attack those gaps by making immediate instructional adjustments. Teachers and administrators felt that frequent assessments allowed teachers to systematically address areas of student weakness and improve student achievement. Without frequent assessments, teachers and students have difficulty targeting weak areas. A 2nd-grade teacher described the effect on student achievement:

> If they're used properly, I think that frequent assessment enables you to determine where your child is, each individual child and what they need to work on. My previous school was a middle school. By the time TAAS [Texas Assessment of Academic Skills] came around, the kids had no idea what they needed to work on, the teachers had no idea what they needed to work on. They didn't know their strong areas, they didn't know their weaknesses and, in that particular middle school, [our test scores] were low every year.

While rapid assessment was used in the short run for remediation, the information also stimulated teachers to redesign instruction so that future students would not need remediation. A high school assistant principal explained how this improved the effectiveness of instruction:

> Especially for the kids who are hard to teach, it just makes the gaps more clear, and it allows you to attack them in a very intentional way. If you didn't have this data, you might not know that was a problem, and you'd just move on. And then, they start to think, "Well, next year how can we teach it right from the beginning? How can we teach it differently?" As time goes on, you're able to make better decisions about what you're teaching. If you go to schools that have this in their culture, they make decisions on a weekly basis about what they're doing, rather than on a 9-week basis. Once you start thinking this way, it's a much better way of teaching.

More Collaboration to Solve Instructional Issues

Second, a majority of teachers (73.5%) reported that partly as a result of the District Assessment tests, teachers are teaming up to identify and solve instructional issues. Teachers reported that the rapid assessment results provided a common benchmark that stimulated dialogue and problem-solving regarding areas where students were weak. A middle school language arts teacher talked about the effect on teacher collaboration:

> Big time. Big impact. We plan together, we assess together, we're collaborating together because of this. [In other schools] you're a

lone wolf. You could hide if you wanted to, or you could shine if you wanted to. There was very little collaboration going on.

Administrators used the assessment information to improve organizational effectiveness. A principal of a Title I elementary school talked about the impact of rapid assessment in helping him to implement flexible grouping and improve teaching and learning:

> It stimulates more discussion and it also gives me the opportunity to look at who's doing a good job. And if someone's doing something really well, I say, "In Dr. Smith's class, all of the kids understood concept A, but next door only 50% of these kids get it. But over in the second class, all of the children understood concept B while only 50% of the kids in Smith's class understand it." Then I'll [regroup the kids]. The only way I can manage the students' learning as well as teachers' learning is if I'm able to utilize that data in a way that changes the way we do business. Change what you're doing. That's what I use the data for.

Rapid assessment pushed teachers to ask for help, work together, and share ideas. A middle school teacher felt that the District Assessments administered every 9 weeks led to more conversation, teaming, and sharing of ideas:

> I think because of the pressure that they may feel from the 9-week assessment—it's forcing those teachers that have been alone in their rooms to get out and ask for help or ask for ideas. It's helped the teaming and the sharing of information, because they realize that we all need to work together. So I feel like that's been a positive thing, that other teachers have created ideas and they're willing to share because they realize that District Assessment reports reflect on all of us. So I think it's been positive.

Continuous Improvement

Third, teachers reported that frequent, rapid assessments stimulated continuous adjustment and improvement of instruction; allowed teachers to improve student achievement in a systematic, proactive way throughout the school year rather than reacting to last year's test scores; and reduced stress. An elementary school special education teacher explained:

> Frequent assessments give you more information, so you're able to adjust your instruction, which means you're meeting the needs of

those students. The stress level at the end of testing time was much higher at [my previous] school. The other school was missing all of that input and not only couldn't make the adjustment, but when it was time to take the state test, it was just, you know, "We hope we've done everything right." Here, we *know* we've done everything we can by the time you get to the end-of-the-year assessment. You adjust your instruction either for the group or for the individuals who need that, to fill in those gaps. It was much more difficult to bring about improvement [at my previous school] because there really wasn't a cycle of continuous improvement. Whereas here, when you have a lot more feedback, you have more opportunities to improve. And as you cycle through that process year after year, I think we get better and better. In my job, working with students with learning differences, it's almost every day that I learn something new. "Ah-ha! I found a new way to show a kid how to do this." You just never quit learning.

More Reflection

Fourth, rapid assessment reportedly caused teachers to be more reflective about their teaching, more consistent, and more accountable for teaching students to higher academic standards. A middle school principal explained:

> [District Assessment has a] positive effect on the curriculum in our district. It has caused teachers and administrators to learn more about what the state of Texas means to "summarize a variety of culturally diverse texts." It's caused us to investigate, what does that mean to "summarize," what does "culturally diverse text" mean? It caused us to go deeper into those things. Previously, we would oversimplify. We would just say, "Oops—we have to teach summarization." It's caused us to be more like curriculum experts, even at the teacher level. Now, we are not just relying on the quality of teacher that you happen to get.

Teachers reported that they felt compelled to react to rapid assessment results by adapting and improving instruction and addressing areas of weakness. A high school assistant principal explained how the rapid assessment results led to higher standards for instruction:

> If we didn't have this, we wouldn't know what kids are missing—we'd just go on thinking that they got it. This makes us stop and look at what students got and what they missed. Once you find out that they're missing it, it's just not natural to [ignore] that. It forces you to make changes to what you're doing, rather than just merrily going along and

teaching the curriculum in a chronological order. That's a change with how traditionally it's done.

Less Isolation

Fifth, teachers reported that rapid assessment reduced teacher isolation by stimulating department-wide analyses of learning difficulties. A middle school language arts teacher talked about the effect on teacher account-ability, operating through teacher feelings of pride and professionalism, rather than coercion:

> Absolutely. I think that prior to Rapid Assessment, teachers could much more easily isolate themselves in their classroom and were not held as accountable for what the students were learning. [Now] we're saying, "Not only do my students have to meet the standards, but so do yours." Therefore, how can we help each other to be successful rather than just speculating, perhaps, that we are successful. [Whereas with District Assessment,] if you have 90% answering the question wrong in your classroom, you have to examine that. I think the accountability factor is very important. It's an analytical process that we go through on a 9-week basis in our departments, our grade levels, about the District Assessment assessments. And we use those. I, for one, don't want my students to perform very low in an area this 9 weeks and have that come up again next 9 weeks. I want to look at that and see why. I want to look good. I want to be a good teacher.

More Accountability

Sixth, interviewees reported that rapid assessment improved teacher accountability. A principal of a Title I elementary school talked about the effect of rapid assessment in providing a benchmark that holds teachers accountable for student learning:

> It's like anything else, whatever you expect you need to inspect, and I see where having the assessment has just made a difference in our school district. It's certainly made a difference in our test scores because we are held accountable. It gives us a real good opportunity to see, "Well, how well are we doing at teaching?" And the only thing that tells me how well I'm teaching is to look at how well my students are learning and if my students aren't learning then I'm not doing a good job of teaching and my motto is that, "You have not taught until someone learns."

The principal argued that rapid assessment provides information needed to analyze problems, improve teaching, maintain student achievement throughout the year, and avoid reflexive, test-driven reactions to low scores on the state-mandated test:

> Absolutely. You're test-driven until you take the results that you're given and do something to enhance the learning of the students. I ask the teachers to tell me, "What trends do you see in this data? What is this data telling you?" I provide the time for them to do that, and then we set goals: what are we gonna do with this data to keep us from just being a test-driven district? I wouldn't have that if I didn't have District Assessment...I see that test as a positive because it holds me responsible and holds my feet to the fire—that I'm going to do what I'm paid to do.

Less Dependence on Extraordinary Teachers

Seventh, teachers and principals reported that Reading Assessment and Math Assessment provided classroom management tools for monitoring student progress and supporting effective teaching practices. Daily feedback quickly alerted teachers to problems and helped teachers to target specific skills with specific students. The rapid assessment system allowed teachers to focus on teaching, rather than the logistics of grading and assessment. Rapid assessment led teachers to analyze and address learning difficulties and helped teachers to qualify as model teachers. A middle school assistant principal talked about the effect of rapid assessment results in stimulating teachers to reflect on the nature of students' difficulties and how they might be addressed:

> With Reading Assessment, the teachers are having to step back and analyze, "What is this child doing? If this child is scoring low on a quiz, what is the problem?" It's making them be better reading teachers. Does he need to take notes while he's reading? Does he need to go back and reread the chapter? Do I need to work with him in a small group when he's reading his nonfiction? It's making him analyze where the problems lie.

Reading Assessment generates leveled book libraries and frequent testing of reading comprehension, so these elements of effective teaching are less dependent on having extraordinary teachers. A master teacher in a Title I elementary school explained:

> The school where I was before this did not have any of the Rapid

Assessment programs. We developed a system that is eerily like Rapid Assessment only it did not have the computer portion to test comprehension. But it was very dependent upon the teachers. The Rapid Assessment program incorporates [independent reading] into the daily teaching. It's not just up to the teacher. And it creates a level playing field where students who may not be reading at home are given that extra attention to all the facets of reading here at school. If you don't have that at home, this really does level the playing field.

The Rapid Assessment program provided the type of checklist that new teachers need to monitor students who need help. A 3rd-grade teacher explained:

I'd say [to new teachers], "You need to have a list of those students that cannot round, you need to be working with those." They'd say, "Where do I get that?" They don't know how to do it. I really think that the frequent assessments [using the Rapid Assessment Programs] are necessary so we know who is lacking what at all times. So we're not surprised when they take that district assessment and that TAAS or TAKS [Texas Assessment of Knowledge and Skills] at the end of the year.

Teachers reported that the combination of individualized curricula and rapid assessment motivated students to read, improving comprehension and fluency for many students with little effort by the teacher, allowing the teacher to focus on students needing extra help. The success of this system supported both novice and experienced teachers in being more effective. A 2nd-grade teacher explained:

A lot of what I see the Rapid Assessment programs doing that I would have to teach without that program is the comprehension. Huge piece. I basically don't [need to] teach comprehension. These kids have it. I mean, you teach them how to do it, but you don't have to dwell on it. Five or six kids had trouble with fluency but half of the class is reading 130 to 150 words per minute [far beyond the state goal of 90] by the end of 2nd grade. That, I attribute purely to the [Reading Assessment] program. The more you read, the better you read, the faster you read. And that's just a huge chunk. It's neat because you can focus with that small group that needs it. And the rest of them, through the [Reading Assessment] program, it's being handled. So there are major chunks of comprehension and fluency that you really don't have to dwell on because of the program.

Another elementary teacher felt that individualized curricula and rapid assessment can have a dramatic impact on teaching, standards, and expectations:

> It's totally changed the way I teach—it takes it to a whole different level. Within the first 9 weeks, [three non-readers] were reading. Your expectations are high across the board. You teach to that. You know what they can do. You expect more, because they can sit down with a book and they can comprehend what's in that book. And I think it is all attributable to what they've done for 3 years now in this program.

Without leveled book libraries and rapid assessment of reading comprehension, teachers may not know how to intervene to help children with their reading. Rapid assessment helps teachers and students to identify and address learning difficulties and to hold students accountable for their learning. According to teachers, individualized curricula and rapid assessment make teachers more efficient, freeing time for creative, higher-level thinking activities. An elementary school special education teacher explained:

> I think it gets back to the fact that you can individualize it. The old way, everybody got the same thing, whether they needed it or not. And so, you spent your time on big quantities of stuff that may not be what everyone needs. [With Rapid Assessment], you, as a teacher, know which kids you need to spend time with. It makes you more efficient. And not having to go through all the grading—we don't have to do that. So, what you've got is this program that's giving you a lot of good information about what the student needs. [And because you're more efficient] you can do a lot of the more creative, higher-level thinking things.

Teachers reported that rapid assessment improved student preparation for critical thinking activities and reduced the amount of time needed for remediation. In addition, the assessments included challenging items requiring students to apply critical thinking skills. As a result, teachers reported less drill and practice and more emphasis on critical thinking. For example, a 5th-grade teacher commented:

> Yes, definitely less drill and practice. I don't do much of that at all, in fact almost everything that I send home is based on word problems and critical thinking and higher-level thinking. Because they have those application-type questions in Math Assessment.

A principal of a Title I elementary school felt that individualized curricula and rapid feedback systems supported master teaching practices:

> When I saw the program come in, I thought, "Oh man, just another program." But then when I got to the training I thought, "This is what we do, but it's organized, it's pulled together." Rapid Assessment is a whole lot of common sense, if you really want to know the truth. I've done many of the strategies as a classroom teacher. Rapid Assessment is just things that I did as a master teacher, but it manages and organizes it, and prior to that we didn't have that organization and management piece.

Motivated Students

As described above, the first process by which rapid assessment reportedly achieves its effects is by making teachers more effective. However, interviewees described a second, motivational process. In the view of teachers and administrators, the feedback provided by the Reading Assessment and Math Assessment programs had positive effects on student self-esteem and engagement, as well as achievement, particularly for low-achieving students. All of the teachers reported that they use Reading Assessment, Math Assessment, or both. Of these teachers, the vast majority (93.9%) reported that the impact of these programs has been positive, citing improvements in motivation to read and do math for all students, including students in special education and with dyslexia. Teachers traced the improved motivation to the individualized curriculum, rapid feedback of results, and opportunities for students to feel successful. Teachers felt that the Rapid Assessment feedback gave children more control over their learning and this control gave them enjoyment. Improved student motivation reportedly reduced behavioral problems and led to improved reading and math achievement.

The classroom observations and student interviews corroborated teacher reports regarding student engagement. In each classroom, approximately 80% of the students were observed to be reading independently, working independently on math problems, or performing self-assessments, according to the Reading and Math Assessment programs. The rest (20%) were observed working with the teacher on specific reading or math skills. Thus, the Reading and Math Assessment programs appeared to be well-implemented in those classrooms and students appeared to be engaged and on task. A majority (85%) of students interviewed responded affirmatively to the question, "How do you like the Rapid Assessment program?" Notably, several students said they "love it" or "it's my favorite part of the day."

Motivated Readers

Teachers and administrators reported that the Rapid Assessment programs motivate students to read more books. A high school history teacher felt that rapid feedback changed the culture of his school:

> When they began the program here three years ago, my observations were that you never saw students just before school sitting in the hall or before school sitting on a ledge somewhere reading. That just *never* happened. It's changed the culture of the school. They have their books with them *all* the time.

A principal of a Title I elementary school traced the effect to rapid feedback:

> I can think of a child who had come in the middle of last school year and the parents said, this child—it was his fourth year—had never read. But for some reason, that instant feedback on how he was doing just gave him a charge. It made him want to participate in the program, and he became a big lover of books and that's what I've seen Rapid Assessment do for children. The mother came to tell me that he asked for a book for his birthday. And he had never asked for a book before.

An indicator that children are motivated by the Reading Assessment program is their eagerness to talk about books, authors, and genres. A middle school language arts teacher described the impact of the program on her students:

> I think it's a very successful program. I think it encourages students to read a lot more. The students talk about their books, they talk about authors that they appreciate, they talk about the genre that they're reading or if they just discovered a new genre. They talk about the characters and how they relate to their lives, and some students will connect with the characters in the novel and it helps them to resolve issues in their own lives.

An indicator that children are motivated is that they bring their books home and ask their parents to listen as they read. A 3rd-grade bilingual teacher talked about the impact of the Reading Assessment program on her son after he transferred to a school in the McKinney district:

> When my son was at another school, I would say, "where's the books that you need to read?" He would say, "I forgot, they're in my locker."

When I transferred him over here, it was such a difference. He was wanting to read on his own, he really wants to read, you just see it. You see them sharing books with each other—when you see that, you know they are just reading for fun. The parents that I've spoken with will tell me, "Oh my child never used to be like that, I mean I never saw anything in his backpack." Now they're seeing books in their backpacks and they're hearing, "Mom, come listen to me read."

Teachers reported that rapid feedback can have dramatic effects on student motivation. A 5th-grade teacher in a Title I elementary school talked about the effect on one of his students:

I've had one student that flunked fourth grade last year. He's not passing any subject except for reading. I asked him at the first of the year, "What's your hardest subject?" and he said, "My hardest subject's reading." Well, now if you ask him—I mean it's only been a few months—he says his favorite subject is reading. It's just totally a switch. He's always going down to the library to get new books.

According to teachers and principals, children are checking out more books from the library. A principal of a Title I elementary school traced this to the impact of the Rapid Assessment programs:

I [compared the number of] library books checked out, and we had quadrupled [the number] for the year. Children were reading like never before. The most important piece is that it makes children want to read. If nothing else, reading is a big topic of discussion in McKinney. Student comprehension is a big topic among administrators in our school. Reading and reading levels, that wasn't something that we talked about before Rapid Assessment. I believe that Rapid Assessment has made the difference.

Independent Learners

Teachers felt that rapid feedback motivated students to immediately seek the source of their errors, promoting independent learning. One teacher talked about the effect as "creating lifetime readers and mathematicians":

The students just absolutely love the programs. With the reading they get that immediate feedback through the TEKS [Texas Essential Knowledge and Skills] report, and the same way with the math. After they scan, a TEKS report tells them which ones they missed, and students can go back and look to see, "Was it something I should've added, when I subtracted?" So students are becoming independent learners, and they're just having such great success with it. Students are loving math more; they're loving reading more. It's creating students who are lifetime readers and not just school-time readers. And lifetime mathematicians instead of just school-time mathematicians. I've had kids who hated math or hated reading, and as long as I'm intervening and making sure they're successful, their attitude changes.

Teachers traced the impact of rapid assessment to the effect of feedback in fostering emotional commitment to work effort. An 11th-grade history teacher explained:

They wanted, they craved that immediate feedback, they had to know immediately. That's the big part of it, getting that emotional buy-in from a student, they're going to be emotionally tied to that result.

Teachers felt that the Rapid Assessment feedback gave children more control over their learning, and this control gave them enjoyment. A 4th-grade teacher in a Title I elementary school explained:

I know the students enjoy that freedom, that ability to be in control of their own learning in reading and math. When I say, "Okay, we need to do Math Assessment," they get excited because it's usually on their own level, they get to go at their own pace, they're not pushed, they're not rushed, and they get to manage themselves. I think that's why they enjoy it.

Teachers were extraordinarily enthusiastic about the effect of the Rapid Assessment programs on student motivation. Teachers felt that rapid feedback can foster pride and excitement about achievement. Students "love" the immediate feedback and control that the assessment programs gave them over their learning. Teachers felt that the key to improved student motivation and engagement was that the rapid assessment program allowed students to monitor their own success and progress from one level to the next and to see when they are successful. Teachers felt that this feedback gave students pride in their achievements. A middle school language arts teacher talked about the effect on one of her Hispanic students:

I have a Hispanic student. And she is a wonderfully bright child. She loves the fact that her reading is improving and she's challenging herself to raise her reading level. She started out on a 4th-grade level of reading this year. She's reading up into mid-5th-grade now. She has challenged herself to do that, and I can see that in her demeanor, that this is an important issue to her. It's a sense of pride, that she's actually elevating herself on a weekly basis with her own challenges for reading.

Consistent with teacher reports that rapid feedback and individualized curricula have improved student motivation, a middle school math teacher reported that with the program she observed fewer behavior problems:

Sue used to be a behavior problem, and she would just come in and be like a little terror. And toward the end of the school year, she started calming down, because she wanted to work on [the Math Assessment] program. She knew that "this is something I can do." So I've gotten very unruly kids, and then by the time school is over at the end of the year, they're well-behaved. [*But do you think that the program contributed to this change in behavior?*] I think so. Because they have to learn to be independent, and they're not depending on you to sit on top of them to get them to work. And their grades have improved, too. Those kids work better if there is a structure and they know what to expect. You know that about Christmastime, they're going to calm down. And then, it's just easy going from there on out, because you don't have to put up with that attitude that they're throwing at you.

Teachers believed that the effect of rapid assessment was dramatic. An elementary school teacher described the effect of implementing the Reading Assessment program on student achievement:

The first year that I was at the other school, they were really struggling with their state test, especially reading. When I went there that year, their reading and math scores were 69 and 78. After the one year that I had been there and we had implemented the Reading Assessment software, our scores went up to 93/93. After that, we went up to 95/97, and then, 97/98. It had a dramatic effect.

All but one teacher (98%) reported that Reading Assessment and Math Assessment had a positive impact on student motivation. Teachers felt that students were empowered by the knowledge that they were strong in certain areas and weak in other areas, and if they focused on the weak areas, they could improve their reading and math skills. Thus, students were less likely to make global judgments about being "stupid" or "not good at math." A principal of a Title I elementary school explained:

> They love it, it's just incredible. The math thing is just incredible to me. The Math Assessment, if you skip it, they just go nuts. They are so motivated by that piece. . . . What I think it does is it empowers the kids. They know what their weaknesses are, know what their strengths are, know what they've got to work on: "I know I need to work on this to make progress." We had kids before that just thought they were bad at math—it's overwhelming, but if you can see where your weaknesses are and how you can shore those up, then it's a whole lot more [manageable]. It's exciting, it's interesting to talk to the kids, because they get really fired up about math and the reading, too. They can tell you exactly what books they've read. They'll talk about authors. Whereas before they just thought they were stupid. They didn't realize that it had anything to do with [their effort]. I really think it makes a huge difference. The reading just happens, it's just so automatic that it just happens.

Opportunities for Success

Teachers traced the impact of the Rapid Assessment programs to the motivational effect of experiencing repeated, incremental success. A 9th-grade algebra teacher explained it as "kids feed on success":

> Kids feed on success, and anything that allows them to be successful, they get excited about, and that program can be developed and operated in such a way that students are going to have success. You start them at a point where they're going to have success, and that is a big motivator. [Whereas before] they were not having success, [they felt that] "I can't do this, I'm a failure, I'm wasting my time," but if they have success, they begin to change that thought.

Teachers felt that the combination of individualized curricula and rapid feedback was especially helpful for low-achieving students, breeding success and confidence by breaking objectives into manageable increments and hiding achievement differentials. A middle school math teacher explained:

> Particularly for low-performance students; they feel they can have success. Let's say I have a 7th-grader who really only performs at a 5th-grade level. So I have him assigned to the 5th-grade library. He really doesn't know that; the other kids don't really know that but he's feeling

success, because he's moving through the objectives successfully. So it gives him confidence. Success breeds success; that gives him confidence in everything.

A recurring theme was the positive impact of the individualized curricula and rapid assessment on children's self-esteem. Teachers talked about the impact on students who previously did not like reading or math. An elementary school teacher traced the effectiveness of the program to the way it provided incremental opportunities for children to experience success:

I've had students who've come in with low self-esteem because they know they are working below grade level. What I like is that Reading Assessment supports all stages of reading. I think it has a positive effect just because there is so much opportunity for them to have success and feel good about themselves. And once they reach that first goal, they're determined to make the next goal as well. The same with math. I've had students who did not like math. But after they've seen that they can [meet] this goal, then they're excited to do it. I think it's just so interesting to see that. I have had only positive experiences with it. I had many students say, "Oh, please give us just 5 more minutes" or "Can I stay in from recess? I want to read instead of go outside and play" or "Can I take my book to lunch, so I can read during lunch?" They want to continue reading. They don't want to stop. They've had success, and they've finally found some good books at their level that they're comfortable with and they're successful. They love that. The math—they're so excited about it and have so much success with it. So you'll have lots of kids wanting to do more, because it is fun and exciting and motivating to them.

Teachers reported that children in special education were also motivated by rapid feedback on incremental gains. A 2nd-grade teacher talked about the progression that occurred:

I've got a special ed child who can barely read on his own. The more he got into the program, he wanted to become part of the program. Now he sits at the computer, and he's pretty much running the show. And that is such a big thing—he just has confidence now, "I can do something."

Rapid feedback can also motivate children with dyslexia. A 2nd-grade teacher talked about the effect of rapid feedback in building her student's self-confidence, independence, and intrinsic motivation to read:

My dyslexic child was just so defiant. So we started using the program. Well, he just took off. . . . Now he's gone 5 to 6 weeks, building that confidence through using the program. He's doing it totally on his own. At reading time, out comes that book, he's going to the library, he's right back. This week alone, he read six books and he's got 100% accuracy. And I truly think it's all because of that program, just the way it's set up that it triggers that intrinsic motivation. Everyone wants to be a winner, and when you see it in black and white, you see yourself progressing, a lightbulb goes on, "Hey, look at me. I can do it."

Teachers felt that a big part of the Rapid Assessment program's success was that differentials in achievement among students were hidden in a way that allowed each child to feel successful. A 2nd-grade teacher explained:

My special ed child is actually in a 1st-grade library. Everyone else is in the 2nd-grade library. But he doesn't know he's in the 1st-grade library. [The program] spits out [problems] just like everyone else's, but it's on a 1st-grade level. He can do it on his own and he is achieving such success with no outside help. So his sense of accomplishment is just huge. He will work through that 1st-grade library and then start on the 2nd-grade, and never know that he's any different than the other kids. So you have a huge impact there, really huge impact.

Teachers of special education and Emotionally/Behaviorally Disturbed (EBD) students felt that the Rapid Assessment programs helped them to handle the logistical task of meeting the needs of different students, and by doing so, freed them to work more effectively. Teachers reported that the combination of individualized curricula and rapid feedback helps them to keep students with learning disabilities with their nondisabled peers. An elementary school special education teacher talked about this as "a wonderful thing":

For students with a learning disability, [our aim] is keeping them with their nondisabled peers to the maximum extent possible. And Rapid Assessment makes that happen. I just got a student who has a learning disability and is in 4th-grade, but is functioning at the 2nd-grade level in math. That student can be with his buddies, in his classroom, doing Math Assessment. He's just in a different [Rapid Assessment] library. It's just wonderful because it keeps that kid with his peers. They like it. I think the biggest thing is every child here in a Rapid Assessment program has the opportunity to be really successful. Every child did not have that chance at my other school, because there was no mechanism to do that. There's no way a teacher can individualize instruction to that extent. And this is a way to individualize instruction in reading and math. It's amazing. It's a wonderful thing.

QUALITY

In the judgment of teachers and administrators, what was the effect of rapid assessment on the quality of curriculum and instruction? A majority of teachers (87.8%) reported that rapid assessment had a positive impact on curriculum and instructional practices. Two teachers (4.1%) expressed concerns about too much testing; the rest were noncommittal. Overall, teachers felt there was a positive effect on the curriculum, with less drill and practice and more emphasis on problem-solving and critical thinking. Teachers felt that the rapid assessment programs reduced pressure to teach to the test by providing the information needed to achieve steady student progress without using worksheets. Teachers felt that rapid assessment reduced the need for remediation, increased the time available for critical thinking activities, and improved student preparation for critical thinking. Although the rapid assessment programs reportedly have more of an impact at the elementary and middle school level, they can also be effective at the high school level in shrinking learning gaps between high- and low-achieving students. As a result, two-thirds of all interviewees supported statewide funding of McKinney's system of quarterly district assessments.

Not Teaching to the Test

Teachers argued that they did not "teach to the test," explaining that they were able to prepare students for the state test while focusing on the intended curriculum. A 3rd-grade teacher in a Title I elementary school described the difference and attributed her ability to maintain breadth in the curriculum to the effect of the rapid assessment programs:

> I think they've had a positive effect. Where I was before, we actually taught to the test. We don't do that here. We teach what's in the curriculum, and we don't focus on the tests because we feel that with the independent reading time, we're teaching them skills that they will be able to use throughout their life and not just teach to the test. We're trying to teach the skills to enable them to pass the test, but having taught at a district where all we did for the entire year was teach to the

test, this is very different and I really enjoy it. [*I think people would say District Assessment is actually designed to help get students ready for the state test, and if you have that as your assessment every 9 weeks and you are focusing on those areas where students are not doing well, it would seem like you are really focusing on getting students ready for the state test.*] You're getting them ready for the test, but in a different way because you're teaching them the skills in good literature instead of constantly doing worksheets that look exactly like the test. You're teaching *toward* the test, instead of *to* the test, using good literature where they're able to do more critical thinking about what they're reading and making those connections to real-life situations.

According to teachers, learning activities involved concrete, hands-on activities designed to improve understanding rather than worksheets. A 3rd-grade teacher in a Title I elementary school described the type of activity she uses:

We do more hands-on activities, not just your basic problem. We create graphs, where the kids take surveys and create charts and graphs. We're doing a probability exercise where we asked how many people drink milk, how many do you think are going to drink chocolate milk. We made a graph and then we'll take that graph and they ask questions about it. So we're teaching things in math, but we're trying to start out with the concrete and go through stages of pictures so they get a better understanding because when they see it and they do it themselves it's so much easier for them to remember than when they're just looking at a graph off of another sheet of paper. It makes more sense to them.

Rather than drill and practice, learning activities were designed to connect to students' prior knowledge. The 3rd-grade teacher explained:

We're looking to see what the problem is and trying to set goals and come up with ideas on what we could do to help them improve—different types of questions, teaching it in a different way, connecting to their prior knowledge. A lot of them haven't even been out of McKinney, so I draw pictures, like I'll start out here with the house: "Here's Grandma's house." And then, "Okay, from here to here, that's three hundred and sixty-two miles." And I relate it to when I go home to visit my mother. "Well, I drive, and I drive so far and then I have to stop. So I've gone from here to here and this was seventy miles. But now you know, I stop to eat lunch, so I get back in my car and I have to go further." And so I try and put it in terms of something that's meaningful to them, something that they will understand.

More Critical Thinking

Teachers were asked whether they had changed the amount of time devoted to critical thinking, drill and practice, or project-based activities, or whether they had eliminated important activities from their curricula as a result of using District Assessment. None of the teachers reported that they reduced the amount of critical thinking activities, while 20.4% reported that they increased time spent on those activities. Although critics of testing are concerned that it "dumbs down" the curriculum, interviewees felt that rapid assessment helped them to be more efficient and created opportunities for them to spend more time on critical thinking activities. Teachers argued that this allowed them to maintain breadth and balance in the curriculum and to avoid narrowing the curriculum to material covered on the state test. An elementary school assistant principal explained:

> I think the Rapid Assessment programs have given us the opportunity to spend more time on critical thinking because the test is taken, and the feedback is very quick, and we can use the results very quickly to reteach children. That gives teachers much more time to really develop children's critical thinking skills. They have more time for planning, instead of having to grade tests. It just freed up some time.

Teachers felt that rapid assessments designed to reflect a challenging state assessment encouraged them to focus on problem-solving, rather than computation. A middle school teacher explained:

> I'm giving them problem-solving questions, whereas before, I may have [used] more computation. So the 9-week assessments have made me reflect on how I test my students, not so much my instruction, but just how I check for their understanding and their mastery of the subject. [*What aspects of the assessment cause you to do that?*] The 9-week assessments are set up to be a reflection of what we expect the TAKS to be. Which is *applying* the computation. The students are going to have a situation, a problem, and they're going to be doing the same math, but instead of just giving them three times four, they have to associate it with a real-life situation. That's been an adjustment because I've always thought, teach them the math, and then we'll teach them to problem-solve. So, it's made me think I need to make sure that we incorporate the problem-solving as we teach.

Only 6.1% of teachers reported that they increased the amount of time spent on drill and practice. Only 6.1% reported that they eliminated important activities from their curricula as a result of using District Assessment. Teachers felt that careful planning avoided the need to sacrifice project activities. Only 8.2% reported that they reduced project-based activities, although many teachers reported that nonessential projects have been replaced with more focused activities. A recurring theme was the need for teachers to be more selective about project activities, focusing on those that are truly educational, not merely enjoyable. Teachers reported that rapid assessment helped them to target instruction and improve effectiveness in a way that freed time for enrichment activities. A middle school principal explained:

> I think it helps us use a rifle approach versus a shotgun approach. We know what the kids do and do not know. You can specialize your instruction and meet the kids where they are. You know what it is that they need help on. At the same time, you don't have to bore them to death with things that they already know. It frees you to spend time on things that you need to spend time on and be able to do enriching things on the items that they already know.

SUPPORT FOR STATEWIDE FUNDING OF DISTRICT ASSESSMENT

An indicator of teachers' summary judgment of the usefulness of the rapid assessment systems is that two-thirds of the teachers (67.3%) reported that they would support statewide funding of McKinney's system of District Assessments every 9 weeks, followed by the state-mandated TAKS assessment at the end of the school year. They felt that without state funding, districts that do not have rapid assessment systems would be severely disadvantaged. Interviewees thought that rapid assessment helped teachers to work more effectively and to avoid cramming for the end-of-year state test. A middle school language arts teacher thought this would be a good investment:

> I think it would be incredible—that's definitely money well spent. Very much so. Very much so. That just seems like a no-brainer. If the state could do it, most definitely. Most definitely.

A high school history teacher thought incorporating rapid assessment into state-mandated testing programs would make state testing more useful and would improve teacher buy-in:

Incorporating the elements of the District Assessment-type program would certainly make state testing more useful. I think it's all any teacher asks for is, "Give me the tools I need to do what I need to do to facilitate learning." And so anytime a teacher sees that sort of benefit coming from a program, I think you're going to see huge teacher buy-in.

Overall, 49% of teachers supported the idea of breaking the state assessment into four quarterly assessments (30.6% were undecided). Teachers felt that the state assessment would be more useful as a diagnostic tool if it provided quarterly snapshots. Although critics of testing worry about the increased stress of additional testing, interviewees felt that increasing the frequency of assessment would help to make them more routine. A 10th-grade English teacher felt that this would reduce the stress of testing:

I think that would be wonderful. It would relieve stress because you could focus on those objectives, and once those were mastered, you'd have a sense of relief that those were done and we can move on to something else. Instead of waiting till the very end of the year and just hoping that they're going to remember it all. I think students would do better. I think it would show a better understanding of what students know.

NEGATIVE EFFECTS

Although interviewee responses were overwhelmingly positive, there was one major problem with the particular software used by McKinney: poor quality control resulted in incorrect grading of a significant number of Math Assessment items. Incorrect grading caused frustration among students and teachers. Some teachers also reported problems in printing reports. However, these problems appear to be correctable and do not appear to be inherent in rapid assessment.

IMPLEMENTATION

Principals and teachers felt that the success of the Rapid Assessment programs depended on leadership by principals, careful implementation by teachers, and support from administrators. Proper implementation required careful planning to fit the Rapid Assessment activities into the school day, careful attention and timely intervention to make sure students benefited from using the programs, and follow-up by principals on the reports that were generated by the system to ensure that teachers were implementing the programs properly. Many teachers were skeptics, at least at the beginning. According to administrators, positive results helped to convert teachers, but strong leadership is necessary to maintain program implementation until teachers can see the results. A middle school assistant principal explained:

> Teachers have gotten on board when they've seen the results and seen kids be successful and be excited. They've seen it work, and now they're getting on board. In the beginning, they did not. They had to analyze their own report for me, and then I would respond and give it back to them. Whereas before, I was just running the reports, analyzing them myself, and giving it to them. Well, they were just throwing it in the trash because it didn't mean anything. So, there's a lot of uncomfortable feelings, and then lots of conversation. Every week, they would turn them in, I would respond, back and forth, back and forth. Finally, when they saw the results, that's when they got on board.

CONCLUSION

McKinney offers a window to answer questions raised by quantitative studies suggesting that the implementation of rapid assessment systems can significantly improve student achievement in reading and math. How did the implementation of rapid assessment systems lead to improvements in student achievement? First, rapid assessment provided diagnostic information to teachers and administrators who previously did not have access to this information on a daily basis and in a form that automatically flags students who need help and areas where they need help. Second, rapid assessment provided instant feedback to students, who previously did not receive rapid feedback on their work. Third, the particular rapid assessment system implemented in McKinney also provided a system for automatically individualizing instruction in reading and math in a way that was not previously available to teachers. As a result of these three changes, teachers and administrators were able to quickly see and address instructional problems, and students reportedly could see themselves making steady progress in individualized curricula.

Did the improvements in achievement reflect broad gains in learning both basic and critical thinking skills, or did they only reflect more efficient learning of the skills on the state-mandated test? According to teachers and administrators, the implementation of rapid assessments allowed teachers to individualize and target instruction, provide more tutoring, reduce drill and practice, and improve student readiness for—and spend more time on—critical thinking activities, resulting in a more balanced curriculum. The majority of teachers and administrators strongly believed that rapid assessment allowed them to improve the quality of education provided to students in McKinney and to counteract pressures to increase drill and practice and reduce critical thinking activities in order to prepare students for the state test. The ability to individualize and target instruction reportedly made teachers more effective and efficient, reducing the need for student remediation, raising the level of preparation for critical thinking activities, and freeing time to spend on critical thinking and enrichment activities. Paradoxically, more assessment—of the right type—may be better assessment. Rapid assessment may offer a way for principals and superintendents to balance the demands of NCLB to improve student achievement with the desire to maintain depth and balance in curriculum and instruction.

What basic principle of teaching and learning can explain the results? In McKinney, rapid feedback on student progress apparently promoted high rates of adaptive responses by teachers and students. Feedback regarding student progress reinforced teacher behaviors of seeking and implementing better ways of teaching. As a result, teachers improved instruction more quickly than they would otherwise. Feedback regarding progress apparently reinforced student behaviors of reading more books, learning reading comprehension strategies, completing more math problems, and learning how to solve math problems correctly. As a result, students reportedly read more books and completed more math problems. According to teachers, reading comprehension improved, and the ability to solve math problems improved. Teachers observed that enjoyment of reading and math increased. In contrast, typical classroom instruction and assessment practices neglect to provide adequate feedback to students and teachers about student progress. Therefore, reinforcement of corrective and adaptive responses is weak and performance is relatively poor.

What specific aspects of feedback are critical? Earlier in this chapter, the review of research suggested the nature of effective feedback systems: nonjudgmental, involving testing, presented immediately after a test. The review suggested the importance of frequent, rapid assessment: two to five times weekly. Other studies suggest additional characteristics that are important. In a carefully controlled experiment, Kahn (1989) demonstrated that feedback is most effective when it is self-initiated by students and paired with external feedback.[10] In McKinney, students self-initiated the feedback by taking reading comprehension quizzes immediately after completing each book, and by scoring their math problem sets immediately after completion. External feedback was provided by teachers who monitored each student's progress. Kahn demonstrated that external feedback alone was no more effective than the no-feedback control treatment. This finding is significant. It strongly suggests that feedback systems that are purely driven by teachers and administrators will be less effective than systems where feedback is initiated, at least in part, by students. In other words, students must have some control over the feedback. The significance of this is explained by the research literature suggesting that feelings of control are strongly associated with student engagement, and engagement leads to improved achievement.

Engaged Students

What were the effects on student engagement and quality of learning? The data from McKinney suggest that rapid assessment may improve student achievement by improving student motivation: individualized curricula adapted to each student's needs and abilities, plus rapid feedback on progress, may be highly effective in improving student engagement and motivation to learn.

What is the mechanism by which feedback achieves its effects? What are the principles? Teachers reported that the feedback provided by rapid assessment gave students the feeling that they were successful and in control of their own learning, engaging students who previously disliked reading and math, including dyslexic children and children in special education, reducing stress and improving student achievement. As Elmore (2004) explains:

> People, in general, enjoy doing what they perceive themselves to be good at, and avoid doing that which they perceive themselves to be unsuccessful at. Low efficacy elicits low engagement; high efficacy elicits high engagement. A successful incentive structure, then, is one that draws the student and the teacher into situations in which they build efficacy and agency. (p. 285)

Individualized curricula ensure that students encounter learning tasks that are within the zone of proximal development—not too easy and not too difficult (Vygotsky, 1978). Rapid feedback regarding progress tells students that they are successful, helping to build self-efficacy. Students who feel successful can therefore enjoy learning (Abrahams, 1987). Thus, individualization of instruction and performance feedback combine to build self-efficacy and control, which improves achievement, and improved achievement feeds back to build self-efficacy and control.

The importance of student control was established as far back as 1966, with the publication of the Coleman Report. Of all of the student attitudinal variables, "sense of control of the environment" was most strongly related to student achievement (Coleman et al., 1966). This result was replicated by other researchers who focused specifically on measures of student control of academic achievement. Brookover et al. (1978; 1979) created a scale of "student sense of academic futility" and found that this measure was the most important predictor, explaining over one-half of the variance in student achievement. Teddlie and Stringfield (1993) replicated the results of these studies using both the student sense of futility scale and scales measuring external and internal locus of control in an academic environment (Crandall, Katkovsky, & Crandall, 1965).

Additional studies suggest that strengthening early academic performance strengthens children's beliefs that they can control their performance. Musher-Eizenman, Nesselroade, and Schmitz (2002) measured the academic performance and beliefs of 4th- and 6th-grade children over time. The results suggest that " . . . there is a feedback loop between performance and control beliefs, with high performance leading to subsequent perceptions of control" (p. 545). In McKinney, rapid assessment reportedly helped to improve student performance, which then strengthened student perceptions that they could control their performance.

Research also suggests that over time, this feedback loop strengthens academic performance. A longitudinal study of 8,802 8th-grade students found that early academic achievement was by far the strongest predictor of achievement in 12th-grade. Path analysis indicated that early achievement influences later achievement primarily by increasing students' sense of personal control (Ross & Broh, 2000). The link between personal control and later academic achievement is supported by a meta-analysis of 78 research studies (Kalechstein & Nowicki, 1997) and path analyses suggesting that children's perceived control over their academic performance predicts future academic achievement (Keith, Pottebaum, & Eberhart, 1986; Skinner, Wellborn, & Connell, 1990). This explains the observations by teachers in McKinney that "success feeds on success." As explained by Ellen Skinner and her colleagues:

> When children believe that they can exert control over success in school, they perform better on cognitive tasks. And, when children succeed in school, they are more likely to view school performance as a controllable outcome. (Skinner et al., 1990, p. 22)

Research suggests that improvements in achievement and feelings of personal control may foster student engagement and resilience. Both path analysis and an experimental study involving children age 9 to 11 suggest that their perceptions of academic competence and control predict intrinsic interest in schoolwork and preference for challenging school activities (Boggiano, Main, & Katz, 1988). A study of 1803 low-income minority high school students found that student engagement is an important component of resilience, defined by the subset of low-income minority students who were academically successful and completed high school (Finn & Rock, 1997).

In McKinney, the key was that students read books and solved math problems at their ability levels, and received immediate feedback on their efforts. Since book and math levels were tailored for each student, students generally experienced success. Success relates to confidence, self-esteem, and motivation to read books and solve math problems. The implication of this finding is that it may be possible to improve student engagement and achievement despite factors that are important but difficult to change: cultural differences regarding the value of education, differences in funding and resources, differences in teacher skills, expectations and rapport with students, and so on. What is under the control of teachers and administrators are curriculum and instruction. This study suggests how those factors can be adapted to improve student motivation and achievement.

Interviewees reported that the process of improving student achievement was relatively simple and straightforward as long as teachers and students had a system that provided adequate feedback regarding student progress, suggesting that the results are not dependent on extraordinary teachers or administrators. In this study, interviewees attributed improved student outcomes to actions by teachers to improve student learning—tutoring, reteaching, and so on. Those actions were attributed to improvements in decision-making about what to teach, how, and to whom. Finally, improved decision-making was attributed to faster collection of diagnostically useful student assessment information through the rapid assessment system. Teachers stated that as they gained experience with this cycle of improvement, they began to anticipate and make changes in curriculum and instruction at the beginning of the school year, instead of waiting until students needed remediation. They believed that the cycle of improvement accelerated when they had rapid access to assessment data. They talked about the effect of rapid assessment in promoting a culture of continuous learning and organizational improvement. According to the teachers and administrators in this study, the implementation of rapid assessment triggered a cascade of changes in every aspect of schooling: the depth and balance of curriculum and instruction, the engagement and achievement of students, and organizational culture.

Toward a Theory of Rapid Assessment

The description of the processes by which rapid assessment achieves its effects moves us toward a theory of rapid assessment. The present results suggest the hypothesis that rapid assessment operates through two paths: improved instruction and improved student motivation. Rapid assessment is more effective if it is embedded in curriculum activities, so that feedback is received by students immediately after finishing a book or a set of math problems. This suggests that the technology supporting the system must allow students—not teachers or administrators—to initiate the feedback. In the district that is the focus of this study, the technology allowed students to initiate the feedback by immediately taking a short comprehension quiz or immediately scoring a completed set of math problems. The logistics of providing immediate feedback strongly suggest the need for supportive technology. Without the technology, schools are forced to rely on the presence of extraordinary teachers working extraordinary hours. The limitations of this approach are obvious.

A second hypothesis concerning rapid assessment is that for most students most of the time, speed and frequency of feedback is, to a large extent, more important than highly personalized but infrequent feedback, such as the type of feedback that teachers can provide through individual conferences with students. At the same time, much of the effect of rapid assessment can be attributed to the increased ability of teachers to spend more time tutoring individual students who need extra help.

Third, the present study suggests the importance of a supportive technology that promotes individualization of instruction. The motivational effects teachers described for rapid assessment may depend on a system where students select books that are graded according to reading level and where math problems are assigned based on student level.

Finally, the results concerning rapid assessment suggest why once-a-year testing is unlikely to have the desired effect of promoting student achievement. Feedback is too slow and infrequent to have much of an effect on either instruction or student motivation.

A "Rapid Cycle" Theory of Organizational Improvement

According to teachers and administrators, rapid assessment facilitated fundamental changes in the organization and culture of schooling, encouraging dialogue among teachers by providing a common point for discussion, increasing collaboration among teachers to improve instruction and resolve instructional problems, reducing teacher isolation, and supporting both new and experienced teachers in implementing sound teaching practices. Teachers suggested that improvement in McKinney is faster and continuous because the rapid assessment information system fosters rapid learning cycles: collecting student assessment information, making decisions, taking action, and evaluating outcomes. In McKinney, cycle time was reduced to the point where teachers made instructional adjustments on a daily basis. The implication is that schools with a faster cycling rate are likely to learn and improve faster and ultimately outperform schools with a slower cycling rate. Schools that rapidly assess student progress may improve instruction at a faster rate, resulting in improved student outcomes—to the degree that the assessments provide instructionally valid information.

Rapid Assessment and Inquiry-Oriented Learning

Some scholars may contend that the type of instruction fostered by rapid assessment may be inconsistent with current trends toward inquiry-oriented, socially-constructed learning. This would be true if rapid assessment led to more drill and practice, less critical thinking, narrowing of the curriculum to material covered by the state-mandated test, and less time for inquiry-oriented activities. However, interviewees reported the opposite effects. They reported that teachers had more time to spend on activities that were not directly tested precisely because rapid assessment made them more effective in teaching the material that *was* tested.

Rapid assessment provides diagnostic information that teachers and administrators in McKinney found useful. If they were inclined, they could have allocated the entire school day to the rapid assessment programs. However, they allocated half an hour per day for the Reading Assessment portion and half an hour a day for the Math Assessment portion—half of the time that is recommended by the Rapid Assessment Corporation. This indicates a desire to spend more time on activities other than the rapid assessment programs. Although teachers and administrators in McKinney clearly found rapid assessment to be valuable, it is also clear that they felt that the vast majority of the school day should be spent on other activities. This is consistent with the conclusion that much of the value of the programs is that they free up time to spend on other activities. It also suggests that it may be premature to conclude that teachers and administrators in McKinney subscribe to a philosophy of instruction that is inconsistent with social constructivism.

If it is true that students in McKinney "love to read" and "love math," this would seem to suggest that instructional approaches in this district go far beyond simple transmission models—unless one wants to argue that transmission models foster a love of reading and math. Clearly, the results of this study raise important questions, but if the findings are confirmed by other researchers, the implication is that funding for rapid assessment programs may enable schools to begin to address the challenge of the No Child Left Behind Act to improve student achievement without compromising educational quality.

The Question of Replication

What is the likelihood that the success of the rapid assessment approach could be replicated in other school districts? Six studies of Math Assessment (see note 9 in this chapter) and three studies of Reading Assessment (see note 8 in this chapter) have been conducted in a range of school districts, both urban and rural, including one study of statewide implementation of Reading Assessment in Idaho. All of the studies concluded that the rapid assessment programs resulted in significant improvements in student achievement. The results suggest that the rapid assessment approach can be successfully replicated in a variety of school districts.

Convergence of Evidence

The best evidence that feedback increases persistence, motivation, engagement, and academic achievement comes from controlled experimental studies.[11] For example, Robinson et al. (1989) randomly assigned 5th- and 6th-grade students to two groups. Both groups of students worked on identical sets of math problems in the same classroom at the same time with the same teacher. In the first session, neither group received feedback. In the second session, Group 1 received feedback, while Group 2 did not. In the third session, both groups received feedback. In the fourth session, neither group received feedback. The results showed that whenever a group received feedback, students in that group completed more problems with greater accuracy, compared to the baseline condition. Whenever feedback was withdrawn, the completion and accuracy rates dropped. The design of this study virtually rules out any explanation other than the conclusion that feedback caused improved student engagement and achievement. It is difficult to attribute the results of this experiment to individual differences in student characteristics, teacher characteristics, classrooms, or schools. The research design controlled for those differences.

The meta-analyses cited earlier of experimental studies that compared classrooms with and without frequent assessment (two to five times per week) suggest that these results are valid in a range of classrooms and settings. What happens when the basic research findings are translated into commercially available curriculum and assessment materials and large numbers of ordinary teachers use these materials without the benefit of special attention from researchers? The best evidence is provided by six evaluations of Math Assessment (see note 9 in this chapter) and three evaluations of Reading Assessment (see note 8 in this chapter). This research suggests that programs based on the feedback principle can produce significant impacts on student achievement. The large number of schools (60,000) that have adopted the programs provides indirect evidence that administrators in those schools have judged that the benefits of the programs justify their cost (Nunnery et al., 2003). This suggests that programs based on feedback principles can be translated into programs that are practical, useful, and affordable.

The convergence of results from both quantitative and qualitative research studies, and basic and applied research, suggests that feedback is indeed central to human learning. The results predict that various policy alternatives will be most effective when they promote feedback to teachers and students regarding student progress. It may be useful to investigate the role of feedback in mediating the effectiveness of class size reduction, recruitment of more qualified teachers, improved professional development for teachers, and whole-school reforms. Such investigations may show that these policy alternatives are most effective when they promote feedback regarding student progress. For example, Finn and Achilles (1999) found that reduction of class sizes in Tennessee improved student achievement by improving the ability of teachers to monitor the progress of low-achieving students. Similarly, it is likely that effective teachers develop effective systems to monitor the progress of their students. Finally, a characteristic of many whole school reforms is an emphasis on developing a system of self-assessment and the use of data to monitor progress (see, for example, Hopfenberg et al., 1993). It may be the case that when these policies fail, such as when class size reduction was implemented in California, the ultimate reason may be lack of feedback regarding student progress. In California, class size reduction necessitated the hiring of inexperienced teachers who apparently did not have the skills of experienced teachers in monitoring and addressing the progress of low-achieving students.

While the importance of feedback has been noted by some researchers, it has largely been neglected by the rest. The net effect is that educational researchers, in general, appear to have overlooked the significance of feedback as a central factor in human learning. For example, the National Academy of Sciences, the nation's most prestigious organization of research scientists, recently published a review of research on human learning and implications for education (Committee on Developments in the Science of Learning, 2000). While the review states that "Studies of adaptive expertise, learning, transfer, and early development show that feedback is extremely important" (p. 140), there is no discussion of the role of feedback in motivating students. The section titled "Motivation to Learn" (pp. 60–61) omits any discussion of feedback. This omission persists in the most recent review of research on teaching and learning that is periodically conducted by the field's leading educational researchers (Richardson, 2001). There is no discussion of the type of rapid assessment programs used in McKinney and evaluative studies suggesting that such programs can have strong positive effects. The impression is that most researchers have overlooked the potential of rapid feedback to motivate students and improve student achievement.

The evidence presented in this chapter suggests that rapid assessment can be an effective approach for improving student engagement and achievement. At the federal and state levels, policymakers may wish to provide funding to implement rapid assessment in districts that otherwise could not afford it, or to direct district staff to existing sources of funding. Funding for rapid assessment programs may enable schools to begin to address the challenge of the No Child Left Behind Act to improve student achievement without compromising educational quality.

2

Less Pressure

Chapter 1 suggested that rapid assessment systems, such as those implemented in McKinney, can have strong positive effects on teaching and learning. But are these effects strong enough to counteract the pressures of high-stakes testing? What happens to the quality of education when rapid assessment collides with high-stakes testing? What can be learned from a case study of this collision? The evidence provided in chapter 1 is suggestive, but how do McKinney teachers and principals respond to direct questions about these issues? How do they describe learning activities in their classrooms? Are these activities consistent with exemplary instructional practices? Chapter 2 addresses these questions.

....

The federal No Child Left Behind Act mandates testing in grades 3 through 8 by the year 2005–2006 and imposes sanctions—including the replacement of school staff—if test results indicate that schools are "in need of improvement." However, research suggests that attaching consequences to test results can cause teachers to narrow the curriculum to material covered on the tests, thereby reducing the balance and quality of the curriculum (Gordon & Reese, 1997; Haney, 2000; Hoffman et al., 1999; McNeil, 2000; McNeil & Valenzuela, 2000; M. L. Smith, 1991; Smith, Heinecke, & Noble, 1999; Smith et al., 1997; Smith & Rottenberg, 1991). Furthermore, if high-stakes testing reduces the quality of the curriculum, the use of those tests to measure improvement in student achievement may be questionable. Test scores may increase, reflecting improved student performance on basic skill tasks, without improvement on higher-order thinking tasks that are not easily tested. However, the number of states adopting high-stakes exit exams is increasing—not decreasing—and 70% of the student population will be subject to this form of high-stakes testing by the year 2009 (Gayler, Chudowsky, Hamilton, Kober, & Yeager,

2004), suggesting that high-stakes testing will remain a central feature of public education for years to come. Therefore, a key issue is to understand how undesired narrowing of the curriculum can be minimized.

Early hopes that portfolio- and performance-based assessments would reduce narrowing proved to be overly optimistic. In Kentucky, a survey of teachers found that 90% agreed that portfolios made it difficult to cover the regular curriculum (Koretz, Barron, Mitchell, & Stecher, 1996, p. 37). Fewer than 45% of principals and teachers reported that Kentucky's portfolio-based assessment program provided a better view of school effectiveness compared to more conventional, commercial standardized tests (p. x). The open-response component was rated as having positive effects on instruction more often than performance events and portfolios (pp. xiv, 56-57). In Vermont, Koretz, Stecher, Klein, and McCaffrey (1994) concluded that the use of portfolio assessment had substantial positive effects on 4th-grade math teachers' teaching practices, but evidence of validity was unpersuasive, and unreliability in test scores precluded most of the intended uses of the scores. In Arizona, Smith et al. (1997) found that teacher opinion regarding the consequences of the state's performance-oriented assessment program was divided. Thus, portfolio- and performance-based assessment systems are not panaceas.

In retrospect, the notion that portfolio- or performance-based assessments might reduce narrowing of the curriculum assumed that the problem is in the assessments—overlooking teacher decision-making processes that ultimately determine what is taught and, therefore, the extent of curriculum narrowing. Thus, it is striking that thousands of schools across the country are implementing performance feedback systems in an effort to improve student achievement in math and reading (Nunnery et al., 2003). These systems directly influence teacher decisions about what to teach, yet no research has been conducted regarding effects on teacher decision-making—until now. The results reported here suggest that the adoption of this type of system may reduce pressure on teachers to narrow the curriculum in response to state-mandated testing, thereby helping to maintain a balanced curriculum while addressing the NCLB mandate to improve student achievement as measured by standardized tests.

STAKES AND PRESSURE

Although stakes may seem synonymous with pressure, they are not. A study by Corbett and Wilson (1991) suggests that this distinction is critical. *Stakes* are defined as formal consequences for students and/or schools that are linked to test results. *Pressure* is defined as communications and informal consequences intended to induce staff to increase test scores (Corbett & Wilson, 1991). In a study of school districts in two states, negative impacts on teaching and learning occurred when stakes were high and pressure to raise test scores was high (Corbett & Wilson, 1991, p. 126). Positive impacts on teaching and learning occurred when stakes were high but pressure to raise test scores was low (Corbett & Wilson, 1991). High stakes and low pressure can occur when students must pass a test to graduate from high school but almost all students pass easily. This type of test is not likely to generate concern among staff or parents or pressure to change the curriculum. Under conditions of high stakes and low pressure, schools responded in a positive way (Corbett & Wilson, 1991). Educators in these schools accepted the test as a valid indicator of student learning and used it as the basis for making improvements in instruction while maintaining a balanced curriculum. Schools had adequate time to respond to student weaknesses indicated by test results. Under this condition, teachers implemented strategies for improving learning in a broad, balanced way that led to a rise in test scores without having to teach directly to the test. Teachers were most likely to adopt, adapt, or invent more effective instructional practices as the best means of improving student learning (Corbett & Wilson, 1991, p. 116).

These findings suggest the importance of reducing pressure on teachers and school administrators to distort curriculum and instruction. The implementation of some type of system that enables teachers to be more effective and enables students to pass the test more easily could reduce pressure to dumb down the curriculum and raise test scores.

RAPID ASSESSMENT

Potentially, one way to reduce the pressure felt by teachers is through implementation of assessment programs that provide rapid diagnostic information about student progress; support more effective, efficient, individualized instruction that keeps more students at grade level with less effort; reduce pressure to drill students on test-related content; and allow teachers to prepare students for the state-mandated test while preserving time and opportunities to teach higher-order skills and a balanced curriculum.

Curriculum-Based Measurement (CBM) is an early form of rapid assessment. In special education classrooms, teachers using CBM demonstrated improvements in instructional quality and student achievement (Fuchs, Deno, & Mirkin, 1984; Fuchs, Fuchs, Hamlett, & Stecker, 1991; Jones & Krouse, 1988; Wesson, 1991) with effect sizes of 0.70 standard deviations (Fuchs, Fuchs, Hamlett, & Stecker, 1991). CBM students liked frequent testing, believed it helped them to learn, saw themselves as more responsible for their learning, and were more likely to attribute their success to personal effort, compared to similar students who were randomly assigned to a control group (Davis, Fuchs, Fuchs, & Whinnery, 1995).

In a quasi-experimental study, Fuchs, Fuchs, and Hamlett (1994) found that CBM helped teachers to manage instructional time efficiently by immediately identifying students who were not making progress and quickly evaluating the efficacy of various intervention strategies. In three experiments, teachers who received computerized CBM skill analyses for their students designed more specific program adjustments, resulting in higher student achievement, compared to teachers who implemented CBM but did not receive the skill analyses (Fuchs, Fuchs, & Hamlett, 1989; Fuchs, Fuchs, Hamlett, & Allinder, 1991; Fuchs, Fuchs, Hamlett, & Stecker, 1990). The development of computer software simplified logistics and training, greatly reduced the time required to implement CBM, and improved teacher satisfaction with the process (Fuchs, Fuchs, Hamlett, & Hasselbring, 1987; Fuchs, Hamlett, Fuchs, Stecker, & Ferguson, 1988). These results suggest that frequent student assessments and rapid feedback of results to teachers may improve teaching effectiveness.

CBM has not been widely adopted, primarily because many teachers believe that CBM measures of numeracy and oral reading fluency are inadequate measures of performance on higher-order thinking tasks (Allinder & Oats, 1997; Hintze & Shapiro, 1997; Madelaine & Wheldall, 1999; Mehrens & Clarizio, 1993; Wesson, King, & Deno, 1984; Yell, Deno, & Marsten, 1992). In contrast, the current generation of rapid assessment systems uses broader measures of performance and, thus, has proven to be much more popular—over 60,000 schools nationwide have adopted rapid assessment systems (Nunnery et al., 2003). The rapid adoption of this type of assessment system suggests that widespread implementation is feasible and that school districts value the information gained from these systems sufficiently to allocate scarce district resources for this purpose. These systems fall into two general categories. Schools may choose to use one or both types of systems in tandem.

The first type of system measures student reading comprehension through computer-scored comprehension tests administered after each book that is read, while math achievement is measured two to five times weekly through computer-scored math assessments. Chapter 1 reported teacher and administrator responses to the implementation of this type of rapid assessment system and concluded that the assessments allowed teachers to individualize and target instruction, provide more tutoring, reduce drill and practice, and improve student readiness for—and spend more time on—critical thinking activities, resulting in a more balanced curriculum. Teachers reported that the assessments provided a common point for discussion, increased collaboration among teachers to improve instruction and resolve instructional problems, and supported both new and experienced teachers in implementing sound teaching practices. The individualized curriculum and rapid feedback on progress reportedly gave students the feeling that they were successful and in control of their own learning, engaging students who previously disliked reading and math, including dyslexic children and children in special education, reducing stress and improving student achievement.

The first type of rapid assessment system is designed to be used by classroom teachers to improve classroom instruction and may indirectly improve performance on the state-mandated tests that are used for NCLB accountability purposes. However, a second type of rapid assessment system is designed to be used by principals as well as teachers. This type of system is aligned with the state-mandated test and aims to provide an early prediction of performance, allowing teachers to modify instruction and improve student performance in advance of the state test.

STANDARDSMASTER

A widely implemented example is the StandardsMaster program developed by the Renaissance Learning Corporation.[1] StandardsMaster is a system for administering district tests customized by the corporation for client school districts to align with district and state curriculum standards, as well as the state-mandated test. This represents an important advantage over CBM for districts aiming to improve student achievement as measured by state-mandated tests. The StandardsMaster tests are often administered on a quarterly schedule with the goal of informing instruction and allowing teachers to reteach material as needed. Each client district selects test items from large item banks and assembles them into appropriate tests. Students take the tests exactly the way they would take the state-mandated test. Tests are machine-scored, with the results available the next day. Reports may be organized by building, classroom, teacher, student, or instructional objective.

A rigorous matched treatment-control pretest-posttest evaluation in the McKinney, Texas, school district (the same district investigated in the current report—see below) found that a sample of 891 students demonstrated significantly higher reading achievement over a 3-year period than 911 students in matched control schools, with effect sizes ranging from .17 to .22 SD in grade 5 on the state-mandated test (effects for 8th-grade students were not statistically significant) (Nunnery et al., 2003). A sample of 898 students demonstrated significantly higher math achievement over a 3-year period than 959 students in matched control schools, with an average effect size of .20 SD in grade 5 and .17 in grade 8 on the state-mandated test (Nunnery et al., 2003).

A previous evaluation during the 1999–2000 school year found that 3,649 McKinney students in grades 1 through 5 improved by 7 NCE points (approximately 0.9 grade equivalents [GE] above a national sample of students) on the STAR Reading test (Smith & Clark, 2001). Together, these results suggest that the StandardsMaster program was effective in improving student achievement in McKinney.

The literature reviewed above suggests that rapid assessment systems can increase instructional effectiveness. Does this reduce the pressure that teachers feel to teach to the state-mandated test, reducing the need to drill students on tested material, and preserving time and opportunities to teach higher-order skills and a balanced curriculum? At the heart of this question is the need for a better understanding of teachers' decision-making processes in response to state-mandated test results *when teachers have rapid access to diagnostically useful information about student progress.* Those decisions determine the quality of instructional activities that are delivered to students, for example, drill and practice or critical thinking activities.

TRACING THE THEORY OF ACTION

How did teachers and administrators in McKinney use rapid assessment results, and how did those results shape their instructional choices? The approach used here is to trace the theory of action backward, looking for disconfirming evidence.[2] The first question is: In the view of teachers and administrators, was the impact of state-mandated testing on the curriculum *positive* or *negative*? Negative views of testing would constitute evidence that the theory of rapid assessment is incorrect—that rapid assessment does *not* lead to positive use of state-mandated test results. The second question is: In the view of teachers and administrators, were district- and state-mandated test results used to improve instruction in a balanced way? If teachers did not use the information provided by the district's rapid assessment system and the state-mandated test, or used it in a way that increased drill or reduced critical thinking activities, that would also constitute evidence that the theory of rapid assessment is incorrect. Finally, the third question is: In the view of teachers and administrators, was there a connection between having rapid access to

Figure 2.1. The rapid assessment theory of action.

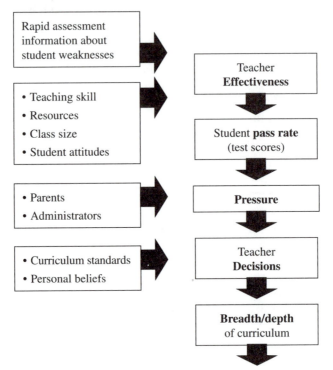

diagnostically useful StandardsMaster results and the way teachers and administrators responded to state-mandated testing? The theory of action for rapid assessment is presented in Figure 2.1.

This theory suggests that rapid assessment information combines with teaching skill, resources, class size, and student attitudes to determine teaching effectiveness and, thus, student passing rates on the state-mandated test. Passing rates combine with parent and administrator actions to determine the degree of pressure on teachers to raise test scores. Pressure combines with curriculum standards and each teacher's personal beliefs to influence teacher decisions about what to teach, thereby determining the degree to which the curriculum is narrowed.

A Positive View of State Testing

In the view of teachers and administrators, was the impact of state-mandated testing on the curriculum *positive* or *negative*? An overwhelming majority of teachers (77.6%) believed that the impact was positive, while a minority of teachers (16.3%) expressed concerns about teaching to the test, time away from instruction, delayed test results, and time spent on test-taking tricks. The majority agreed that the state-mandated test encouraged teachers to focus instruction in a positive way on important skills and knowledge. This suggests that the theory of rapid assessment passes the first test: in a district where rapid assessment has been implemented, teachers and administrators judged that state-mandated testing has a positive impact on the curriculum.

Was this view limited to newer teachers, suggesting that the district may be selecting teachers with positive views about testing? Surprisingly, teachers with fewer than 5 years of experience were not more likely to have positive views than teachers with 5 or more years of experience. Furthermore, all of the administrators—who had significantly more experience in the district than the average teacher—held positive views about testing, suggesting that experienced teachers and administrators were just as likely to hold positive views as newer teachers.

Three themes dominated positive views. First, teachers and administrators expressed the belief that state-mandated testing improved accountability for teachers, although it decreased teacher autonomy, and this increased accountability benefited students by ensuring that more students master the district curriculum. A veteran middle school principal weighed the trade-offs:

> I would say that it is very positive. I have been teaching in Texas for 20-plus years and before we had the TAAS test in our state, teachers had complete freedom on what they could teach. That was nice as a professional educator, that you had so much autonomy there was no one telling you what you had to do. It was good from a teacher's standpoint but it was bad from a student's standpoint. I didn't like teaching fractions so my kids graduated from the 5th grade without learning fractions because I didn't like to teach them. So what I think the TAAS has done for us is made us more purposeful about what we teach. Teachers are more aware of what we have to teach and the standard to which we're expecting our kids to master our curriculum, so it has had a very positive impact on everyday practices in our schools.

A second theme is that teachers and administrators felt that the impact of the state-mandated test is positive because the test is perceived to be appropriate, focused on skills that students need to know, and aligned with the intended school curriculum. Therefore, teachers and administrators felt that the changes made to instruction as a result of the test results benefited their students. This view is illustrated by the response of a middle school assistant principal:

> Yes, I think this is exactly what we need to be focusing on. I don't think the state is doing anything to us. I think this is a good thing for kids, and now there's accountability where there needs to be. Before, we were testing such basic skills, and now we're requiring that they know so much more. So I think it's a good thing. We are no longer teaching—I don't like to use the word "irrelevant," but we don't just teach whatever we want to anymore; we are teaching what needs to be taught and what's going to be tested.

Furthermore, teachers and administrators felt that the state-mandated test encouraged teachers to teach the intended curriculum to all students, reducing the tendency to give up on hard-to-teach students. This view was captured by a high school assistant principal who felt that the resulting changes in curriculum and instruction prepared more students for college:

> Much of what's being tested on TAKS is the curriculum that they're learning in high school, which is good because at the high school level, people weren't necessarily teaching the specified curriculum, because there was no accountability. So this forces schools and teachers to teach what they're supposed to be teaching, which is, in the end, preparing students for college. And the most positive thing, I think, is that it makes you narrow your focus and realize that all students have to learn this, not just the easy-to-teach students. And that's the hardest job we have, is to teach all kids.

A third theme was that teachers and administrators felt that the state-mandated test results provided objective data that stimulated teachers to be more reflective about what they are doing in the classroom. This view was captured by the response of a high school principal who felt that in the past, teachers had attributed poor student performance to socioeconomic factors, but the test data now forces them to examine their own contribution to student outcomes:

> The reason that I like it, and it's been a good thing and it's been a positive is, for the first time, we as teachers had to really look at data that said, "Am I successful?" And I am only successful as a teacher based on the success of the kids in my classroom. Prior to that,

[judgments were] based on subjective criteria. "This kid has a bad home life." Now we have information that we get from TAAS/TAKS data. As instructional leaders, we use that information, and we really dig deep [to understand] how well our kids know the information that we're teaching them. For the first time, it's making an impact on our teachers because it makes them become more reflective about what they're doing in the classroom. For that reason it's been positive.

Increased reflection reportedly led to changes in instructional practices. Secondary schoolteachers and administrators realized that they could not simply teach literature, but had to teach reading skills in combination with literature because many students were not fluent readers. Writing teachers had to shift away from formulaic writing instruction in order to prepare students for the state test. Teachers found that they needed to replace textbook and worksheet activities because students were not adequately prepared for the challenges presented by the test. Finally, administrators reported that teachers were using more projects in social studies and science.

Use of Test Results

If a majority of teachers in McKinney believed that the high-stakes state-mandated test had a positive influence on curriculum, instruction, and student learning, is it possible to trace this positive assessment to the implementation of McKinney's system for rapidly assessing student progress? The first step is to investigate the extent to which teachers used StandardsMaster and state-mandated test results. Therefore, it is significant that an extraordinarily high percentage of teachers (89.8%) reported that they use test results to systematically improve instruction. For example, a high school principal described how the 9-week StandardsMaster results were used to identify particular instructional objectives where students needed focused attention:

I am passionate about this. We use the 9-week assessments along with the state test to drive our instruction: where their gaps in learning are, where they are strong. We have our teachers break up into subject teams to go through all of the incoming TAAS/TAKS data of the 8th graders. We look at where our kids have gaps and need to be taught or retaught. That dictates how much time we spend on it. It doesn't dictate what we teach because the state curriculum tells us what to teach, but it does dictate to us how much time we plan on teaching certain TEKS objectives—the Texas Essential Knowledge and Skills. So it does dictate how much time we spend on planning and how much time we spend in the classroom on objectives that were not passed or were passed on the previous year's standardized tests.

Influence on Teaching Practices

If teachers use test results, the next question is: How does that influence teaching practices? Teachers were asked to describe how the availability of test results prompted them to change their instructional practices. Significantly, teachers asserted that the StandardsMaster test results did not cause narrowing of the curriculum, since the curriculum is specified by the state. However, the results helped teachers to diagnose areas of difficulty and influenced the amount of time teachers devoted to particular topics. Teachers noted the importance of having professional development to interpret the results and implement more effective instruction. For example, a 2nd-grade teacher described the impact of a weeklong reading institute in helping her to improve oral fluency:

> The test results specify what you need to work on. I didn't know what to do with the results last year. I did the testing and I never looked at it again, to be honest. [But] I went through a weeklong reading institute, and my world changed. I came back in February and looked at fluencies. They wanted the kids to be reading 90 words per minute. And I had tons of kids down there in the 55 range. They said that poetry was one of the best ways to get the fluency up, the repetition, the sing-song. Well, I came back, dug my data out, and started working on fluency. By March, those kids were already there. Without the data and knowing what to do with the data, I wouldn't have had a clue, because it would've sat there. So it's greatly impacted the way I teach.

When teachers used test results, the majority (65.3%) reported that they used the results to identify and teach missing skills, including higher-order thinking skills as well as basic skills. For example, test results were used to monitor the progress of a lead group of students. If the lead group missed a concept, then it was retaught to the entire class. Otherwise, it was retaught selectively by tutoring students who missed it.

If teachers had reported that testing pressured them to narrow the curriculum to material covered on the state test, leaving important content out of the curriculum, this would also be evidence against the theory of rapid assessment. But this was not the case, for two reasons. First, teachers felt that the skills they focused on to prepare students for the state test were entirely appropriate. Teachers argued that the skills needed for the test were aligned with skills needed beyond school. For this reason, they felt positive about what they had to do to prepare students for the state test. For example, a middle school math teacher felt that the skills he was teaching were intrinsically important for students to know:

> To be honest with you, I don't focus on those skills to prepare students for state tests. The name of the state test—TAKS or TAAS—is rarely mentioned in class. Because it's life. It's not just about passing this test. You need to know this because you've got to get through high school, you've got to get a job, and you just need to know. That really keeps my attitude pretty positive, because there's more at stake here than just a score on a test. We just do what we need to do.

The teachers also perceived the state test to be aligned with the state and district curriculum. A high school principal explained:

> The state assessment and what we are supposed to be teaching are aligned. If we were not testing what we were supposed to be teaching—that would be an issue. Or if we were testing what we were not supposed to be teaching—that would be an issue. But now that they are aligned, I think that it's exactly the way it should be.

Second, teachers did not perceive negative narrowing of the curriculum because they believed they had the time and freedom to maintain breadth and depth in the curriculum. This is consistent with the theory that rapid assessment improves teaching effectiveness to the point where it relieves the time pressure that teachers ordinarily feel in preparing students for the state test. Teachers asserted that they went beyond basic skills and worksheets, and felt that it was possible to maintain breadth and depth while preparing students for the state test. For example, a master teacher in a Title I elementary school explained:

> While they are basic skills, one of the things that we are *really* working on is integrating the curriculum, and adding meat and depth to *all* of the things that we teach, still staying in the realm of what we *must* teach. So what I see is, as I move around in all the different classrooms—because I work with all the different teachers in different classrooms—what I see is not just basic skill teaching. I have seen it before. I've seen it in other places, where, "Here's the worksheet. Here's the basic skills. Test, test, test."

Reduced Time on Projects?

A common complaint by teachers in districts that do not use rapid assessment systems is that high-stakes testing places so much pressure on teachers that they are forced to eliminate project activities that do not directly teach the type of knowledge and skills tested on the state-mandated test. In McKinney, while half of the teachers (49.0%) reported that they have reduced the amount of time they spend on projects, almost all (91.7%) of these teachers reported that they eliminated unimportant projects and refocused the remaining projects in a way that benefited students. This is consistent with the theory that rapid assessment preserves time for important project activities, but it also suggests the role of high-stakes testing in focusing those activities according to priority. Overall, teachers felt that the changes were positive. For example, a middle school principal responded to the question of whether teachers reduced time spent on projects:

> Yes and no. We scrutinize our projects more completely, and we make sure that the projects are aligned with the state curriculum objectives. Before we had the accountability in our state testing, we would make up projects just because they sounded like they would be fun. We lost sight of why we needed kids to make a salt map. Well, it's because we needed them to know the regions of Texas. We focused more on product rather than process. We've gotten smarter about our projects and we're focusing more on what we want the kids to learn and be able to do after they finish the project than just projects for projects' sake, because the kids might think it's fun.

Although the vast majority of teachers in this district had positive views about the impact of testing, a minority of teachers reported concerns about lost enrichment activities. Significantly, teachers reported that the problem is not testing *per se*, but having to cover too many Texas Essential Knowledge and Skills (TEKS) instructional objectives.

Quality of Instruction

What about the quality of instruction in McKinney classrooms? The theory of rapid assessment predicts that quality would not be compromised because teachers have adequate time to teach critical thinking as well as basic skills. Two researchers with substantial experience in evaluating teachers conducted observations in 10 randomly selected classrooms to assess the quality of instruction. Both researchers agreed that the quality of instruction would, according to their experiences, be characterized as consistent with best teaching practices. To triangulate these observations and to determine if teachers in the research sample expressed views about teaching that were clearly contrary to generally accepted "best practices," teachers were asked during each interview to "describe a lesson or activity that is representative of your teaching approach." Significantly, teachers described creative, hands-on lessons that seemed consistent with best practices, suggesting that at a minimum, they knew how to create such lessons, even though the study was not designed to determine how often those lessons were implemented. Examples of these lessons included the following:

- An elementary school special education teacher vividly demonstrated the concept of air pressure by having students inflate a garbage bag using straws, showing that air pressure can lift the weight of a human body.
- A 2nd-grade teacher used a memorable hands-on activity where students tabulated and charted their preferences for various types of pie, noting that students spontaneously began writing mathematical statements to summarize the data.
- A 3rd-grade teacher in a Title I elementary school taught students the relationships among multiplication, addition, and division by having students count pennies and group them into cups, explaining that multiplication is a way to add equal groups, and that some numbers of pennies can be evenly divided among cups, while other numbers result in a "remainder."
- A middle school math teacher taught the concept of circumference by having students blow soap bubbles on their desks, measure the diameters, use the formula for circumference, measure circumference using string, then compare the results from the formula with the measurement.

CONCLUSION

The vast majority of teachers believed that the impact of the state-mandated test on curriculum and instruction was positive. The results contradict several previous studies of Texas's high-stakes testing program where teachers and administrators suggested that the impact of the state-mandated test is negative (Gordon & Reese, 1997; Haney, 2000; Hoffman et al., 1999), although recent studies suggest that McKinney is not the only Texas school district where teachers report positive effects (Scheurich, Skrla, & Johnson, 2000; Skrla, Scheurich, & Johnson, 2000; Skrla, Scheurich, Johnson, & Koschoreck, 2001).

How can the results be reconciled with earlier research? One possibility is that the teachers and principals interviewed for this case study happened to be exceptionally talented in their ability to juggle the demands of testing and high-quality instruction. However, the interviewees unanimously identified the use of the rapid assessment system as a key factor in their ability to improve student achievement in a way that promotes balanced instruction, without the excessive stress and pressure that might otherwise lead them to narrow the curriculum and focus on drill and practice. Thus, the interviewee responses suggest that rapid assessment was a key factor in reducing the pressure that teachers felt and appeared to be a key factor in the teachers' positive responses to Texas's high-stakes test.

A second possibility is that Texas has responded to critics and improved the state-mandated test to the point where their main concerns have been addressed. This view is supported by teachers who compared the new TAKS test with the older TAAS and concluded that the TAKS addressed most of their concerns with the TAAS. Previous research regarding teachers' views of testing may be outdated, at least in Texas. However, the TAKS had not been implemented at the time of the interviews—the comparisons of TAKS and TAAS were based on sample items and descriptions, not on actual experience with TAKS. Thus, interviewee responses were primarily based on experiences with TAAS, not TAKS.

The explanation that best fits the data is that the rapid availability of diagnostically useful assessment results through the StandardsMaster program reduced the pressure felt by teachers to drill students in order to improve student achievement. According to the teachers, the rapid assessment program helped teachers to quickly, efficiently identify and address areas of student weakness. This improved efficiency allowed teachers to prepare students for the state-mandated test *and* teach a balanced curriculum that included learning activities that would otherwise be squeezed out of the curriculum. According to the teachers, rapid assessment permits carefully targeted instruction and improved their effectiveness and efficiency in teaching certain core skills and knowledge that are tested on the state-mandated test. Thus, it appears that rapid assessment reduced pressure on teachers to raise student achievement by providing a technology that improved teacher effectiveness, mobilizing teacher capacity for higher-quality instruction—the missing link, according to Elmore (2004), in the theory of educational accountability.

This suggests that one way to tilt the balance so that high-stakes testing programs have positive, rather than negative, effects on curriculum and instruction is to fund and implement a technology—rapid assessment—along with professional development that would give teachers more control over student achievement and thereby reduce the pressure teachers feel to boost test scores through whole-class drill and practice. Conversely, it appears that negative effects on teaching occur when teachers do not have adequate tools and professional development to improve student achievement through balanced instructional practices. While there may be other ways to reduce the pressure that teachers feel (such as lowering standards and passing scores), teachers in this study strongly supported the use of rapid assessment as a means to achieve this end without lowering educational standards.

The theory of action described by the teachers in this study suggests that systematic use of student assessment data can greatly improve teacher effectiveness in improving student achievement. If this theory is correct, then we would expect teachers in this study to report that they regularly use test results to inform instruction. This is exactly what occurred: an extraordinary 90% of teachers in this study reported using the state-mandated TAAS and StandardsMaster test results to guide instructional improvement. The interview results suggest that the use of the results was extremely systematic, targeting students and areas where students needed help. The results suggest that the teachers' positive views of state-mandated testing resulted from the implementation of a system that supported effective teaching by improving teacher knowledge about where to focus instruction.

The results of this study are consistent with the conceptual framework presented at the beginning of this chapter. Based on earlier research (Corbett & Wilson, 1991), this framework suggested that high-stakes tests can have positive effects on curriculum and instruction when pressure on teachers to improve student achievement is low. That research indicated that under conditions of high stakes and low pressure, schools responded in a positive way, with educators using test results as the basis for making improvements in instruction while maintaining a balanced curriculum. Under this condition, teachers implemented strategies for improving learning in a broad, balanced way that led to a rise in test scores without having to teach directly to the test. Teachers were most likely to adopt, adapt, or invent more effective instructional practices as the best means of improving student learning (Corbett & Wilson, 1991, p. 116).

In this study, it appears that pressure was reduced because the use of rapid assessment enabled teachers to teach more effectively. Teachers used test results to diagnose areas where students needed help. Teachers selectively retaught concepts that were missed or provided tutoring. In this way, teachers aimed to reduce the number of students who fell behind. Thus, the use of rapid assessment is the most likely reason that teachers in McKinney reported that testing had a positive influence on curriculum and instruction.

However, a second factor appeared to be significant. Teachers reported that the state test was properly aligned with curriculum and instruction. Clearly, this contributed to the sense that preparing students for the state test was consistent with teaching the state and district curriculum. This suggests a two-factor model: high-stakes tests may have positive effects when pressure on teachers to improve student achievement is low and when tests are properly aligned with curriculum and instruction. Pressure on teachers can be reduced in a number of ways, including lowering standards, lowering passing scores, or—in this study—implementing a system that helps teachers to teach more effectively. Proper alignment of tests with curriculum and instruction involves both breadth (topic coverage) and depth (balance of critical thinking and fact-oriented questions) and minimization of unwanted trickiness.

The policy implication of this study is that the implementation of the No Child Left Behind Act is more likely to be successful if it is accompanied by funding and resources needed to implement the type of rapid assessment system that was used in McKinney, and if tests are properly aligned with curriculum and instruction. In addition, implementation of the Act is more likely to be successful if state tests are designed and implemented in a way that fosters the type of balanced teaching that McKinney teachers appear to have achieved. A careful reading of the interview excerpts reveals clues about test design and implementation details that influenced teacher judgments about the worth of tests:

- Do tests provide diagnostic information?
- Do they avoid contrived writing prompts?
- Do they focus on substance, rather than essay format?
- Are they sufficiently challenging?
- Do they focus on analysis and evaluation, rather than simple summarization?
- Do they require students to use multiple sources of information to answer questions?
- Do they avoid questions that require memorization?
- Are they fully aligned to the state curriculum standards?
- Do they avoid excessive quantities of instructional objectives?
- Do they help teachers to prepare all students for college?
- Are test results available promptly, and in a format that helps teachers to identify areas of student weakness?

Incorporating these features into state tests may be essential to secure the support of teachers and foster successful implementation of the No Child Left Behind Act.

The interview excerpts also reveal the importance of professional development. Teachers mentioned participation in the New Jersey Writing Project, a reading institute, and a math conference, where they learned teaching skills that helped them to teach students in creative, engaging, and powerful ways. Successful implementation of the No Child Left Behind Act probably requires funding for this type of professional development. It may also require changes in the preparation of new teachers and principals in the skills of using data to improve instruction while maintaining depth, breadth, and balance.

This study may offer hope to those who are concerned about the consequences of the move toward increased testing. There appear to be certain conditions under which a results-driven approach to instruction is compatible with high-quality teaching. Two key conditions may be the presence of a system for rapidly obtaining diagnostically useful assessment results, and proper alignment of tests with curriculum and instruction.

3

Less Frustration

Chapters 1 and 2 focused on changes that can be implemented by local school districts in order to improve student achievement and improve chances that the federal No Child Left Behind (NCLB) Act will have positive consequences. Chapter 3 addresses a change in federal policy that could greatly reduce the frustration that many students feel when forced to take the type of standardized tests required by NCLB.

As noted in chapter 2, NCLB substantially increases testing requirements and sets demanding accountability standards for schools, districts, and states (Linn, Baker, & Betebenner, 2002). A key assumption is that results of state-mandated tests provide useful information to school superintendents, principals, and teachers about areas where changes in professional development, funding, and teaching approaches may improve instruction and student achievement (Smith & O'Day, 1991). However, current forms of annual testing may not provide sufficient information to improve instruction. Furthermore, results that are reported over the summer, after students have moved on to the next grade level, are too late to help those students. A second assumption is that state-mandated tests do not cause harmful stress for students. However, previous research suggests that this assumption is incorrect (M. L. Smith, 1991). There is a need to investigate NCLB's assumptions, to understand how test results do—or do not—provide useful information to administrators and teachers, and to address possible flaws.

A promising approach is to integrate computer-adaptive testing technology into state-mandated tests. Computer-adaptive tests adjust the difficulty of the test so that each student receives a form of the test that is at an appropriate level of difficulty, reducing test-related stress, while collecting achievement information on a constant scale (Kingsbury & Hauser, 2004; Weiss, 2004). In addition, the tests provide more diagnostic information, information about individual student growth, and rapid reporting of results. Thus, the use of computer-adaptive tests may address flaws in current state-mandated tests. Adaptive technology has been mainstreamed into the Graduate Management Admission Test, the Graduate Record Examination, and a growing number of other tests (see http://www.psych.umn.edu/psylabs/CATCentral/ for more information).

Unfortunately, the U.S. Department of Education has interpreted language under section 1111(b)(2)(A) of NCLB to rule out the use of computer-adaptive tests for NCLB purposes. This language specifies that each state must develop and implement "a single, statewide State accountability system" (NCLB, 2002, p. 1445). The U.S. Department of Education ruled that the "use of levels assessments"—including computer-adaptive tests—"would not allow all schools and students to be held to the same high standards required by the NCLB Act," presumably because adaptive tests individualize the items that are presented to each student (CTB/McGraw-Hill, 2004; Title I—Improving the Academic Achievement of the Disadvantaged, Final Rule, 2002, p. 45044). While testing experts agree that a well-designed computer-adaptive-test would constitute a uniform means of assessing student performance against a given standard, and would allow all schools and students to be held to the same standard, Education Department officials assert that adaptive tests would not provide a uniform test: "The regulations are very clear in saying all students have to be held to the same standard" (Trotter, 2003, p. 17). Testing experts believe that the department's stance stems from a misunderstanding regarding adaptive testing (Trotter, 2003). Despite the department's position, it appears that the use of adaptive tests is consistent with the language of the law, suggesting the possibility that the department could change its policy if desired.

A critical question is whether the advantages of computer-adaptive tests outweigh their disadvantages, according to the perceptions and values of administrators and teachers—the key actors who would be responsible for implementing those tests and managing their consequences. A path analysis indicates that teacher attitudes toward state-mandated tests strongly influence whether they change their instructional strategies (Pomplun, 1997). Thus, it is critical to examine teacher attitudes toward computer-adaptive testing in order to understand how the implementation of adaptive testing might influence instructional strategies.

However, the existing research literature is silent regarding the views of K–12 teachers and administrators about adaptive testing for accountability purposes. The literature offers neither an empirical nor theoretical understanding of the influence of test characteristics on teacher and administrator instructional decisions (see Elmore, 2004, for a related point). Researchers have not studied what matters to teachers and administrators and therefore can only speculate about changes in test design and implementation that would meet their needs. This gap in the literature limits the ability of researchers to make effective policy recommendations regarding testing.

PURPOSE OF THE STUDY

I conducted a study to fill this gap by investigating what matters to teachers and administrators: how teachers and administrators use tests and how test characteristics influence the value of tests, with regard to both computer-adaptive tests and current versions of state-mandated tests. This study proposes a theoretical framework for understanding how test characteristics influence teaching and learning, examines the fit of this framework with empirical data about teacher and administrator decision-making processes, and provides policy recommendations.

KEY TEST CHARACTERISTICS

What are the key characteristics of state-mandated tests that influence the quality of the information that is provided to teachers? One important characteristic is the degree of alignment with the state curriculum. Research suggests that poorly aligned tests provide poor information and may lead teachers to narrow the curriculum in a negative way (Corbett & Wilson, 1991; Gordon & Reese, 1997; Haney, 2000; Hoffman, Pennington, Assaf, & Paris, 1999; M. L. Smith, 1991; Smith & Rottenberg, 1991). In response, states have worked to ensure proper alignment of curriculum and instruction (Rothman, 2004).

Although tests may be properly aligned in terms of the topics that are covered, researchers have also raised concerns that multiple-choice assessments may not emphasize and foster active learning and critical thinking. One suggestion is to use performance-based or portfolio assessments. These assessments are believed to shape instruction in desirable ways, encouraging teaching that promotes active learning, compared to multiple-choice assessments (Baron & Wolf, 1996; Rothman, 1995). However, evidence regarding this hypothesis is mixed. A qualitative study of the effects of testing in Maine and Maryland found that performance-based assessments have limited effects on changing basic instructional strategies when stakes are low or moderate (Firestone, Mayrowetz, & Fairman, 1998). As noted in chapter 2, Koretz, Barron, Mitchell, and Stecher (1996) surveyed teachers and principals in Kentucky and found that 90% of the teachers agreed that portfolios made it difficult to cover the regular curriculum (p. 37), and portfolios were cited as having negative effects on instruction almost as often as having positive effects (p. xi). Fewer than 45% of principals and teachers reported that Kentucky's portfolio-based assessment program, the Kentucky Instructional Results Information System (KIRIS), provided a better view of school effectiveness compared to more conventional, commercial standardized tests (p. x). Recall also that Koretz, Stecher, Klein, and McCaffrey (1994) studied Vermont's portfolio assessment system and found that evidence of validity was unpersuasive and that unreliability in test scores precluded most of the intended uses of the scores. Thus, the literature regarding performance- and portfolio-based assessments suggests that the limitations of these tests prevent them from meeting the requirements of state-mandated assessments.

There are four other characteristics of testing that have received less attention but have great potential to influence the usefulness of state-mandated tests: 1) the level of detail that is provided regarding areas where students are strong or weak, 2) whether teachers receive the results in time to use them to improve instruction with their current students, 3) the degree to which each test's level of difficulty is appropriate for students, and 4) whether information is provided regarding individual achievement growth, as well as level of achievement. Research suggests that current state-mandated tests do not provide useful diagnostic information to teachers, report results so late that they cannot be used to help students, are often inappropriate in terms of level of difficulty for low achieving students (M. L. Smith, 1991; Smith & Rottenberg, 1991), and do not measure progress in achievement (Corbett & Wilson, 1991; Gordon & Reese, 1997). Lack of diagnostic information and slow reporting of results prevents teachers from using test results to improve instruction, while the use of nonadaptive tests causes frustration and stress for students because each student receives exactly the same test, regardless of individual differences in developmental levels (Clarke et al., 2003; Gordon & Reese, 1997; Haney, 2000; Hoffman et al., 1999; Pedulla et al., 2003). Lack of growth information leads to invalid inferences about school performance (Elmore, 2004; Linn, 2004). Since test scores are associated with family income, low scores may simply reflect that a school or district serves a low-income population, not that the quality of instruction is poor (Linn, 2004).

THEORETICAL FRAMEWORK

The theoretical framework for the current study is presented in Figure 3.1. The degree to which state-mandated tests provide diagnostic information

Figure 3.1. Framework for understanding effects of four test characteristics.

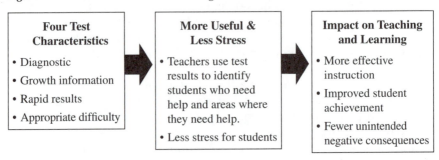

about areas of student strengths and weaknesses, information about individual growth in student achievement, and rapid results is hypothesized to influence the value of testing—specifically, the ability of teachers to use the results to revise and improve instruction. Tests that are adjusted in difficulty for each student would be less stressful for low-achieving students. Tests with these characteristics may result in improved student achievement with fewer unintended negative consequences.

RESEARCH QUESTIONS

The study focused on three research questions: 1) In the view of administrators and teachers, how do the characteristics of Minnesota's state-mandated tests influence their usefulness? 2) In the view of administrators and teachers, how do the characteristics of computer-adaptive tests influence their usefulness? 3) How does the usefulness of Minnesota's state-mandated tests compare with the usefulness of computer-adaptive tests?

BACKGROUND

The Northwest Evaluation Association (NWEA) is a nonprofit organization founded specifically to develop improved standardized tests.[1] NWEA's computer-adaptive tests, called the Measures of Academic Progress (MAP), are not state-mandated in Minnesota. However, they are of interest because they demonstrate the feasibility of computer-adaptive tests, which have certain desirable characteristics not available in conventional tests. The adaptive tests have been implemented in over 900 school districts. The distinctive feature of this type of test is that the computer scores a student's responses as the test is being administered and, based on the results, selects additional items with difficulty levels matched to the student.

Computer-adaptive tests ensure that low-achieving students are not subjected to a frustratingly difficult test that is beyond their ability, and that high-achieving students are not subjected to a test that is too easy and provides limited information about their abilities (Hardwicke & Yoes, 1984; Schinoff & Steed, 1988). In addition, the technology permits the test to be shortened, reducing fatigue and reducing the time lost to instruction. The increase in efficiency has been estimated to be 50%, that is, it takes on average half as many items to achieve the same level of accuracy as a conventional test (Wainer, 1993). Significantly, the tests provide information about each student's criterion-referenced level of achievement, even though students receive different forms and test items. This is achieved through a process that accounts for the difficulty of each test item as well as whether each item is answered correctly. The tests also provide information about growth in individual student achievement, unlike most state-mandated tests.[2] Accountability systems based on growth information provide a more accurate measure of the contribution of a school or teacher, compared to current testing programs that simply report whether achievement is high or low.

Adaptive tests are designed to provide more diagnostic information than state-mandated tests. The tests can efficiently zero in on exactly the areas where students are weak and are designed to provide test results quickly (as quickly as the same day), and results can be organized by building, teacher, student categories, or curriculum standard. Some Minnesota schools took advantage of this capability to administer the adaptive test at the beginning of the school year and then used the results to diagnose and address areas of student weakness.[3] Interviewees were specifically asked about their views regarding this option.

Thus, adaptive tests demonstrate many features that could be incorporated into state-mandated assessments: quick results in a user-friendly format, more diagnostic information, and information about individual growth in achievement, in forms that avoid student frustration. Unfortunately, the U.S. Department of Education does not permit states to use fully computer-adaptive tests for NCLB purposes, apparently because federal government officials believe that the use of a uniform test is the best way to collect reliable information on the progress of all students (Olson, 2002).

Adaptive tests demonstrate the technical feasibility of an alternative approach to testing that has several virtues. However, they are multiple-choice tests, whereas the trend has been away from such tests and states such as Minnesota that have created state-mandated tests have opted for greater use of constructed response formats. Interviewees were asked to compare the advantages and disadvantages of the state-mandated and adaptive tests.

At the time of the research study, Minnesota's state-mandated tests were typical of state-mandated tests across the United States, except that Minnesota required all districts within the state to administer two types of tests. The Minnesota Comprehensive Assessments (MCAs) were high-standards tests and were administered at grades 3 (reading and math), 5 (reading, math, and writing), 10 (reading and writing), and 11 (math). The MCA tests will also be implemented in grades 4, 6, 7, and 8 beginning in 2005–2006. The reading and math tests were composed of multiple-choice and short-answer questions. The writing test required a written essay.

At the time of the research study, the Minnesota Basic Standards Test (MBST or BST) was a minimum competency exit exam administered in grades 8 (reading and math), 10 (writing), and 12 (for seniors who needed to retake the MBST).[4] Students were required to pass the test in order to graduate from high school. The test was designed to ensure that all graduates possess basic skills in reading, writing, and math, and was composed of multiple-choice questions and a written essay.

METHODS

The methodological approach in this study is qualitative, specifically, *phenomenology*—the study of how participants understand their experiences—in this case, how teachers and administrators understand and value the differences between computer-adaptive and state-mandated testing, and the decision process through which assessment information is translated into instructional choices. As with all research, the value of the study depends on the degree to which the lessons learned can plausibly be extrapolated to the larger universe of individuals who are public school teachers and administrators. However, the *logic* of extrapolation in the phenomenological approach depends less on the *quantity* of data than it does on *insight* into teachers' and administrators' decision-making processes, in the same way that insight into how a particular puzzle may be solved can provide a generalizable understanding of how an entire category of similar puzzles may be solved. Thus, the researcher collected information from teachers and administrators—the individuals who are arguably most knowledgeable about how they use test results—then analyzed the data with the goal of gaining insights regarding teacher and administrator decision-making processes. The data from this study are not intended to be understood as a random sample of all teachers and administrators in Minnesota.

Grounded Evidence

The evidence that I offer is grounded in two ways. First, it is based on the responses of teachers and school administrators—the end users of the information that tests provide—regarding characteristics of tests that promote appropriate use of the results. Second, the evidence offered in this chapter is grounded in what is currently feasible. Thus, the present study focuses on a comparison of a current state-mandated testing program with an alternative that has demonstrated its technological, social, and economic feasibility (hundreds of school districts across the country have elected to allocate scarce resources to purchase and implement the alternative testing system).

Sample

Data reported here come from a qualitative study of teacher and administrator responses to a set of questions about computer-adaptive and state-mandated testing in Minnesota. Minnesota was selected for two main reasons. First, the state testing program is "high stakes"—students must pass the Basic Standards Test, administered beginning in 8th grade, in order to graduate from high school. It was expected that the relative advantages and disadvantages of computer-adaptive and state-mandated tests would be especially salient to teachers and administrators in a high-stakes testing environment. Second, several school districts in Minnesota have implemented the adaptive tests, so it was possible to ask respondents to compare the effects of computer-adaptive tests with the state-mandated tests in order to establish the relative merits of computer-adaptive and state-mandated tests. It was hypothesized that computer-adaptive tests would be viewed as more appropriate for students and more appropriate for instructional improvement, providing quicker results and information about individual growth that would be highly valued by teachers and administrators.

Four school districts were selected that were representative, in terms of student demographics, size, and distance from major urban centers, of four major categories: one large urban (40,000+ students, 74% minority, 68% free/reduced lunch), one small urban (<2,000 students, 62% minority, 37% free/reduced lunch), one suburban (11,000 students, 28% minority, 8% free/reduced lunch), and one semirural district (<2,000 students, 2% minority, 4% free/reduced lunch). In each district, interviews were obtained with the superintendent or assistant superintendent, director of research, and the principal and four teachers at one high school, one middle school, and one elementary school (except in one district that only had two schools). Schools were selected that represented the socioeconomic characteristics (ethnicity and percentage receiving free/reduced-price lunch) of each district. One elementary school declined to participate after learning that teachers would not be compensated for the interviews (a second elementary school was substituted).

Teachers were selected using criterion sampling (Creswell, 1998), focusing on the tested grades. All participants had bachelor's degrees and approximately one-third also held masters' degrees (6 administrators held doctorates). Years of experience in the classroom ranged from 1 to 29. Approximately 60% of the participants were female, and 40% were male. A total of 61 individuals were interviewed. Table 3.1 presents the distribution of the research sample.

The interview protocols included general questions about the impact of testing as well as questions about specific policy alternatives: "Overall, is your opinion about the impact of the state testing program positive or negative? Why? What are the strengths and weaknesses of the computer-adaptive test, compared to the state-mandated test? Would you favor the use of a computer-adaptive test that adapts the difficulty of the questions to the student's level? Would you favor, at every grade level, giving the test before the school year, as a pretest to diagnose students, and at the end of the school year, as a posttest to determine how much students improved during the year?"

Each interview was audio-recorded, and lasted about 50 minutes. Specific questions asked respondents to compare the efficacy of the NWEA assessment with the state-mandated assessment. The comparison was expected to provide a better understanding of the possible impact of substituting an assessment similar to the NWEA assessment for current state-mandated assessments.

In-depth interviews were selected over surveys primarily because surveys do not permit follow-up questions to clarify exactly what is intended by each response. While random sampling is desirable, surveys are not necessarily the answer because even with the most sophisticated survey strategies, the response rate is unlikely to be much higher than the 33% rate achieved in a recent nationwide survey (Pedulla et al., 2003). With a low response rate, response bias is almost certainly a problem, negating the value of the random sample. In-person interviews may be more representative because the response rate is much higher—100% in the present study. While fewer participants can be sampled, the results may be more valid, accurate, detailed, and useful because follow-up questions were possible.

Table 3.1. Distribution of sample.

Interviewees	District Type				
	Large Urban	Small Urban	Suburban	Rural	*Total*
Superintendent	1	1	1	1	4
Director of Testing	1	[a]	1	[a]	2
Principal or Ass't Principal	3	2[b]	3	3	11
Elementary School Teacher					
Regular	3	3	4	4	14
Special education	1	1	1	0	3
Middle School Teacher		[a]			
Math	1		1	3[c]	5
Language arts	1		1	3[c]	5
Science	0		1	3[c]	4
Special education	2		0	1	3
High School Teacher					
Math	1	2[c]	1	1	5
Language arts	1	2[c]	1	2	6
Science/social studies	2	0	1	1	4
Special education	0	1	1	0	2

[a] Not employed here.
[b] Single middle/high school.
[c] Teachers teach multiple subjects.

Analysis

Interviews were transcribed and coded to identify primary themes. The themes were identified jointly by two raters and cross-checked by a third researcher. Discrepancies were resolved through discussion.

RESULTS

Four themes dominated interviewee responses about the state-mandated tests: 1) concern that inadequate diagnostic information prevented teachers from using the results to improve instruction, 2) concern that delays in reporting state-mandated test results prevented teachers from using the results to improve instruction, 3) concern about lack of information about growth in student performance (lack of baseline information about student performance prevented teachers from using test results to target instruction, and lack of growth information prevented administrators from taking into account student growth when making accountability decisions about schools), and 4) concern that tests designed for average students were not appropriate for low-achieving or high-achieving students.

Four themes dominated interviewee responses about the computer-adaptive tests. These themes mirrored the concerns interviewees expressed about the state-mandated tests. But since the computer-adaptive tests addressed those concerns, interviewees were extremely positive about incorporating the computer-adaptive features and technology into state-mandated tests. The four themes were: 1) the adaptive tests provided much more diagnostic information that teachers could use to inform instruction, 2) the adaptive test results were reported much more quickly than the state-mandated test results, sometimes the same day the test was administered, and were therefore more useful for improving instruction, 3) the adaptive tests provided information about growth in student progress—teachers used the baseline information to target instruction, and teachers felt the use of growth information would be more accurate and fair as an indicator for accountability purposes, and 4) the adaptive tests were much more appropriate for low-achieving and high-achieving students, since the level of difficulty was adjusted for each student.

State-Mandated Tests: Inadequate Information and Reporting Delays

Overall, 91.8% of interviewees expressed major concerns about inadequate diagnostic information. Test results were not broken down by type of problem or instructional objective, and therefore teachers lacked the information needed to identify and address particular areas of student weakness. Furthermore, results were typically organized and reported by the previous year's classrooms, making the results marginally useful to teachers as they looked back and considered areas of instruction needing improvement, but of no use to teachers seeking to understand the weaknesses of their current students and how those weaknesses might be addressed.

Interviewees weighed the cost of state-mandated testing in terms of the time it took away from instruction. They felt that current state tests did not provide the type of diagnostic information that would be useful in designing curriculum and instruction—information that might justify the cost. Interviewees complained that test results were reported in a way that did not provide diagnostically useful information that would help to identify specific areas where students performed poorly and where teachers needed to improve their instruction. Interviewees wanted much more specific information, such as an item analysis, rather than the vague subscores that were reported to them. Without this information, they were at a loss as to how to improve instruction. A principal in a semirural middle school described the dilemma:

> They don't break it down so we know what we need to do for that one child . . . that's real frustrating. They need to be more diagnostic. With the MCAs, there isn't any item analysis. We can say, "Oops, we have a problem in literal comprehension," but what kind of a problem do we have? Or "literary passages," what does that really tell us? It doesn't really tell us anything that we have found to be useful.

Although test-makers point out that improving the diagnostic capability of a test usually requires increasing its length, interviewees indicated that they would support longer tests if the tests provided more diagnostic information. A principal in an urban elementary school felt so strongly about this that he and his staff pieced together elements of different assessments and created an assessment system completely separate from the state test that provides detailed diagnostic information on 43 skills, tracked from kindergarten through grade 6:

> [The state-mandated test] needs to be diagnostic. . . . You spend so much money . . . they could have had this done [by now] . . . If they want to really tell us what we're doing wrong and right, then they need to start at kindergarten and tell us what needs to be taught, what needs to be tested. This is a really simple answer but no one seems to be doing it. It's not a hard thing; it's not rocket science.

By saying that "it's not rocket science," this interviewee indicated his belief that it is feasible, practical, and desirable to make the state-mandated test more diagnostically useful. All interviewees unanimously agreed that while the stated purpose of the state-mandated system is *accountability*, the system would be much more useful and effective in achieving accountability if it provided more diagnostically useful information. While measurement specialists typically reply that this is not feasible or practical, the widespread use of computer-adaptive tests at the district level suggests that it is indeed feasible and practical to implement more diagnostically useful state-mandated tests.

Overall, 50.8% of interviewees expressed concern about slow reporting of state test results, which prevents teachers from using the data to improve instruction. Tests were typically administered in March or April, but results were sometimes not received until teachers returned in September. A superintendent in a semirural district felt so strongly about this that she wrote a letter to the state legislature. Interviewees explained that state-mandated assessments, as currently designed, do not provide rapid feedback to teachers. They identified rapid feedback as key to the use of test results to improve instruction. A superintendent in an urban school district argued that:

> If you really wanted to impact somebody during the year that you had them, you would do the assessment early on, you'd get the feedback fast, and then teachers could use some of the data to say, "Here's how my class falls out and here's how I want to rearrange my instruction to deal with that." . . . I think that the key piece is feedback as quickly as possible.

Adaptive Tests: Diagnostic Information and Faster Results

Is it feasible to design a state-mandated test that provides rapid feedback of diagnostic information to teachers? Responses of interviewees who used adaptive tests suggest that the answer is "yes." Interviewees were asked to compare the adaptive tests with the state-mandated tests. Interviewees were impressed by the diagnostic capability and the unusually quick reporting capacity of the adaptive tests—results were reported within 1 to 2 days.

All (100%) of the interviewees emphasized the importance of rapid feedback of diagnostic information. An assistant superintendent in a suburban school district explained: "The [adaptive test] does a great job meeting our purposes, of giving instant feedback, diagnostic and growth [information]." A 5th-grade teacher in an urban elementary school said: "Another strength [of the adaptive test] is that the results are back to us that day. As soon as the student is done taking it, we have the results in front of us." A 3rd-grade teacher in an urban elementary school wished that the state test provided the same rapid diagnostic capability:

> I do find it valuable and I do use the information from the [adaptive test] to . . . say, "Okay, a good percentage of our students are not scoring well in reading a table or in reading a graph and making [it]," so we're able to adjust our teaching. If that could be done with the state test then it would be valuable.

The reason the adaptive tests were more useful is because the scores were broken down into subscores that were more specific than subscores from the state test. An elementary school principal in a suburban district explained:

> The [adaptive test] has strands in it, so I can break the test down in the math strands and say, "It's really his number sense that this child really fell down on in this test," or whatever . . . that's more of a useful diagnostic tool to me than waiting for the spring MCAs. . . . I'd rather do the [adaptive test] and not have to do the MCAs. . . . Generally speaking, the MCAs are not something that I tend to use to design instruction very much.

Interviewees directly compared the adaptive tests with the state-mandated tests and concluded that the immediate feedback from the adaptive tests made them much more useful for improving instruction. An elementary principal in a suburban school district described the advantage:

> I like the adaptive tests a lot. The nice thing is that a kid takes it today, finishes it, I have the results tomorrow. That's a real advantage—I don't have to wait. We took these [MCAs] two weeks ago . . . We won't get the results until July. Everybody's gone . . . So I like the idea of computer-adaptive tests.

State-Mandated Tests: No Growth Information

For several reasons, almost all interviewees (96.7%) agreed that state tests should be designed to deliver information about individual growth in student achievement, rather than simply reporting whether students met a given proficiency level. First, it is unfair to judge schools according to fixed proficiency levels of achievement because test results reflect the socioeconomic background of students as much as they reflect the quality of instruction. Measures of growth would address this issue, since schools with predominately low socioeconomic student populations could demonstrate growth in achievement even if many students do not achieve at the same level as more affluent peers. Second, student performance varies from cohort to cohort. Measures of individual growth would account for these differences. Third, a test designed to measure growth would be administered annually and could be designed to provide diagnostic information needed by teachers at the beginning of each year to identify and address areas where students are weak. The feasibility of this approach is demonstrated by schools that administered the adaptive test, which is designed to measure individual growth in student achievement.

Interviewees complained that the state-mandated tests were not designed to provide information about growth in student achievement, either psychometrically or in regard to the way test results were reported. A principal in an urban middle school talked about the problem of calculating growth when data are reported for successive cohorts, rather than following each cohort over time:

> If you look at the MBST, it's made to measure where a particular student is at a particular point but it is not made to measure how we as a school are doing this year as opposed to last year, because it's a different group of students that you're testing. So you're not measuring growth. You have a different group of kids; obviously they're going to test differently.

Teachers wanted to have the type of information about growth in student performance that would be obtained through pretest and posttest measures at the beginning and end of the school year. This information could be used for student placement decisions, as well as to evaluate the effectiveness of instructional interventions. When asked, "Would you like to have pretest and posttest measures of student academic growth, if test results are available within 7 days?" a Title I reading coordinator in an urban middle school was extremely enthusiastic about this possibility:

> Yes! Of course! And in 7 days? I don't know; can that be done? Yes, we would love that. Right now, we're looking at some reading interventions, and if we could screen all the 5th-graders we can just plug them right in to the intervention program. Whereas now, we don't get their scores right away and we waste a lot of time.

A 2nd-grade teacher in an urban elementary school suggested that it would be helpful if this capability were built into the state test:

> Well finally! What a great idea. I think that's the way assessments are supposed to be used. We need to assess what you don't know, let's teach you, now let's find out what you have retained and learned, and here's what you know. Guess what? What you don't know, we're going to come back and finish teaching you. That makes a lot of sense.

Teachers believed that the use of pretests and posttests would help them to focus instruction effectively throughout the school year. Teachers also felt that measuring growth in student achievement would be a fair way to increase accountability, both for students and for teachers. This suggests that teachers are not opposed to accountability as long as it is implemented in a way that they consider to be fair. A 4th-grade teacher in a semirural elementary school supported the use of test scores for diagnostic and accountability purposes:

> Yes, definitely. Because then you know where your job lies, what things you need to cover. . . . I think pretesting, posttesting would be great. It's accountability for kids, it's accountability for teachers.

Currently, state-mandated test results fluctuate from year to year because the results measure different cohorts of students who vary in ability. The tests are not designed to measure the progress of each cohort of students as they progress from grade to grade. This creates invalid indications of progress. Educators were opposed to the use of this type of indicator for teacher and school accountability purposes. A superintendent in an urban school district explained the problem:

> The way in which the assessments are currently reported makes it difficult to know if kids are really making progress, because the state-mandated tests are looking at different cohorts of kids. And so, one year it looks like you've done a phenomenal job, you move up several points, and the next year, it looks like everybody went to sleep at the wheel, without recognition that the next cohort of kids may have entered with English barriers or other kinds of problems.

Adaptive Tests: Measures of Individual Growth

By measuring growth in student performance, adaptive tests provide an indicator of progress, whereas current state-mandated tests only indicate the level of achievement. Students can demonstrate growth even if their absolute level of performance is low. At the same time, measures of growth can reveal problems that are not apparent through measures of absolute performance. By providing measures of individual growth as well as measures of absolute achievement, adaptive tests provide more accurate, valid, and useful information for both educational improvement and accountability. Of the interviewees who used the adaptive tests, all (100%) agreed that they provided useful measures of student growth. For example, an elementary school principal in a suburban district described the advantage:

> With the [adaptive test], I can measure growth [and] find problems in my school. . . . Last year one of the things I found is that only 30% of

my 2nd-grade kids made their growth goals in math. . . . The adaptive tests demonstrated what I suspected. I think the adaptive tests are much more useful to me as a building administrator than the MCAs are.

Educators argued that measures of individual academic growth were more accurate and valid for the purpose of evaluating the effectiveness of instruction, grouping methods, and educational interventions, and facilitate early intervention so that teachers, parents, and students have enough time to make whatever changes are necessary to improve student achievement before students face the exit exam. An assistant superintendent in a suburban district explained:

> I think [growth is] a better measure of the effectiveness of your system. . . . We took this student from point A to C. I think the beauty of the adaptive test is not just for the kids who are challenged academically, but what we've found on the high end is that our 4th-graders were not making adequate progress. So, [we asked], what is it in our instruction, grouping methods, or teacher training that is not creating that growth opportunity? I think [the adaptive test] works on both ends for us . . . we now have a history of each child, we know, starting in 2nd grade to 3rd grade, that the child made X amount of progress on the test. And we're able to diagnose: did the interventions work? But with the [state-mandated test] it's a test at a point in time. The adaptive test is a predictor, [scores are] correlated to your chances of passing the [state graduation test]. So I think there's a fair amount of power in that for families, which gives you the grace of time leading up to that to say, "What can I do to affect my child's chances?"

State-Mandated Test: One Level of Difficulty

The state-mandated test is difficult and frustrating for low-achieving children because the test's level of difficulty is geared to average children. All of the interviewees (100%) agreed that this was a problem and undermined support for testing among teachers. Furthermore, the validity of the test results is undermined when children become so frustrated that they give up. While special education teachers feel that there are benefits when their students participate in testing because it provides goals and because the students feel good about being included with their peers, they are concerned about the impact of a test that is too difficult for their students.

Teachers described devastating effects on student self-esteem. According to teachers, low-achieving students felt embarrassed and humiliated by the state-mandated tests. A 2nd-grade teacher in an urban elementary school described the effects:

> If you test a student who is a low achiever with the same measurement that you give to others, any person would know that self-esteem would bottom out in that child. A low-achieving student thinks, "This is a second grade assessment and I can't do it?" I'd be angry, embarrassed, sad—same as an adult would when asked to do something they couldn't do.

Teachers were extremely disturbed by the degree of frustration felt by low-achieving students. Teachers felt that it was unfair and unreasonable to expect students to struggle through a long test with no support, and the testing experience threatened to undermine everything that teachers have done throughout the year to build up their students' self-esteem and confidence. A 5th-grade math teacher in a suburban elementary school described the frustration that students felt and his own response:

> For [some] students, it is sheer frustration for 5 days. And it is absolutely impossible to not feel sympathetic, because they're so frustrated. And short of them having an extreme disability, they're expected to take the whole test for the whole time with no support. It's very difficult to watch a student go through that. Because [it undermines] everything that you've done during the year to help improve their self-esteem. . . . Some of those kids, if you talk to them after the test, you know that they're just shocked. They'll say, "I didn't understand it. I didn't understand any of those problems."

Teachers linked poor student attitudes and behavior to student beliefs that they won't pass the state test. Teachers believed that the test, as currently designed, had negative effects on students' self-esteem. An 8th-grade teacher in an urban high school explained:

> I've had a few students who have basically had horrible attitudes in my class and when I finally get a chance to talk with them one on one, I find out it's because of this test. I've had students who [are] just very negative because they're starting off with the idea that there's no way they'll pass. . . . I definitely believe it affects the low-functioning students. I think it affects their sense of self-worth.

Teachers observed that low-achieving students gave up and did not attempt to finish the state-mandated test because the problems were too difficult or the text was too difficult to read. This threatens the validity of the test results, which are scored on the assumption that students did their best to answer the items correctly. An 8th-grade math teacher in an urban high school described his observations:

> I would say particularly with low-functioning students they don't even choose to try. . . . Low-functioning students generally can't read, or have very low reading skills. So, they are going to look at a word problem and say, "I'm not going to get this anyway." When I give a practice test I would say probably 10 students per test will just go through and bubble in whatever answer. They'll be done with the test in five minutes, because they figure, "I'm not going to be able to pass it anyway so who cares."

Special education teachers supported the basic idea of testing their students because the goal of passing the test provides a tangible incentive. However, the teachers were also concerned that the test was too difficult for their students and discouraged them. A special education teacher in an urban high school described her ambivalent feelings:

> I think it's positive, looking at it as a special ed teacher. [It is] an incentive, a reality check, a goal. . . . [But] for some of my kids it's an unattainable goal. We can modify the passing percentage that's required. . . . But that modification becomes ridiculous when I'm modifying the passing percent to 30%. I had a senior girl take the math test seven times. Then I start to think, how does this make this child feel? I could have told you before test one that this was unattainable even at a 30% mark. [On the other hand] it's been a good thing, because it's been a standard, an expectation, a goal. It makes them feel good because they feel, "I'm just like everybody else, I have to take this," and in that way it's a good thing for those kids.

Adaptive Tests Adapt to Each Student

Computer-adaptive tests adjust the difficulty level of the test to each student. Teachers believed the adaptive technology reduced the frustration felt by low-achieving students, increasing the probability of completing the test and improving test validity. At the same time, the tests provided more challenging and interesting questions for high-achieving students, generating diagnostic information that helped teachers to identify areas where those students needed help. Thus, the use of adaptive tests helped teachers to meet the needs of all students. Teachers also appreciated that the adaptive test only took 2 days to administer, compared to the 2-week disruption of classes for the state-mandated test. From the teacher's perspective, this is a major advantage since they may be asked to administer several tests within the 9-month school year. All (100%) of the teachers who used the computer-adaptive test agreed that it provided a much better experience for low-achieving children because it adjusts the difficulty of the test items for each student. For example, a 5th- and 6th-grade special education teacher in an urban elementary school compared the effect of the state test and the effect of the adaptive test on her students:

> [For low-achieving children, the state-mandated test] is a reminder that they are failing, that they aren't up to standard, which they already know. . . . I just think that it affects their self-esteem in a negative way. . . . [The adaptive test] is much better—much, much better. The kids don't come out of it with such a feeling of failure. A much better experience.

A 5th-grade teacher in an urban elementary school explained:

> I like the adaptive test. . . . I like the fact that they have a better chance of answering questions at their ability. . . . There are kids at a 2nd-grade reading level in my class taking a 5th-grade MCA test and they feel, "Why don't I know that stuff?" They are hard on themselves about it. Whereas if the test is adapting to their level, they can at least answer some of them successfully and feel, "I did fine."

An 8th-grade math teacher in an urban high school thought that the adaptive feature addressed a major motivational barrier for many students:

> I think [computer-adaptive testing] would be a great idea. That way, students would be able to find more success. I think a lot of the problem, especially in math, is that students have found no success throughout their whole schooling. . . . So if they were given an opportunity where, "Okay, you didn't quite understand this question, so we'll give you one that's a little bit easier," and allow them to be successful, I think that would help a lot. If I didn't feel successful in something, I would never want to do it. So if they could find success, that would be wonderful.

A 3rd-grade teacher in a suburban district felt that adaptive tests provide a more valid indicator of achievement:

[In regard to the state test], if they struggle with reading, if they struggle with phonics, they stress out, and they say, "Forget it. I can't read this. I'm not going to do it." . . . Because the state test is for the average 3rd-grader. Some of these kids are [far below] 3rd-grade level; some of these kids are way beyond 3rd-grade level. [Whereas the computer-adaptive] test adjusts to their level and I think that's more accurate.

A 5th-grade teacher in an urban elementary school framed the validity issue in terms of her sense of an appropriate test:

When I look at the questions that the students are receiving on the adaptive test, I see that they're questions that are being taught, are being covered, and I know that those questions are either getting progressively harder for those students that need to be challenged more, or they are getting easier for those students that are struggling. To me, that is a very appropriate test.

Finally, teachers felt that the adaptive test would take less time away from instruction because it is more efficient than standard tests. A special education teacher in a suburban school district explained:

I feel the adaptive test is much better. . . . I think the fact that it's on a computer, kids think it's more fun. They do it starting in 2nd-grade and they do it every year. It doesn't take 2 weeks' worth of time to take it; it may take 2 days to take the whole thing. That was a huge issue with the [state-mandated] testing. I had to basically cancel [instruction for] all of my kids, K–5, just to do the [test] accommodations and to get my special ed kids to take the MCAs. That was a huge sacrifice and I feel like I'm still catching up from it because it puts all the kids on hold.

DISCUSSION

In this study, teachers and administrators described four major problems with Minnesota's state-mandated tests: 1) lack of diagnostic information, 2) reporting delays, 3) lack of information about individual growth in student progress, and 4) a single level of difficulty that is inappropriate for low-achieving and high-achieving students. These issues undermined the ability of the state-mandated tests to provide useful information to teachers and administrators about areas that need attention.

It is important to note that these problems are not limited to Minnesota's tests. The researcher noted the same problems during interviews with approximately 100 administrators and teachers in Michigan, Massachusetts, and Kansas, and the same problems have been noted by other researchers as well (Clarke et al., 2003; Corbett & Wilson, 1991; Gordon & Reese, 1997; O'Day, 2004; Pedulla et al., 2003; M. L. Smith, 1991; Smith & Rottenberg, 1991). These problems appear to be systemic due to the limitations of current paper-and-pencil tests. The Minnesota results are merely illustrative of these problems.

Teachers suggested that test results should be used to diagnose and address areas of weakness. This would require redesigning the state tests to provide more diagnostic information and to provide it quickly. According to teachers, a diagnostic approach that provides rapid results would greatly reduce their concerns about testing. This approach would address many teacher concerns and could be expected to increase the value of test results. Teachers interviewed for this research study were favorably impressed by the diagnostic capability and the unusually quick reporting capacity of the adaptive tests—in some instances, results can be available to teachers within seconds. From the teacher's perspective, this is a major advantage.

For several reasons, interviewees agreed that state tests should be designed to deliver information about growth in student achievement, rather than simply reporting whether students met a given proficiency level. First, it is unfair to judge schools solely according to fixed proficiency levels of achievement because test results reflect the socioeconomic background of students as much as they reflect the quality of instruction. Measures of longitudinal growth for individual students would address this issue, since schools with predominately low-socioeconomic-status student populations could demonstrate growth in achievement even if many students do not achieve at the same level as more affluent peers. Second, student performance varies from cohort to cohort. Measures of individual growth would account for these differences. Third, a test designed to measure growth would be administered annually and could be designed to provide diagnostic information needed by teachers at the beginning of each year to identify and address areas where students are weak (see note 3 in this chapter).

The frustration that low-achieving children encounter when taking standardized tests has received little attention. But this issue undermines support for testing among teachers, as well as undermining the validity of the test results when children become so frustrated that they give up. While computer-adaptive tests would address this issue, the U.S. Department of Education prohibits the use of fully adaptive tests for NCLB reporting purposes,[5] apparently assuming that only a fixed test can provide scores for every student on the same scale. However, modern testing technology provides a method for determining how students perform relative to each other, even when they take computer-adaptive tests. The use of adaptive tests would help teachers to meet the needs of all students. Given that some students may be frustrated by a test that is meant to be challenging and foster teaching to high standards, it may be important to design tests in such a way that the difficulty level is adjusted to each student. Such tests may also reduce pressure to narrow the curriculum by challenging all students at a range of difficulty levels, rather than focusing the attention of 8th-grade teachers on the minimum competency level of the basic standards test. This could help to avoid a watered-down curriculum for advanced students.

It might be argued that significant improvements in the design or implementation of state-mandated tests would be expensive and impractical. However, over 1000 school districts across the country have voluntarily purchased adaptive tests that incorporate many characteristics desired by teachers. This investment indicates a judgment that the advantages of those tests outweigh not only their financial costs but also the possible disadvantages of using multiple-choice tests. Districts that have purchased and adopted the adaptive tests evidently believe that the benefits outweigh the costs. Therefore, it appears that computer-adaptive tests demonstrate an attractive alternative that addresses several problems with current state-mandated tests.

Another argument is that the role of state-mandated tests should be limited to accountability. However, teachers, principals, and superintendents interviewed for this study overwhelmingly wanted the state test to deliver diagnostic information that would allow them to identify and address areas of weakness by improving curriculum and instruction. Interviewees repeatedly questioned the value of testing unless it provides diagnostic information. It is difficult to see how state-mandated testing can have a positive influence on curriculum and instruction if the intended users—teachers, principals, and superintendents—find the test results to be of little use.

Currently, the U.S. Department of Education bans computer-adaptive testing for accountability purposes, requiring instead that all students within each state receive exactly the same test items in order to ensure that every school's performance is judged on a common scale (Trotter, 2003). In spite of the department's position, testing experts agree that computer-adaptive tests can individualize testing while meeting the department's requirement to provide information about achievement on a common scale (Trotter, 2003).

The department's position is especially puzzling because nonadaptive tests are much less accurate (technically, "precise") than adaptive tests, for any student whose performance is either above or below average (Weiss, 2004). In essence, the department's rejection of adaptive testing ensures that measurements for "non-average" students are less accurate, less fair, and less useful than scores for average students.[6] In contrast, adaptive tests measure all students with the same degree of accuracy and the scores are equally fair and useful.

The main recommendation for the U.S. Department of Education is to lift the prohibition against the use of computer-adaptive tests for NCLB accountability purposes, allowing states to use computer-adaptive tests that adjust the difficulty of test items for each test-taker while providing information about achievement on a constant scale, more diagnostic information, measures of longitudinal growth, and quick results. The department should also provide resources to implement computerized testing.

CONCLUSION

The design of current state-mandated tests assumes that the role of state-mandated tests should be limited to accountability rather than diagnosis, and that the tests can foster improved student achievement by providing information about general *subject* areas where improvement is needed, rather than specific *topics*. The assumption is that the responsibility to diagnose specific areas of weakness should be allocated to local district- and school-level assessments.

The evidence presented in this chapter suggests that these assumptions are incorrect. According to teachers and administrators, state-mandated tests are only useful and only assist teachers to improve instruction if the tests provide diagnostic information and information about individual student growth, are adjusted in difficulty for each student, and provide assessment information rapidly so that it can be used to improve instruction. If so, the basic assumptions underlying NCLB are flawed and it is unlikely that NCLB will achieve the improvements in student achievement that are desired.

However, additional evidence presented in this chapter suggests a possible solution to this problem: a proven type of test that uses computer technology to adjust the difficulty of the questions presented to each student, thereby reducing the frustration felt by low-achieving students. Computer-adaptive tests are much more efficient than regular standardized tests, allowing them to provide more diagnostic information (Wainer, 1993). They are also designed to provide the type of information about student growth that is desired by many teachers and school administrators, and deliver the results on demand—quickly enough to be used to improve instruction. Computer-adaptive tests offer a potential solution to problems that cause many teachers to oppose testing.

Inexplicably, federal policy bans the use of computer-adaptive tests for NCLB purposes—the type of test that arguably would be the most helpful to teachers and administrators and most likely to help improve student achievement. This chapter strongly recommends that federal policy should be changed and the federal government should allow the type of computer-adaptive test design that is currently banned.

This chapter has provided specific recommendations to address four critical concerns about current state-mandated tests that undermine their usefulness. The potential of the standards and testing movement to exert a positive influence on teaching and learning is likely to be undermined to the extent that the following issues are not addressed: lack of diagnostic information, slow reporting of results and inappropriate format, lack of individual growth information, and lack of computer-adaptive features that ensure that students receive test forms at appropriate levels. The recommendations in this chapter would address these concerns and could be implemented if the U.S. Department of Education relaxed its prohibition against computer-adaptive tests.

Unless these concerns are addressed, there is a risk that the growing backlash against testing will cause educators to abandon efforts to implement high standards. This point has been expressed forcefully with regard to Kentucky's KIRIS testing program:

> As teachers begin to realize that the test has no legitimacy and that it is too technically deficient to be influenced by how they teach, they will stop paying attention to it. . . . Measurement driven instruction does not work when teachers fail to see the connection between measurement and instruction. (Cunningham, as cited in Mehrens, 1998, p. 20)

4

Less Narrowing

The evidence presented in chapter 3 suggests that a relatively simple change—allowing states to use computer-adaptive tests—could reduce stress on students as well as strengthen the signals that help teachers to diagnose student difficulties. This change would affect almost every student and teacher. By reducing stress on students and helping to make test results useful to teachers, computer-adaptive testing could help to address some of the key objections to NCLB.

However, another objection is more basic. Critics charge that high-stakes testing compels the use of multiple-choice standardized tests that may be fundamentally incompatible with high-quality instruction. These critics charge that high-stakes testing narrows the curriculum and causes teachers to "teach to the test." This concern is unlikely to be addressed simply by switching to computer-adaptive state-mandated tests. Therefore, a critical question is whether it is possible to avoid excessive narrowing of the curriculum in a high-stakes testing environment. Can this be achieved with state tests that rely primarily on a multiple-choice format? Is it really possible for multiple-choice tests to be well aligned with instruction if teachers wish to emphasize critical thinking?

This chapter presents evidence from a case study of Minnesota that high-stakes standardized tests and high-quality instruction are not necessarily incompatible. This chapter examines the characteristics of Minnesota's testing program that appear to reduce unintended narrowing of the curriculum, suggesting that other states could minimize narrowing by redesigning their testing programs along Minnesota's model. Surprisingly, it appears that multiple-choice tests are not necessarily inconsistent with instruction that emphasizes critical thinking when the tests are well-aligned with the intended curriculum and pressure on teachers is low.

....

Initial estimates are that 80 to 90% of all schools receiving Title I funds may be found "in need of improvement" by the federal government and subject to NCLB sanctions (Bracey, 2002). A concern is that this type of high-stakes testing may be fundamentally flawed, that it may narrow the intended curriculum—defined as the knowledge, skills, and habits of thought teachers believe are important for students to learn—causing teachers to "teach to the test" (McNeil, 2000). This concern is supported by a recent study, based on a nationally representative sample of school districts, which reported that 71% of the districts shifted instructional time to reading and mathematics from at least one other subject (Center on Education Policy, 2006).

However, narrowing of the curriculum may not always be undesirable (Smith & O'Day, 1991). Alignment of state standards, tests, curriculum, and professional development may be necessary to ensure that students are taught and tested on the content and skills they are expected to know and be able to do. Well-designed tests could help teachers to identify and address areas of weakness, improving the quality of instruction as well as providing accountability information. It may be reasonable to narrow the curriculum by focusing teachers' efforts and emphasizing topics that are valued (Smith & O'Day, 1991). This reasoning has engendered broad support and a decade of bipartisan legislative initiatives culminating in NCLB (Jennings, 2000). Whatever its flaws, NCLB seems unlikely to be repealed (Elmore, 2004). Currently, however, there is an opportunity to modify the legislation and its implementation to reduce unintended negative consequences. The focus of this chapter is to understand what can be done to avoid unintended, negative consequences due to narrowing of the curriculum in a high-stakes testing environment.

In Minnesota, high-stakes testing was implemented in 1998 and diplomas were withheld from students who failed the state Basic Standards Test (BST) beginning in 2000 (sample tests and items are available at http://education.state.mn.us/mde/Accountability_Programs/Assessment_and_Testing/Assessments/index.html). Surprisingly, however, an overwhelming 85% of Minnesota teachers support the state's exit exam (Draper, 2000). It is important to understand what may contribute to these positive views. It is unlikely that teachers would support the exit exam if they believed that it forced them to eliminate valuable chunks of the curriculum. If teachers in Minnesota do not feel pressure to narrow the curriculum in a way that reduces educational quality, it is important to understand their reasoning. This reasoning is likely to explain their choices about what to teach in their classrooms—choices that ultimately determine the extent to which the curriculum may or may not be narrowed. If we understand their reasoning, perhaps we can understand the conditions under which the curriculum may be narrowed—and how excessive narrowing can be avoided. The study reported below suggests that the unique design of Minnesota's testing program may be well aligned with teachers' expert judgment about what should be emphasized. This design may contribute to teacher satisfaction with high-stakes testing, and may provide lessons about how to implement high-stakes testing in a way that minimizes unwanted narrowing of the curriculum.

FOUR CONCERNS

There are four main concerns related to narrowing of the curriculum and the fear that improved test scores merely reflect teaching to the test, rather than broad gains in learning. One concern is that non-tested subjects, such as art, may be deemphasized (McNeil, 2000; McNeil & Valenzuela, 2000; M. L. Smith, 1991; Smith & Rottenberg, 1991). This might be addressed by requiring schools to provide elective or required instruction in those areas.

A second concern is that even within tested subjects, particular topics or skills not included on the test may be deemphasized (McNeil, 2000; McNeil & Valenzuela, 2000; M. L. Smith, 1991; Smith & Rottenberg, 1991). This might be addressed by ensuring that the most important topics and skills are covered by the state-mandated test.

A third concern is that testing narrows curriculum and instruction to memorization of bits of factual knowledge (McNeil, 2000; McNeil & Valenzuela, 2000; M. L. Smith, 1991; Smith & Rottenberg, 1991). This may occur if state curriculum standards and tests aligned to those standards attempt to cover too much factual knowledge. An unanticipated consequence is that teachers may feel it is necessary to drill students on the universe of factual items that may appear on the test, in the hope that students will correctly answer those items that actually appear. Addressing this issue may require changes in state curriculum standards as well as the state test.

A fourth concern is that testing may cause teachers to spend excessive time on test-taking tricks and strategies that have little value outside the testing situation (McNeil, 2000; McNeil & Valenzuela, 2000; M. L. Smith, 1991; Smith & Rottenberg, 1991). For example, students may be taught to make sure that bubble sheets are correctly completed. This issue might be addressed through tests designed to minimize unwanted trickiness.

The first concern might be addressed through policy and the last concern might be addressed through proper test design. The focus of this chapter is the second and third concerns: the construct underrepresentation that occurs when tests only assess aspects of the intended curriculum that are easy to measure (Baker & Linn, 2004). The question is whether it is indeed possible to design and implement large-scale assessments, suitable for state-mandated testing, that are properly aligned with the curriculum in order to reinforce intended learning outcomes (Linn, 2004; Rothman, 2004). A review of state-mandated tests and state curriculum standards found that while there is superficial alignment of test content with state curriculum standards in many states, a more careful analysis suggests that lack of alignment may indeed be a problem (Rothman, 2004; Rothman, Slattery, Vranek, & Resnick, 2002).

KEY RESEARCH FINDINGS

Two reviews of research found that in some cases—but not others—state-mandated tests narrow the curriculum (Cimbricz, 2002; Mehrens, 1998). To a certain extent, variation in findings reflect individual-, school-, and district-level differences in experiences, training, and attitudes with regard to high-stakes testing (Cimbricz, 2002; Grant, 2000). Some individuals have positive attitudes, feeling that testing can be used to diagnose and address weaknesses, and are well-trained to use test results in this way (Massell, 2001). Others have negative attitudes and are not trained or have little experience in using test results for formative purposes. A path model suggests that both teacher attitudes and professional development mediate the effects of testing programs on instructional practices (Pomplun, 1997). However, it seems unlikely that all of the variation in outcomes is due to individual differences. Each state has control over the design and implementation of its state test, and it seems likely that those decisions systematically influence the degree to which the curriculum is narrowed. Unfortunately, existing research does not provide a strong basis for specifying exactly what factors or conditions are important.

Stake Levels

A common supposition is that differences in stake levels explain variation in outcomes. It is hypothesized that low stake levels are associated with little or no narrowing, while high stakes are associated with greater pressure on teachers and more narrowing of the curriculum. There is some evidence in support of this hypothesis. During a period of low stakes, when the results of state-mandated tests were rarely tied to decisions about student promotion or graduation, or threats to reorganize schools, Porter, Floden, Freeman, Schmidt, and Schwille (1986, p. 11) concluded that: "Another myth exposed as being only a half truth is that teachers teach topics that are tested. Little evidence exists to support the supposition that national norm-referenced, standardized tests administered once a year have any important influence on teachers' content decisions." Kuhs et al. (1985) concluded that Michigan teachers' topic selection was not significantly influenced by the state minimum competencies test or the district-used standardized tests.

In contrast, several studies of Texas's high-stakes testing program concluded that preparing students for state-mandated tests narrows the curriculum (Gordon & Reese, 1997; Haney, 2000; Hoffman et al., 1999; McNeil & Valenzuela, 2000). Smith and Rottenberg's (1991) study of two elementary schools in Arizona also concluded that high-stakes testing causes narrowing of the curriculum as teachers align instruction with test content (Smith & Rottenberg, 1991).

However, high stake levels do not always result in narrowing of the curriculum. Grant (2001) compared the teaching of two high school teachers in New York, where passing the state Regents exams entitled students to a prestigious Regents diploma, and passing the easier Regents Competency Test was necessary to obtain a regular diploma. In this high-stakes situation, Grant found little direct influence of testing on content or pedagogical decision-making and concluded instead that the teachers' personal beliefs governed their teaching (see Grant, 2000, 2001). Similarly, a study of Kentucky's reform efforts concluded that teachers' responses to these efforts in four exemplary schools were shaped by the participants' shared vision of curriculum and commitment to children, rather than by high-stakes testing (Wolf, Borko, Elliott, & McIver, 2000). Notably, in both of these cases, it could be argued that while stakes were high, pressure on teachers was low. In New York, students who failed the Regents exams were not denied a diploma as long as they passed the minimum-competency Regents Competency Test. And in the four exemplary Kentucky schools, it appears that strong administrative leadership deflected pressure from teachers and strong teaching served to raise test scores and allay parent concerns. In other words, effective teaching may have reduced the number of students who failed the state-mandated test and reduced pressure to narrow the curriculum.

Performance-Based and Portfolio Assessments

If individual differences and differences in stake levels do not adequately explain variation in the impact of state-mandated tests, what about characteristics of the tests themselves? Some researchers suggest that multiple-choice tests are inherently poorly aligned with sound teaching practices, causing teachers to "dumb down" their instruction (McNeil 2000; McNeil & Valenzuela, 2000; M. L. Smith, 1991; Smith & Rottenberg, 1991). It has been suggested that performance-based or portfolio assessments are more likely to shape instruction in desirable ways, to encourage teaching that promotes active learning, compared to multiple-choice assessments, and to avoid negative narrowing of the curriculum (Baron & Wolf, 1996; Rothman, 1995). In principle, well-designed performance-based and portfolio assessments could be aligned with sound teaching practices and would provide information about student progress regarding important basic and critical thinking skills that teachers would use to improve instruction.

However, the evidence reviewed in chapter 2 suggests that performance- and portfolio-based assessments are unlikely to be panaceas for negative consequences of testing (Firestone, Mayrowetz, & Fairman, 1998; Koretz et al., 1994, 1996; Mehrens, 1998; Smith et al., 1997). To the extent that it occurs, narrowing of the curriculum may happen independently of the format of the test (Haney & Madaus, 1989; Mehrens, 1998). Thus, it may be fruitful to search for factors other than the test's format that influence the manner and degree to which state-mandated tests narrow the curriculum.

....

Minnesota provides an instructive case study. Using interview methods, the following research questions were addressed:

1. What are the views of teachers and administrators in the four Minnesota districts regarding state-mandated testing?
2. In what ways does Minnesota's state-mandated testing program influence teacher and administrator choices about what is taught in their classrooms and schools?

Details of Minnesota's state-mandated tests are provided in chapter 3. The Minnesota Comprehensive Assessments (MCAs) are designed to be aligned with the Minnesota Academic Standards, but no information is available about the actual degree of alignment. The Minnesota Basic Standards Test (MBST or BST) was not intended to be aligned to the Minnesota Academic Standards and no alignment review had been conducted (Gayler et al., 2004). Cumulative passing rates on the MBST (after five attempts) for all Minnesota students were high: 99.1% in math and 99.5% in reading/language arts (Gayler et al., 2004).

The dual system of using high-standards tests as well as a basic skills exam was a reflection of the desire to test both levels of skills but to make high school graduation contingent on passing a basic skills exam. At the time of the study, there were no accountability consequences or rewards for teachers, schools, or districts linked to student performance on the MCAs or exit exam. The state did not provide special programs of support to schools and teachers in the form of professional development aligned to the assessments and standards. Sample tests and items are available at http://education.state.mn.us/mde/Accountability_Programs/Assessment_and_Testing/Assessments/index.html.

Data reported here come from a qualitative study of teacher and administrator responses to state-mandated testing in four Minnesota districts during the 2002–2003 school year. Minnesota was selected for two reasons. First, the state testing program was "high stakes"—students had to pass the Basic Standards Test, administered beginning in 8th-grade, in order to graduate from high school. Therefore, it was possible to investigate the effects of a high-stakes testing program on curriculum and instruction. Second, Minnesota had an unusual system where the Minnesota Comprehensive Assessments (MCAs) were challenging high-standards tests, but the 8th-grade exit exam was a minimum competency test. Unlike systems that rely primarily on minimum competency tests, Minnesota's dual approach may have been less susceptible to narrowing of the curriculum.

The interview protocol included general questions about the impact of testing as well as specific questions about the influence of testing on teaching and learning: "Overall, is your opinion about the impact of the state testing program positive or negative? Does the state testing program influence the type of skills and knowledge that you focus on? Are these skills and knowledge important? Is the test designed so you feel a need to drill students on factual material?" Details of the sample, data collection, and analysis are provided in chapter 3.

Limitation of the Study

A limitation of this study is that it relies on teacher and administrator judgments regarding the effect of Minnesota's tests on curriculum and instruction. These judgments may be biased. However, two recent studies suggest that in some cases, self-report data may be a reliable indicator of actual instructional practices. One study compared teacher self-reports and independent observations of teachers' enacted curriculum and found strong agreement between the two measures (Porter & Smithson, 2001). A second, national study involving 25,000 teachers found close agreement between teachers' self-reported instructional practices and students' perceptions of those practices (Shim, Felner, Shim, & Noonan, 2001).

EVIDENCE FROM MINNESOTA

What were the views of teachers and administrators in the four Minnesota districts regarding state-mandated testing? By an overwhelming two-to-one margin, most interviewees answered that the overall impact of state-mandated testing was positive. This margin was consistent across district type (urban, suburban, and rural) and grade level. All administrators answered that the overall impact of testing was positive. The results are consistent with a random survey of teachers across the state, which found that 85% supported the basic standards exit exam (Draper, 2000).

Interviewees who viewed testing positively exhibited four patterns when responding to this question. First, teachers felt that testing improved the quality of the curriculum, although they initially feared that testing would have a negative impact, causing teachers to focus only on basic skills. According to interviewees, test results force teachers to acknowledge that many students are below grade level in math and reading, prompting greater collaboration among teachers and administrators to improve the quality of the curriculum and to align the curriculum vertically from grade to grade. For example, a principal in a suburban middle school explained:

> The negative part about it would be if teachers and staff were simply addressing the basics for the kids—teaching the basics, not taking them to the next level because that test has become so important, and that would be their only focus in the classroom. I think there was a lot of initial talk about that when the testing first started. I don't see that happening here in our middle school now that I have that opportunity to be in classrooms. . . . The positive part is that we are looking at education differently and that we're not working in isolation. Things are on the table, so to speak, and so we can work cooperatively as a team and make differences in the curriculum that really enrich the curriculum and enrich the teaching for the kids and the staff. So I see that as the positive side of it. There's more dialogue, there's connection between K–12 curriculum, there's connection between the levels of high school, middle school, [and] elementary.

Interviewees in the majority group asserted that teachers prepare students for the test by integrating the skills needed to pass the test into the school curriculum throughout the year, rather than through isolated test preparation that narrowly focused on the types of items expected on the test. A principal in a semirural elementary school explained:

> I think the test forces us to look at what's important . . . it's not in a

way that the teachers teach to a test, but I think they each in their own way make sure that they bring to the forefront in their instruction the skills that enable kids to take the test without a high level of anxiety. I think they do a great job of that, and they don't do it a week before or two weeks before; I think they do it in a timely fashion so that we can honestly say that we're not teaching to the test. We're teaching in a way that children can learn.

Second, interviewees in this group felt that testing has made them more accountable and improved the quality of instruction. Teachers believed they were more focused, goal-oriented, and reflective about what they needed to teach. Teachers reported more dialogue and communication among themselves. Professional development and staffing are said to be more focused on improving student achievement. Teachers reported that after-school intervention programs have been initiated and focus on the needs of low-achieving children. For example, a high school science teacher in an urban school suggested that testing has impacted instruction through a number of different ways:

I think it has been wonderful. I think it has raised a number of eyebrows, and it has caused people to step back and ask themselves, "What is it that I'm doing in the classroom that they're asking me on a test, and why are they asking." In other words, it's causing a lot of self-reflection that teachers often don't have time to do. [They do] a lot of planning but often not a lot of time reflecting. . . . It's impacting professional development such that now our professional development is geared more toward the impact on the classroom, not just on me going out to a meeting of the National Science Teachers Association meeting in Hawaii. Now I have to relate it to how it's going to impact the class. So it's impacted the professional development as well. Obviously it has impacted funding at the district level. We now have specialists in the classrooms or in the buildings. And I think it's also raised awareness that you have some kids that are special ed and kids that are not, and those kids that are outside of special ed still need help, and we're seeing that help is made available to them.

Third, teachers felt that testing improved student attitudes, engagement, and effort by holding students accountable for learning. Teachers noticed that more children are seeking help and participating in after-school programs. An 8th-grade math teacher in a suburban middle school explained that her view of testing is positive because it causes students to adopt a new attitude toward learning:

Overall, positive . . . [because] it is finally something that the kids are accountable for. Up through middle school, you are not accountable for anything in Minnesota really. You can fail, fail, fail, fail, and still go into high school. In high school, you're accountable. So this is finally something where the kids say, "Oh my gosh, this counts." So I like that; I like watching the attitude change because for the first time, it counts.

Fourth, teachers felt that testing resulted in greater efforts to ensure that all children succeed and improved student achievement. For example, a 4th-grade teacher in a semirural elementary school described a program to identify children with low reading scores and to refer them to a special after-school program:

Here in [district name] our children coming out of 3rd grade and into 4th grade that have scored low in the reading area, they are identified and are given the opportunity to be in an after-school program called "Soar to Success." I think it's an 18-week program, runs from 3:00 to 4:00. I've seen a lot of kids have great success with the program. . . . It's one of the programs that have come out of the low scores from the state testing. [So you view that as a positive?] Yes, very, very much so, very much so a positive. If nothing else, their self-esteem while they're in that program, they're getting their homework done, they're learning different ways to attack reading.

EFFECTS OF MINNESOTA'S SYSTEM ON THE CURRICULUM

In the previous section, interviewees reported that testing led to focusing of the curriculum. Given the concern among educators about the effects of narrowing of the curriculum, the second question addressed in this study is the following: In what ways did Minnesota's state-mandated testing program influence teacher and administrator choices about what is taught in their classrooms and schools? The themes reported below characterized the views of the majority of interviewees who felt, by a two-to-one margin, that state-mandated testing had a positive impact on the curriculum. These themes were consistent across district type (urban, suburban, and rural).

A Focus on Basic Skills at the 8th-Grade Level

As might be expected, interviewees stated that teachers focused on basic skills at the 8th-grade level, consistent with the emphasis of the Basic

Standards Test on minimum competencies. Teachers also focused on particular topics that were emphasized on the state test. What was unexpected was that teachers in the majority group—across suburban, urban, and rural districts—felt that this focus was appropriate. An 8th-grade math teacher in a suburban middle school explained:

> Absolutely! The first year we took the test, we spent that summer rewriting our curriculum to align with [it]. We broke it down; we took the eight strands and we analyzed which strands [our district's] 8th-graders did the poorest on. We took those strands and we put them in the front of the year, so that we had them done by February. Ratios, proportions, and percents were the weakest area, so we did that right before the test. [Do you feel that these skills and knowledge that you teach are important?] Yes, all of those eight different strands are necessary skills for kids. So it's not like I'm teaching surfing or something totally irrelevant. It is relevant to their daily lives.

Although teachers focused on basic skills, they did not feel overly constrained. Both English language arts and math teachers in the majority group viewed the state test as well aligned with their instructional priorities and believed that they were teaching vital skills that were applicable beyond the test. An 8th-grade English teacher in an urban secondary school explained:

> I teach them basic skills that I know will be helpful. . . . For example, making sure that when you're reading an article, that you look at some of the questions first so that you're not just reading random information. . . . They're good skills to have. . . . I don't necessarily teach to the test so much as I teach some skills that I think will be beneficial for the test [as well as] in other areas.

A math teacher in a semirural high school added:

> As an adult, and as an educator, yes, I feel [that the skills measured by the Basic Standards Test are] important, because without those skills, most people are not going to be able to make good judgments throughout their lives. With those skills, they have more of an equal opportunity to make good judgments and decisions. . . . [And] I think the grad standards in mathematics as a whole have done a lot to improve math education in the state of Minnesota. I think without it, there'd be many school districts still doing what they did twenty to thirty years ago, because why change if you don't have to?

Teachers in this group believed that the test covered basic math skills that all students should learn. As an 8th-grade teacher in an urban elementary school added, "It's all part of our curriculum. . . . Those things are supposed to be basic skills that everyone would have. So I really don't have a problem with the test." An 8th-grade math teacher in an urban secondary school put it succinctly: "The topics on the test are, I think, topics that students should know."

These views were shared without exception by all of the administrators who were interviewed, across rural, suburban, and urban districts. Superintendents agreed that the test has focused the curriculum on important skills and knowledge at every grade level. A superintendent in a semirural district said:

> Definitely in math and reading. . . . It certainly has influenced what we're looking at, what's being taught in the curriculum, and then where we have gaps, we're purchasing additional curriculum resources and materials. [Do you think that the skills and knowledge that you teach to help kids prepare for the state test, are those the important things that they need to know?] I think I would agree, and most of our teachers would agree, and principals in the area agree.

Principals believed that as a result of focusing the curriculum on important basic skills, fewer students are failing to learn those skills. As a principal in a suburban middle school explained:

> Some of those fluffy extraneous things [have been eliminated from the] curriculum— people just doing what they want to do because it's fun. So I think that's been a plus, and I think that we're focusing on what needs to be done for kids to have their skills for future lifelong use. Focusing on the basics is one of them, and having students be able to be successful and function is a basic. Kids aren't as easily dropping through the cracks as they used to be. So I think that's important that we have kind of solidified some things that we need to address with students for their success. . . . And it definitely has focused more [attention] on the skills that the kids need.

Interviewees in the majority group agreed that testing focused instruction on reading and math—the tested subjects—and felt that this focus over non-tested subjects was appropriate. As a principal in an urban middle school explained:

> Teachers do focus on reading and on math, and our students,

approximately half of whom are special needs students because they're either special ed or English language learners new to the English language, they have to learn it. . . . You have to learn how to read. You can't learn anything if you don't.

Science teachers agreed with the focus on reading and math, welcomed the opportunity to integrate reading and math into science instruction, and asserted that integrated instruction in these areas was desirable. A high school science teacher in an urban school reported:

It has [influenced the type of skills and knowledge that I focus on] because now I have to teach math and reading in my science classroom. I cannot just assume that by giving a textbook at the 10th-grade reading level that these kids know how to read at the 10th-grade reading level. [How do you feel about having to teach reading and math?] I love it! If I had my way, reading, writing, arithmetic would never have come out of anybody's curriculum. It would be early childhood family education through grade 16. It would be in every single classroom, every single day. It would not be compartmentalized. The thought is totally silly for me that it's even fragmented; it makes no sense.

Teachers in the majority group did not feel that they needed to focus on test-taking tricks and strategies to prepare students for the state test. Instead, they asserted that they prepared students by teaching skills that are broadly useful. For example, a Title I reading coordinator in an urban middle school said: "It's just general reading skills . . . what we focus on is just good reading instruction and helping the kids with test-taking skills, because some kids really need help with that. Good test-taking skills, ironically enough, are also good reading strategies."

All of the principals in this study asserted that they are opposed to teaching to the test—meaning isolated drills on the types of items expected on the test—and that their teachers understand this. The principals said that they would sanction any teacher caught teaching to the test. As a principal in an urban middle school put it: "We don't look at the test and focus on what's on there, and if I ever find a staff member who does, they're in deep trouble." This suggests that the principals in this study provided countervailing pressure against teaching to the test.

Teachers in the majority group asserted that in any case, drill is not useful in preparing students for the state tests. For example, a special education teacher in an urban high school said:

I find with the math test in particular, the Basic Standards math test, drilling is very little help, because I see the math test is essentially a reading test. My kids have great difficulty comprehending what the question is. Drill to me is helpful when you're drilling on the same thing—for instance, addition facts over and over, or multiplication facts over and over. Well, that test doesn't focus on drill at all, because each question is totally different in the expectation or the skill that it requires. Drill to me means repetition and that isn't one of the things in the math test.

Interviewees in this group felt that testing did not interfere with their ability to provide a balanced educational experience for students. Teachers and administrators felt that they could balance the need to prepare students for the test while maintaining student interest and encouraging students to be self-motivated learners. A curriculum coordinator in an urban middle school explained:

We have to focus on the strands in both reading and math. We don't teach to it in this building directly although I know that there's a balance, that you have to because it is high stakes. We'd be doing a disservice not to. But I think we try to balance the appropriateness of [instruction]. We're not going to teach the whole year from the strands primarily or solely. [Do you feel that the skills and knowledge in the strands are important?] Yeah, I do. I feel they're important. . . . I think there's a way to teach [the strands] to make it interesting. And I think there's a way to teach to interest a student to become more of a self-learner. I think some programs take it to the extent that, "We're going to design everything around the test and we're going to teach to it," and I think you lose students easily in that type of environment. Whereas if you create an environment where you view the strands as what we're going to focus on, and then create a unit or a project where they're going to use those skills, I think that's more of a creative way to approach it.

A Focus on Critical Thinking in Elementary Grades

Of the teachers who felt (by a 2-to-1 margin) that testing had a positive impact on the curriculum, the comments of the elementary-level teachers suggest that the more challenging MCAs test administered in the elementary grades prompted a greater focus on critical thinking skills. For example, a 4th-grade teacher in a semirural elementary school explained that the test was well aligned with her goals of teaching reasoning skills:

Yes, very much so. [Do you feel that the test focuses on important skills and knowledge?] Yes. I think it teaches children to look differently at a question, it teaches children how to answer questions with reasoning. It's not like a multiple guess or multiple choice; they actually have to explain how they arrived at things, and I think that's really good. I think more of it should be done in classrooms.

Elementary-level teachers in the majority group believed that the influence of the state test on instruction was positive because it involved challenging multistep problems, and teachers were required to prepare students to reason through that type of problem. As a 3rd-grade teacher in an urban elementary school explained:

I would say the state test is a very challenging test. I think that one thing that my colleagues and I always comment on in 3rd-grade is that these are multistep problems, when I think about the math. That's a very challenging thing for 3rd-graders. You begin to do one-step problems and you feel pretty good. Two steps, okay; beyond that it's really challenging for them. I'm glad that they have exposure to that; it gives us a high mark to shoot for.

The emphasis of the state test on complex, higher-order thinking in the elementary grades presented a challenge for low-achieving students. A 3rd-grade teacher in a semirural elementary school described the challenge:

My perception is the test is geared more for the higher-level thinker. It's kind of stressful for the lower student. One, it depends on if they can read well, because whether it's math or reading, they have to read alone unless they have a special [education] plan. So reading can enter into it. And then if they've got the organizational skills to prepare themselves—how to set up problems or methods. And then the actual thought process involved, I think it's difficult. So I think it's very difficult for the low-end student. I'm thinking of the ones not in special ed. However, I have to say with our practice testing, they don't seem to have anxiety at the time of testing, which is good. They seem to just accept it and they're proud of themselves. . . . I think it's designed more for the higher-level thinkers, not for the average 3rd-grade student. It gets complex pretty quickly on the test.

Teachers felt that the challenging nature of the state test has raised standards and improved outcomes. A 2nd-grade teacher in a semirural elementary school described the effect on teaching and learning:

We noticed some years ago that our math scores were generally low, so it's like, "Okay, we've got to do something about this." But we have really upped our standards for all our math. *Whoa.* We have really raised our standards, and so our math scores are coming up.

The focus of the test on critical thinking skills reportedly has had a positive influence on the curriculum in non-tested subjects such as science. In both science and math, the curriculum now emphasizes real-life situations and higher-order thinking. A 5th/6th–grade special education teacher in a semirural middle school described the changes in the curriculum:

Our curriculum has changed in science and math so that we're teaching the children life skills, real-life situations, higher-level thinking, math strategies, and science items. . . . It seems to make more sense to them that they're learning something that they can use in the future, rather than to just work on a page of multiplication facts.

NEED FOR SEGMENTED TESTS

Interviewees who were critical of testing suggested a change in the design and implementation of state tests that could address multiple concerns: administering state tests in short segments spread throughout the school year. Segmented testing would allow the number of topics covered to be increased (because the total amount of testing could be increased), reducing the pressure to narrow the curriculum, without forcing students to sit for long periods of time for any single segment. Multiple testing checkpoints throughout the school year could also improve the delivery of diagnostic feedback to teachers, creating opportunities to help students who need assistance.

DISCUSSION

The results suggest that teachers and administrators in the four Minnesota districts felt, by a 2-to-1 margin, that the overall impact of state-mandated testing in Minnesota was positive, consistent with survey results showing that 85% of teachers statewide supported the state's exit exam (Draper, 2000). Within this majority group, teachers and administrators felt that the impact of the state tests on curriculum—focusing attention on basic skills at the 8th-grade level and critical thinking skills at the elementary level—was appropriate.

Their reasoning explains their choices about what to teach in their classrooms and, thus, the nature of curriculum narrowing in Minnesota due to high-stakes testing. Teachers and administrators reasoned that students need to know basic skills in math and reading as well as critical thinking skills in order to succeed in the world outside school. In their judgment, the state-mandated tests were well aligned with key instructional priorities and well designed to avoid construct underrepresentation. In their view, Minnesota's state-mandated tests assessed students on skills that students should know. Teachers in the majority group felt that it is appropriate to emphasize these skills and to deemphasize less important outcomes. This suggests that a properly aligned, well designed testing system can avoid excessive narrowing of the curriculum.

The teachers' claims that drill-oriented instruction was not helpful in preparing students for the state-mandated tests suggests that the tests may have been consistent with inquiry-based teaching that emphasizes the learner as an active constructor of knowledge. Whether the Minnesota teachers endorsed inquiry methods was not directly addressed in this study, but the evidence from this study does not support the hypothesis that state-mandated testing in Minnesota was inconsistent with an inquiry-oriented approach.

Three additional features of Minnesota's system contributed to proper alignment and sound design. First, Minnesota's unique testing system encouraged a focus on basic skills as well as critical thinking, maintaining breadth and depth in the curriculum. The high-standards MCA exams offset pressure to narrow the curriculum to the basic skills tested on the MBST exit exam. In contrast, states that only use minimum competency tests inadvertently risk encouraging teachers to focus only on the basic skills needed to pass those tests. Second, Minnesota's decision to select a minimum competency exit standard resulted in a high cumulative passing rate—over 99%—and low pressure on teachers to teach to the test. Thus, teachers felt that they could prepare students for the exit exam without drilling students on the types of items expected on the exam. Third, administrators reportedly discouraged teaching to the test, providing countervailing pressure against any tendency to drill students on narrow, test-focused skills.

The implication of this study is that well-aligned, well-designed tests that emphasize basic skills and critical thinking, plus minimum competency exit standards that reduce pressure on teachers to teach to the test and administrators who discourage teaching to the test, can avoid much of the curriculum narrowing that reduces the overall quality of education received by students in a high-stakes testing environment. To the extent that excessive narrowing of the curriculum occurs in other states, the cause may be state-mandated tests that are not well designed or well aligned to the intended curriculum.

The results of this study highlight the importance of aligning the design of state-mandated tests with the intended curriculum, and are consistent with prior research regarding the importance of alignment (see Fuhrman, 2001). In some instances, this requires changing how tests are designed. In other cases, it requires changing state curriculum standards so that they are not excessively oriented toward factual knowledge and do not inadvertently lead to tests that emphasize recall of such knowledge. The results of this study also suggest the importance of *not* linking the compensation or job security of administrators to test scores through bonus systems and performance reviews because this may inadvertently undermine the motivation of administrators to provide the type of countervailing pressure noted in this study, possibly creating an environment where teachers feel intense pressure to raise test scores. It may also be desirable to explore the feasibility of segmenting state-mandated tests into several shorter tests and spreading their administration throughout the school year. Segmented testing would allow the number of topics covered to be increased, reducing the pressure to narrow the curriculum.

The main finding of this study—that it is possible to avoid excessive curriculum narrowing when stakes are high—may seem surprising if high stakes are equated with high pressure. However, this finding is consistent with research that makes clear that *stakes*—formal consequences for students and/or schools that are linked to test results—are not synonymous with *pressure*—communications and informal consequences intended to induce staff to increase test scores (Corbett & Wilson, 1991). In a study of 300 school districts in 2 states, negative impacts on the curriculum occurred when stakes were high and pressure to raise test scores was high (Corbett & Wilson, 1991, p. 126). Positive impacts on teaching and learning occurred when stakes were high but pressure to raise test scores was low (Corbett & Wilson, 1991). Recall that high stakes and low pressure can occur when students must pass a test to graduate from high school but almost all students pass easily. This type of test is not likely to generate concern among staff or parents, or pressure to change the curriculum. Under conditions of high stakes and low pressure, schools responded in a positive way (Corbett & Wilson, 1991). Educators in these schools accepted the test as a valid indicator of student learning and used it as the basis for making improvements in instruction while maintaining a balanced curriculum. Schools had adequate time to respond to student weaknesses indicated by test results. Under this condition, teachers implemented strategies for improving learning in a broad, balanced way that led to a rise in test scores without having to teach directly to the test. Teachers were most likely to adopt, adapt, or invent more effective instructional practices as the best means of improving student learning (Corbett & Wilson, 1991, p. 116).

Thus, although there are clearly many factors that influence whether state-mandated tests have positive or negative effects, Corbett and Wilson's study suggests that in high-stakes situations, the degree of pressure that teachers feel to improve student achievement is paramount. The current study suggests that teachers feel less pressure when state-mandated tests are well designed and properly aligned with curricular and instructional priorities, the exit exam focuses on minimum competencies rather than high standards, and administrators provide countervailing pressure against the urge to teach to the test.

This framework can be extended to incorporate other factors, such as the dropout rate of minorities and ESL students—these factors may be understood as influencing the pressure that is placed on teachers to improve student achievement. A high dropout rate places more pressure on teachers. Similarly, teachers with a higher level of pedagogical content knowledge may feel less pressure to teach to the test, providing a countervailing force against pressures to narrow the curriculum. The Corbett-Wilson theoretical framework suggests why the impact of testing may be positive in one school district and negative in another. It suggests, for example, that despite strong consequences for students, testing *may* have a positive impact on curriculum and instruction *if countervailing factors reduce the pressure on teachers.* Conversely, a lack of countervailing factors may cause teachers to resort to drill and practice.

The role of pressure in causing inadvertent narrowing is significant because many states are rushing to implement high-standards exit exams that are likely to generate tremendous pressure on teachers to raise test scores (Gayler et al., 2004). The present study suggests that this move may be premature. Minnesota's system of testing offers an alternative way to raise educational standards without creating excessive pressure on teachers to sacrifice the breadth and depth of the curriculum. State and federal policymakers can increase the probability that high-stakes testing will have positive, rather than negative, effects on teaching and learning by drawing upon Minnesota's model and ensuring that tests are properly aligned and pressure on teachers is reduced.

5

Less Failure

The evidence presented in chapter 4 suggests that the type of multiple-choice tests that are being implemented in response to NCLB are not necessarily inconsistent with instruction that emphasizes critical thinking, when the tests are well-aligned with the intended curriculum and pressure on teachers is low. However, NCLB raises yet one more serious concern: high-stakes testing can cause high failure rates if standards are set too high. Chapter 5 compares Arizona, which implemented a high-standards exit exam with a 39% failure rate, with Minnesota, which used a minimum competency high school exit exam with a failure rate of less than 1%. This comparison suggests the value of using minimum competency exit exams—but poses the dilemma that such exams may ultimately cause teachers to dumb down the curriculum. Chapter 5 suggests a potential solution that up to now has largely been ignored.

....

Increasingly, high-stakes testing policies are shaping American education (DeBard & Kubow, 2002; Fusarelli, 2004; Kornhaber, 2004). By 2009, half of all states (25) will require students to pass a state test in order to graduate from high school; this requirement will affect 70% of students nationwide (Gayler et al., 2004). These policies have been adopted in an effort to signal students that learning matters and that working hard pays off. International comparisons of homework completion, absences, and time on task in school strongly suggest that students in the United States devote less time and energy to the task of learning (Bishop, 1990; Roderick & Engel, 2001). These comparisons suggest that poor student effort contributes to the relatively poor performance of American students (Bishop, 1990; Heyneman, 1990; Powell, 1996; Steinberg, Brown, & Sanford, 1996; Stevenson & Stigler, 1992; Tomlinson & Cross, 1991). The adoption of high-stakes testing, where consequences are linked to student performance, aims to make the link between effort and achievement abundantly clear and to motivate students to study harder: "American education is not fashioned in such a way as to motivate students, and this must be changed if the United States is to compete with other countries" (Jennings, 2000, p. 12).

A growing body of research suggests that high-stakes testing is, *on average*, associated with modest improvements in student effort (Jacob & Stone, 2005; Jacob, Stone, & Roderick, 2004; Roderick & Engel, 2001) and achievement (Bishop, 1990, 1998; Braun, 2004; Carnoy & Loeb, 2002; Frederiksen, 1994; Grissmer & Flanagan, 1998; Hanushek & Raymond, 2005; Powell, 1996; Roderick, Jacob, & Bryk, 2002). One study found that older children may benefit more than younger children, presumably because older children are better equipped to regulate their effort and respond to high-stakes testing (Roderick, 2002). However, a second study using the same data but a different methodology found the reverse (Jacob & Lefgren, 2004). Significantly, there is evidence that the achievement of retained students remains low and these students lose ground academically relative to similar students who have been promoted (Heubert & Hauser, 1999; Roderick & Nagaoka, 2005; Shepard & Smith, 1989), although one study finds a positive effect of retention (Greene & Winters, 2006). While negative effects seem to be confirmed by studies finding that high-stakes testing may be associated with higher student dropout rates for low-achieving students (Allensworth, 2004, 2005; Jacob, 2001; MacMillan, Balow, Widaman, & Hemsley, 1990; Reardon, 1996; Reardon & Galindo, 2002), several studies fail to find a significant relation between the existence of exit exams and higher dropout rates (Catterall, 1987; Greene & Winters, 2004a; Lillard & DeCicca, 2001; Muller, 1998; Muller & Schiller, 2000) or rates of diploma acquisition net of covariates including poverty rates, proportions of minority students, and levels of academic achievement (Warren & Edwards, 2005), or find no difference in dropout rates between low-achieving students who pass and those who fail an exit exam (Griffin & Heidorn, 1996).

Several troubling studies suggest that school staff may hold back low-achieving students or exclude more students with disabilities from testing in an effort to boost average scores—raising questions about the validity of reported gains in student achievement (Amrein & Berliner, 2002a, 2002b, 2003; Amrein-Beardsley & Berliner, 2003; Haney, 2000). However, after correcting for methodological limitations of those studies, other researchers concluded that higher test scores are associated with reduced dropout rates (Carnoy, Loeb, & Smith, 2001) and improvements in student achievement due to high-stakes testing are real, not illusory (Braun, 2004; Hanushek & Raymond, 2005; Rosenshine, 2003).

This review of the research literature suggests three conclusions. First, the effects of high-stakes tests are neither uniformly positive nor uniformly negative. Second, effects that are averaged over all students, including those who do not experience test failure, may hide negative effects on student motivation and achievement for a smaller group of students who fail the tests. Third, there is a need for research regarding policy-relevant factors that can be manipulated in order to minimize negative outcomes for low-achieving students and maximize the positive effects of high-stakes testing.

In this chapter, I propose a policy-oriented framework to understand variation in the effects of high-stakes testing. This framework seeks to explain why high-stakes tests do not have uniform effects and why effects on student motivation and achievement can vary dramatically, depending on how the tests are designed and implemented. In particular, this framework suggests how some high-stakes tests are inadvertently designed in a way that negates intended effects on the motivation and engagement of low-achieving students, and how the design and implementation of current high-stakes tests can be manipulated to improve the ratio of benefits to educational costs.

KIND AND WICKED LEARNING ENVIRONMENTS

High-stakes testing may be considered a form of feedback to students. Under what conditions is this type of testing supportive of teaching and learning? Hogarth (2005) distinguishes between kind and wicked learning environments. In a kind learning environment, feedback is accurate, providing accurate signals about expectations. In a wicked environment, feedback is inaccurate, providing confusing signals. Reviews of controlled experimental studies suggest that accurate performance feedback increases persistence, motivation, engagement, and academic achievement in school settings (Black & Wiliam, 1998a, 1998b; Fuchs & Fuchs, 1986; Kluger & DeNisi, 1996). Inaccurate feedback has the opposite effect because it sends inaccurate signals about the relationship between effort and achievement. If students work hard but inaccurate feedback provides false signals that the effort is not paying off, students will reduce their effort and performance will decline. If students do not work hard, but inaccurate feedback provides false signals that performance is adequate, poor effort will be reinforced and students will maintain poor effort. Thus, inaccurate feedback sabotages effort and achievement.

Research on motivation also suggests the importance of designing learning tasks that are within each student's zone of proximal development, that is, tasks that are neither too easy nor too difficult, given each student's stage of development, and that are most likely to engage students and elicit greater effort and learning (Vygotsky, 1978). Tasks that are too difficult are likely to frustrate students and result in reduced effort and achievement. Thus, exit exams that are too difficult for low-achieving students may discourage rather than encourage them.

The framework that I propose suggests that particular decisions that are made regarding test design and implementation details can greatly influence the accuracy of the feedback that is provided to students, the degree to which a given exit exam is within the zone of proximal development for low-achieving students, and thus, the degree to which the learning environment is kind or wicked. Tests that are appropriate in difficulty, well aligned with important learning objectives, with accommodations for students in special education, where students are given adequate opportunities to improve performance, are more likely to provide accurate feedback to students and to provide a kind learning environment.

It seems obvious that tests with wicked properties can have negative effects on student motivation and, thus, teaching and learning. A test that is too difficult provides inaccurate feedback to students about their performance and can discourage students whose performance may otherwise be adequate. A test that is poorly aligned with curriculum and instruction does not measure what students have been taught, provides inaccurate information about student performance, and is negatively associated with student achievement (Gorin & Blanchard, 2004). A test that does not provide adequate accommodations for students with disabilities can prevent students from displaying their skills and knowledge and thus provides inaccurate information about what students know and can do. A testing system that does not provide ample opportunities for students to improve performance can incorrectly suggest that ability levels are fixed, that effort is not rewarded, and that performance improvement is not an important goal. Thus, tests with wicked properties provide inaccurate feedback that undermines engagement and achievement.

Significantly, it appears that many state-mandated tests exhibit one or more of these wicked properties. Fourteen states have already adopted high-standards exit exams, and seven more will adopt high-standards exams by the year 2009 (Gayler et al., 2004). Evidence from states such as Massachusetts, which has implemented a high-standards exit exam, suggests that the relatively high difficulty of this type of test can be especially discouraging for low-achieving students (Clarke et al., 2003). Variation in the difficulty of state exit exams is reflected in wide variations in passing rates. In math, for example, initial passing rates range from 36% to 91% across 12 states (Gayler, Chudowsky, Kober, & Hamilton, 2003).

Low passing rates generate intense concerns that exit exams may unfairly deny diplomas to large numbers of students whose performance is adequate according to other indicators (Gayler et al., 2004).

Research also suggests that many state testing programs exhibit three other wicked properties. Lack of curricular alignment is a problem in many states (Porter, 2002; Rothman, 2004; Webb, 1999). Tremendous variation across states regarding accommodations for students with disabilities suggests that students who need accommodations have uneven access to the content of high-stakes tests (Lehr & Thurlow, 2003). Finally, there is significant variation in how test results are used: 57% of teachers randomly sampled across the country reported that test results were used to identify students for tutoring, summer school, or other remedial programs, suggesting that the remainder—43%—taught in schools where test results were not used for those purposes (Pedulla et al., 2003). These variations in test design and implementation may explain variation in the effects of high-stakes tests.

To illustrate, Arizona's high-stakes exit exam, called AIMS (Arizona's Instrument to Measure Standards), was characterized by Arizona State University's Education Policy Studies Laboratory as a "brutal" test (Glass, 2003, p. 1). After reviewing the items on the test, researchers concluded that AIMS requires knowledge of advanced algebra, trigonometry, analytic geometry, probability, and statistics, and is "an examination so difficult that only a minority of college graduates could pass it" (Glass, 2003, p. 1). A range of Arizona employers were asked to review representative items from the test. Ninety percent of the employers reported that they did not require, and their employees did not use, such skills in their daily work (Glass, 2003), suggesting that the test was not well aligned with the skills and knowledge needed outside school. In addition, district curricula throughout Arizona are poorly aligned with the state's curriculum standards and the AIMS test (Arizona Education Association, 2003). Furthermore, the state does not require school districts to provide remediation services for students who do not pass AIMS (Gayler et al., 2004), suggesting that students may not have adequate opportunities to improve performance. Finally, there is no process in place for students to request a waiver or appeal the exit exam requirement (Gayler et al., 2004), suggesting a lack of flexibility in cases where student performance may be judged adequate according to other indicators.

Largely as a result of these factors, passing rates on Arizona's high school exit exam were the lowest of any state that has implemented an exit exam (Gayler et al., 2004). In 2003, only 36% of all Arizona students passed the math portion, and only 59% passed reading/language arts (Gayler et al., 2004). Passing rates for Hispanic students were far lower—18% in math and 38% in reading/language arts. Only 7% of English language learners passed math, while 13% passed reading/language arts. Since students have multiple opportunities to take the test, cumulative passing rates are higher. However, after three attempts, only 61% of all students in the class of 2006—the first class that must pass AIMS to receive a diploma—have passed all three portions of AIMS, leaving 16,500 students who must pass in their final two attempts (Eyewitness News 4, 2005). Repeated failure leaves many of these students feeling discouraged and hopeless (Kossan, 2004).

As the scale of the problem became clear, implementation of the high stakes aspect—denying diplomas to students who fail—was delayed several times (Gayler et al., 2004). Passing scores were lowered (Kossan, 2005) and for the 2006 and 2007 cohorts, letter grades will now be factored into scores in an attempt to reduce failure rates (Fischer, 2005). However, researchers questioned the legitimacy of the exam and suggested that the test is so badly flawed that it should be abandoned (Glass, 2003; Smith et al., 1999). Legislation was proposed to completely dismantle the high-stakes component (Scutari, 2005).

While Arizona's experience may suggest that there are severe drawbacks associated with high-stakes testing, what is unclear is what happens if five design factors are changed: 1) the exit exam focuses on minimum competencies, rather than advanced skills, 2) the test is well aligned with key learning objectives, 3) modifications are available to students with disabilities and students can request a waiver or appeal the exit exam requirement in cases where student performance may be judged adequate according to other indicators, 4) test results are used in a way that provides ample opportunities for students to improve performance, and 5) results are used to recognize multiple levels of achievement through the use of multiple diploma options. These design factors may significantly alter the effects of high-stakes tests on key outcomes (Figure 5.1).

MINNESOTA

For several reasons, Minnesota presents an intriguing case example. High-stakes testing was implemented in 1998 and diplomas were withheld from students who failed the state Basic Standards Test (BST) beginning in 2000 (sample tests and items are available at http://education.state.mn.us/mde/Accountability_Programs/Assessment_and_Testing/Assessments/index.html). Unlike Arizona, however, reaction has been muted, suggesting the possibility that accountability policies have been implemented in a way that is relatively benign. Based on a random sample, 64% of all Minnesotans say that there is about the right emphasis, or not enough emphasis, on achievement testing in Minnesota's public schools,

Figure 5.1. Influence of selected test design and implementation decisions on key outcomes.

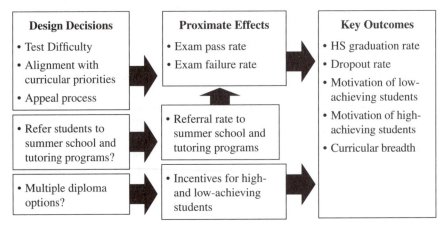

while 28% say there is too much (Lonetree, 2003). Sixty-seven percent of Minnesota parents agree that there is about the right emphasis, or not enough (Lonetree, 2003), and an overwhelming 85% of teachers support the state's exit exam (Draper, 2000). These results suggest that Minnesotans and Minnesota parents reject, by a 2-to-1 margin, the notion that there is too much emphasis on testing, and there is even stronger support among teachers for the exit exam. If Minnesotans are, in general, satisfied with the state's testing system, it is worth investigating the extent to which this is due to particular decisions about how the system was designed and implemented.

The first design factor that contributed to extraordinarily low passing scores in Arizona was the decision to make AIMS a high standards test, rather than a minimum competency exam. Minnesota chose, instead, to adopt an exam that only required students to know basic reading, math, and writing skills.[1] Second, Minnesota—unlike Arizona—provided greater flexibility for English language learners and students with disabilities who had an IEP (an Individualized Education Program, for students who require specialized education), or a 504 plan (for students who require test accommodations). The IEP team could reduce the scale score needed to pass (Gayler et al., 2004). Students then received a diploma with a "Pass Individual" designation. Third, Minnesota—unlike Arizona—required school districts to write a remediation plan and to provide remediation for students who failed the state's exit exam in 8th or 9th grade, and to give all students a total of 11 opportunities to take and pass the BST between 8th and 12th grade (compared to the 5 opportuni-

Table 5.1. Initial passing rates on state exit exam.

| | Initial Passing Rates (% Passing) | | | |
| | Arizona | | Minnesota | |
Group	Math	Reading	Math	Reading
White	49	74	78	87
Hispanic	18	38	38	52
Black	21	44	31	50
English learners	7	13	29	36
Disabled	10	26	28	40

Source: The data are from Gayler, Chudowsky, Hamilton, Kober, & Yeager, (2004). Arizona data are from 2003; Minnesota data are from 2004; data from equivalent years are not reported.

ties that Arizona students received) (Gayler et al., 2004). On top of these basic structural differences was one more important difference, revealed in the interview data reported below. According to the interviewees, Minnesota's tests were relatively well aligned with the interviewees' views of the skills and knowledge that students should possess when they leave school. All of these structural differences were designed and, therefore, represent aspects that potentially could be manipulated through careful design of testing programs by policymakers in other states who seek to reduce the unintended negative consequences of high-stakes tests.

The key point is that the basic structure of Minnesota's high-stakes testing program was very different from Arizona's and could be expected to have very different effects. Those effects were striking: cumulative passing rates (after 5 attempts) for all Minnesota students were extremely high: 99.1% in math and 99.5% in reading/language arts (Gayler et al., 2004), compared to 61% in Arizona (Eyewitness News 4, 2005). Examination of passing rates for key groups of students suggests that these differences were not attributable to differences in the composition of the student populations in the two states. While cumulative pass rates were not available for those groups, it is possible to compare initial pass rates (Table 5.1).

The data in Table 5.1 demonstrate that every group of students passed each subject at a substantially greater rate in Minnesota, compared to Arizona. Passing rates in math for Hispanic students were twice as high, and for English language learners quadruple the rates in Arizona. As a result, students were far less likely to experience exam failure and were much more likely to graduate in Minnesota, compared to Arizona, due to differences in the design of Minnesota's testing program. To the extent that Minnesota obtained the presumed benefits of high-stakes testing with regard to improved student motivation, while minimizing the educational costs of exam failure, discouraged students, and increased dropout rates, Minnesota's design may be preferable to Arizona's, and may serve as a model for other states as well. Thus, knowledge of the differences in the program designs and an understanding of their differential effects provide practical knowledge as well as a theoretical lens for understanding how differences in program design may produce dramatically different results.

What is needed is an expert judgment about the value of Minnesota's design. Ultimately, however, judgments depend on the experience of the individuals making the judgments. One approach is to rely on judgments by researchers or measurement specialists. However, the approach used in the current study to assess the value of Minnesota's model was to draw upon the expert judgments of a sample of Minnesota teachers and administrators, because they were the most experienced observers of the effects of the state testing program in their classrooms. Unlike researchers and measurement specialists, they observed on a daily basis how students responded to the standards, policies, and consequences that constituted Minnesota's model. Thus, they were likely to be especially attuned to unintended, as well as intended, consequences of this model. What did they observe about the design of this model? Were the effects kind? What can be learned from Minnesota's experience? What did teachers recommend, and what are the implications for designing a kind testing environment? To what extent can Minnesota serve as a model for accountability policies in other states?

The data reported below come from the qualitative study of teacher and administrator responses to state-mandated testing in Minnesota reported in chapter 4 (which examined reactions related to curriculum and instruction that are not discussed in this chapter). Details regarding the study's methodology are reported in chapters 3 and 4.

The interview protocol (see the Appendix) included questions about the interviewees' views about testing, with particular emphasis on factors that potentially could be changed in other states through modifications in test design or implementation, including how test results were used.

The data were analyzed using a grounded theory approach (Bogdan & Biklen, 1992; Strauss, 1987). Thus, the framework presented in Figure 5.1 was developed after the data were collected and analyzed. Interviews were transcribed and coded to identify primary themes (Strauss, 1987). The themes were identified jointly by two raters and cross-checked by a third researcher. Discrepancies were resolved through discussion. Initial analyses indicated that interviewee responses did not differ significantly across grade level, teachers as opposed to administrators, or district type, so responses were collapsed across these categories.

POSITIVE EFFECT OF TESTING

How did teachers and administrators in the four Minnesota school districts view Minnesota's testing system? Fifty-six percent of interviewees stated that the overall effect of testing was positive, 28% of interviewees responded negatively and 16% were noncommittal regarding the impact of state-mandated testing on curriculum, instruction, student engagement, and student achievement. Thus, positive responses outnumbered negative responses by a 2-to-1 margin. Preliminary analyses indicated that there were no significant differences in responses across districts, grade levels, position, age, or years of experience, so responses were collapsed across categories.

Why did teachers and administrators have positive views? Teachers believed that the test fostered student accountability and motivated students to work harder, consistent with Roderick and Engel's (2001) finding that high-stakes tests improve student work effort. Interviewees talked about their students studying and working harder in school in order to pass the exit exam, even students diagnosed as EBD (emotionally/behaviorally disturbed). Thus, teachers believed that students were responding to the exit exam by working harder. As a Title I reading coordinator in an urban high school explained:

> I think that the high stakes is okay, because we want our kids to stay motivated. Just like to learn to drive, to get that driver's license, you need to pass a couple of tests. And as a society, before we put you on the road, we want to make sure that you can at least do the basics. . . . I have seen over the last 7 years or 6 years, however long we've been doing it—I've seen over the years the buy-in and the incredible amount of energy and focus that the kids exert. And they take it seriously. Even our kids who are behaviorally disturbed will sit for one day while they're taking that test. I mean, it's amazing, and I think that kids who need to have that kind of focus will. I've changed my mind on that over the years. [You mean you've changed from not supporting it to supporting it?] Yes. [And that's because of?] Because of how I've seen the kids respond. They've responded positively, they've risen to the occasion.

This response captures the views of all of the special education and Title I teachers interviewed for this study. It is remarkable because these teachers work closely with students who are most at risk of failing the exit exam. Therefore, one might expect that the teachers would be especially sensitive to negative effects on their students' engagement and motivation. However, the teachers believed that the effect on student motivation was positive, not negative.

How can this result be reconciled with results from states such as Arizona? It seems likely that the relatively easy passing standard in Minnesota placed the exit exam within the zone of proximal development for precisely those students who were most in need of external consequences to motivate greater work effort. In contrast, Arizona's exit exam was far above the zone of development for those students. It was simply too difficult and, as a result, discouraged the very students it was meant to encourage. This analysis suggests that setting the passing standard and level of difficulty of the exit exam is critical in maximizing the motivational effect of high-stakes tests.

Teachers and administrators in Minnesota felt that the difficulty of the test was appropriate for an exit exam. In general, teachers felt that the basic skills test was relatively easy, based on student reactions after taking the test. As a 5th-grade teacher in a semirural middle school said:

> A lot of the 8th-graders, they'll take that test and they'll go, "That wasn't very hard." I think they should be able to pass that. I don't think those tests are so hard. Isn't it a basic minimum requirement? It's not like you're trying to challenge the top kids. I think the top kids will probably whiz through those pretty well. If it's just a basic skills test, then I think everybody needs to pass it.

The view that all students should be able to pass the exit exam was shared by all interviewees at every level, from high school down to the elementary grades. As a 3rd-grade teacher in an urban elementary school stated:

> I think they need to pass it. I think that's very important. . . . When kids leave the public education system, they need to leave with certain things under their belt. And if they're not able to pass the Basic Skills Test, then I don't think they should pass. You need those for life skills. You need a lot of those things, and it's important that you have them.

Each interviewee agreed that the Basic Skills Test covered essential skills and knowledge needed outside school and, thus, was well aligned with key learning objectives. The contrast with Arizona's test, which required proficiency in skills and knowledge that are not needed in the workplace, is stark. The difference explains why Minnesota teachers and administrators strongly supported Minnesota's exit exam and rejected the suggestion that the high-stakes aspect be dropped. As a math teacher in an urban middle school said:

> I wouldn't change it, no. I think that the Basic Standards Test is just what it states; on the math part, those are survival skills. Those are math operations that they should acquire and they should know. And to graduate from high school as a senior, those are pretty basic skills. So I think it's important. It's something that holds schools a little bit accountable and then holds the students accountable for learning it.

This view was also supported by special education teachers who work closely with students who have learning disabilities and who are most at risk of failing the exit exam. Significantly, these teachers emphasized their ability to provide appropriate accommodations and modifications for students with disabilities. As a special education teacher in an urban high school stated:

> From my vantage point, no [I would not delay the exit exam], because I have so much flexibility in what I can do in terms of accommodating and modifying [the test for special education students]. So speaking for my special ed population, no. . . . You know, in looking at the test over the years I've seen it, I don't feel it's too hard.

The ability of special education teachers in Minnesota to provide accommodations and modifications for their students meant that, unlike in Arizona, teachers could modify the passing score for their students and avoid setting a task that was beyond the ability level of their students. This ability to individualize the passing score allowed teachers to preserve the motivational aspect of the high-stakes test without frustrating students. A special education teacher in an urban elementary school explained:

> I think that kids need to get the message that you have to have certain skills to graduate. I think that's a good message and I think it's a good standard. [You even feel that way as a special ed teacher?] Yes. [Do you think many of your students will need waivers?] Of my students right now . . . I would say about a third of my students may need to have [the passing score] brought down. But I think the majority of students

with learning disabilities . . . are going to be living in a functional world when they're out on their own, and they need those basic skills. . . . [But individualize the passing score] so you say, "We aren't going to make you be at 90% on these skills, we'll let you be at 80% on these skills," which says that you've developed a lot in them.

CONCERNS

Of the interviewees who were opposed to the exit exam, three regular education teachers were concerned about denying diplomas to students with learning disabilities or students in special education, especially if those students have worked hard and made great progress. These teachers suggested an alternative assessment or modifications to the criteria for passing the test, apparently unaware that this flexibility was already available to special education teachers. One teacher expressed concern about the validity of using a single test to determine graduation and suggested that it should serve as one of several indicators. One teacher and a principal wanted the exit exam to provide formative information for improving curriculum and instruction.

CREATING KIND ENVIRONMENTS

Reducing the difficulty of the exit exam primarily serves to bring the task within the zone of proximal development of low-achieving students. Within that zone, the exam reportedly served to motivate those students. Thus, reducing the difficulty level reduces the probability that students will be discouraged by a task that is far beyond their abilities, and reduces the unintended negative consequences of denying diplomas to students who are working hard but are simply unable to raise their performance to a higher level.

Reducing the difficulty of the exit exam is necessitated when large numbers of students advance to the upper grades without the preparation necessary to pass a more difficult exam. Thus, it is a stopgap measure that does not address the larger issue: how to improve student performance in the earlier grades so that students are at a more advanced level by the time they reach the exit exam. If it were possible to accelerate student learning at an earlier age, more students would be prepared to pass an advanced exit exam. What role can high-stakes testing play in accelerating student learning well before the exit exam?

Some school districts, such as the Chicago Public Schools, are experimenting with the use of high-stakes tests to determine whether students are promoted to the next grade. Research on the effects of promotion exams suggests that they have modest positive effects on the engagement and achievement of students who are not retained (Jacob & Stone, 2005; Jacob et al., 2004; Roderick & Engel, 2001; Roderick, Jacob, & Bryk, 2002). However, there are negative effects on the achievement of students who are retained (Heubert & Hauser, 1999; Roderick & Nagaoka, 2005; Shepard & Smith, 1989). Thus, there is a need to develop testing programs that motivate students without relying on retention. What consequences can be attached to test results that do not involve retention?

Two consequences that have been widely implemented by schools across the country include the use of test results to refer students to summer school, and to refer students to after-school tutoring. Research suggests that both of these interventions can improve the performance of low-achieving students (Cohen & Kulik, 1981; Cooper, 2001). Thus, increased use of summer school and tutoring potentially can accelerate the performance of low-achieving students.

Although many schools offer summer school and after-school tutoring, the effectiveness of these interventions is frequently undercut by lack of attendance. Thus, some mechanism is needed to encourage participation by students who need help. This could be accomplished through mandatory referrals based on test scores. What did Minnesota teachers and administrators say about this use of test results?

Putting Teeth into Summer-School Referrals

Interviewee responses indicated that roughly two-thirds (63%) of all interviewees supported the use of test results, in combination with teacher recommendations, to refer students to summer school. In general, teachers felt that mandatory referrals based on test results would improve student accountability, would put teeth into summer-school referrals, and would increase the chances that students who need help would get it. Both regular and special education teachers supported this view. A special education teacher in an urban high school explained why this type of high-stakes testing may be beneficial:

> [Would you require students who fail a promotion exam to attend summer school or be retained?] I would like to see that required. We frequently suggest [summer school], and we offer that. But for a number of reasons parents opt "no." Or the student opts "no" by

skipping, coming only occasionally, to the point where it's ineffective. If it was a statewide requirement, that might give it more force and we might get better results. If we're saying, "These are eighth grade skills," then it makes sense that you need to have these skills in order to move on. So I like that idea.

This suggests why many teachers approve of attaching stakes to test results. They feel that the opportunities that schools currently provide to students are not adequately utilized. They feel that the capacity of schools to assist students is limited when students and parents do not do their part to take advantage of those opportunities. High-stakes testing is viewed as a means of compelling students to attend summer school and compelling parents to plan summer vacations so that they do not conflict with summer school. Teachers pointed to the need for this type of assistance in the early and middle grades, to prevent as many children as possible from falling behind and risking failure at the exit level. But perhaps the most important reason, articulated by a 4th-grade teacher in a semirural elementary school, is that mandatory referrals are needed to break a culture of complacency:

> Personally, I think that the school district needs to provide that for children. If we want everybody to read, we want everybody to be accountable, let's do something about it. Let's not just keep passing them on, and saying, "You're in the low percentile on this but we're going to keep passing you on." [If they don't go to summer school, should they be retained?] I agree with that. I totally agree with that.

Teachers provided many suggestions to ensure that summer programs are effective. They urged that the assessment be designed to provide diagnostic information for identifying areas of weakness and tailoring summer programs to address those weaknesses. Teachers also addressed the logistics of requiring students to attend summer school. A big issue is what to do if students do not attend. As a last resort, schools may retain students or, alternatively, may simply require students to participate in after-school tutoring programs if they had been identified as needing summer school but did not attend. A second issue is funding to hire teachers. Teachers agreed that the district or state would have to provide those resources. A third issue is how to accommodate children with learning disabilities or in special education. Teachers felt that summer school would have to provide carefully tailored interventions for those students in order for it to be helpful. Some teachers suggested that summer school not be limited to students scoring low on assessment tests, which would reduce the risk that students participating in the summer program would be labeled as failures.

Concerns About Summer School

A third (34%) of the interviewees were opposed, and 4% were undecided, when asked about using test results for mandatory summer-school
referrals. Teachers opposed to requiring summer school for students who
score low on assessment tests were concerned about the availability of
resources, the potential for student burnout, the compulsory aspect of
such a requirement, enforceability, and low test reliability and validity,
especially if students do not take the test seriously. Teachers were concerned that students who did not want to attend would misbehave and
be expelled, although some teachers felt that retention in grade would
be appropriate and helpful in that situation and would improve student
accountability. All of these concerns suggest the need for careful implementation of summer programs and alternative provisions for students
for whom summer school would not be beneficial.

Improving Attendance at Tutoring Sessions

By an overwhelming margin (80%), interviewees supported the use of
test results to refer students for tutoring. The teachers' reasoning is basically the same as the reasoning used to justify test-based referrals to summer school and the overall principle of attaching stakes to test results.
Teachers felt that a test-based requirement would improve attendance at
tutoring sessions that are already offered and help to ensure that students
who need help receive it. A special education teacher in an urban high
school described attendance at voluntary programs as "abysmal":

> Yes. I think that [mandatory referrals] would be helpful. . . . We've
> tried many, many, many things to try to raise student's scores. We've
> had homework clubs for kids after school, we've had Honor Society
> students tutoring [but] I see very few kids taking advantage of it. . . .
> Our attendance is abysmal.

Teachers felt that this type of early intervention was essential to prevent children from falling behind. Some teachers recommended that students be assessed at the beginning of the year so that they could receive
tutoring throughout the year, avoid the stigma of being identified as in
need of help at the end of the year, and avoid being referred to summer
school. Another recommendation is to allow students who do not need
the tutoring to participate, as a way of reducing the labeling that occurs
when the programs are limited to low-achieving students and encouraging students to view the programs positively. Teachers wanted diagnostic
assessments that would provide information about areas where students

are weak. Concerns included lack of funding for tutors and the availability of busses to transport students who stay after school for tutoring. Teachers felt the state would need to provide resources to support this type of requirement.

Concerns About Tutoring

A minority (14%) were opposed, and 5% were undecided, about using test results to refer students for tutoring. Teachers who were opposed cited concerns about the compulsory aspect of this approach, a preference for teacher recommendations, the need for funding to hire teachers, a need for transportation, a concern over labeling students (which could be addressed by offering tutoring to all students), and concern that poor student performance reflects behavioral issues rather than a need for tutoring, suggesting the need to temper mandatory referrals with teacher judgments.

DISCUSSION

By a 2-to-1 margin, teachers and administrators in the four Minnesota school districts believed that the exit exam fostered student accountability and motivated students to work harder, consistent with Roderick and Engel's (2001) finding that high-stakes tests improve student work effort. Interviewees talked about their students studying and working harder in school in order to pass the exit exam, even students diagnosed as EBD (emotionally/behaviorally disturbed). Thus, teachers believed that students were responding to the exit exam by working harder. This finding is consistent with survey research showing that 85% of Minnesota teachers supported the state's exit exam (Draper, 2000). These survey results suggest that the interviewees' positive views about state-mandated testing were not due to selection effects.

While the current results are consistent with prior research regarding the effects of high-stakes exams on student motivation and achievement, they are remarkable for two reasons. First, the motivational effects described by interviewees were achieved with a minimum competency exam. It appears that the exit exam does not need to be a high-standards exam in order to exert a motivational effect, at least for the group of low-achieving students who are presumably most in need of motivational consequences.

Second, the motivational effect was reportedly achieved without the unintended negative consequences associated with high-standards exit exams such as Arizona's AIMS test. This suggests that the benefits of a high-stakes test can be obtained without many of the costs, if the test is designed and implemented according to the Minnesota model.

Key Features

What were the key features of that model? First, Minnesota chose to adopt a minimum competency exit exam that only required students to know basic math, reading, and writing skills. According to the teachers and administrators interviewed for this study, the test was relatively easy, and it was not unreasonable to expect that students pass the exam before receiving a diploma. Second, the content of the exam was aligned with essential skills and knowledge that are important in the world outside school. Teachers and administrators expect students to have these skills and knowledge. Third, special education teachers had the flexibility to adjust the passing score on the exam for students with disabilities, ensuring that students who were working hard were not denied diplomas. Fourth, schools were required to write a remediation plan and provide remediation services for all students who failed the exit exam the first time they encountered it in 8th-grade, ensuring that students received the help they needed in order to improve their performance. Students were given a total of 11 opportunities to pass the exam.

As a result of these design features, cumulative pass rates exceeded 99%, meaning that very few students were denied diplomas as a consequence of failing the exit exam. Thus, the costs of high-stakes testing associated with students failing the exit exam were limited to less than 1% of the student population—far lower than the 39% who failed Arizona's exit exam. These differences explain why the effects of Minnesota's program were relatively benign compared to Arizona's.

The gap between initial and cumulative passing rates at the state level suggests that many students benefited from the supportive features of Minnesota's testing system that ultimately contributed to the 99% cumulative passing rate. In 2005, statewide initial passing rates were 85% in reading and 74% in math (in comparison, initial passing rates averaged 76% in reading and 64% in math across the 4 districts included in the study; unfortunately, district-level cumulative passing rates are not available).

Thus, supportive features are important, and they are arguably even more important when the exit exam is difficult. For example, Massachusetts has a high-standards test with unlimited opportunities for students to retake the exam and an appeals/waiver process for students meeting certain eligibility criteria (Sullivan et al., 2005). Massachusetts also provides an alternate assessment for severely disabled students and funding for tutoring (Sullivan et al., 2005). As a result, cumulative passing rates are higher in Massachusetts—96% (Sullivan et al., 2005) than in Arizona—61% (Eyewitness News 4, 2005). Supportive features, however, may not be sufficient to offset all of the "wicked" consequences of a high-standards exam. While the passing rate in Massachusetts is relatively high, the cumulative failure rate (4%) is quadruple the failure rate in Minnesota (under 1%), and this difference is likely to be greatly magnified for minority and ELL student groups that are most greatly affected by the implementation of a high-standards exam and whose initial failure rates, in Massachusetts, range as high as 52% (Sullivan et al., 2005). Thus, it is important to ensure that exit exams do not require a level of skill and knowledge that exceeds the level needed by the majority of students once they leave school. For this purpose, a minimum competency exam may be sufficient.

Given the benefits of using minimum competency exit exams, how can policymakers ensure that all students have incentives to achieve at high levels? It is notable that, in addition to the minimum competency exit exam that is first administered in 8th grade, Minnesota (at the time of the research study) required all districts within the state to administer "high-standards" Minnesota Comprehensive Assessments (MCAs) in grades 3 (reading and math), 5 (reading, math, and writing), 10 (reading and writing), and 11 (math). There were no consequences linked to MCA test results. However, the dual system of using high-standards tests as well as a basic skills exam aimed to ensure that teachers did not narrow the curriculum to basic skills—and may explain why interviewees felt that the effect of Minnesota's minimum competency exam on the breadth of the curriculum was relatively benign (see chapter 4).

Mandatory Referrals

Despite the advantages of the Minnesota model, it could be improved in two ways. First, there is a need to ensure that students take advantage of opportunities to improve their performance in the early grades, well before they reach the exit exam. Teachers and administrators recommended that students who fail an end-of-grade exam be required to attend summer school and after-school tutoring. This requirement could be enforced by retaining students who fail to attend. However, unlike most high-stakes promotion exams, where students are retained if they do not pass the end-of-summer exam, students would only be retained if they do not attend the remedial programs. Thus, students would not be punished as long as they seek out the help they need. This feature would maximize the benefits to students without retaining students who may be working hard but unable to pass the exam.

This approach reflects teachers' views about the benefits of high-stakes testing. When teachers talked about the positive side of testing, they emphasized that consequences are needed to compel students to accept help. According to this view, students currently have opportunities to learn, but they are not taking advantage of those opportunities. Teachers see education as a joint task that requires a partnership among teachers, schools, parents, and students (Bishop, 1990; Powell, 1996). What they observe is that without stakes—meaning consequences for students—many students and parents do not make adequate efforts to ensure that students get the help that is needed and offered by teachers. While many states require schools to provide remediation services, very few require students to attend (Gayler et al., 2003). Compulsory attendance potentially could ensure that students receive the help needed to improve performance.

Multiple Diploma Options

A second change in Minnesota's program would address two major criticisms: minimum competency exams do not motivate students to reach for high standards, and they can inadvertently foster narrowing of the curriculum (McNeil, 2000; McNeil & Valenzuela, 2000; M. L. Smith, 1991; Smith et al., 1999; Smith & Rottenberg, 1991). How can states such as Minnesota retain the benefits (for low-achieving students) of a minimum competency exam, yet encourage all students to strive for high standards and avoid narrowing of the curriculum to basic skills? One approach, currently used on a limited basis by 34 states (primarily with regard to students with disabilities), is to give students multiple diploma options (Johnson & Thurlow, 2003). This approach could be adapted so that students who pass the minimum competency level are awarded a regular diploma, while those who exceed higher levels of performance receive more prestigious diplomas. The multiple diploma approach aims to counteract pressure to dumb down the curriculum since teachers are expected to prepare students at high, as well as low, levels of achievement. A multiple diploma system would clearly distinguish high and low levels of achievement, unlike single diploma systems, and could serve to restore the meaning of high school diplomas.

In New York, for example, students who pass five Regents exams with a score of 65 or above receive a prestigious Regents Diploma, while students who are unable to meet that standard but are able to pass five exams with a score of 55 or above are eligible to receive a local diploma

(University of the State of New York, 2005). This type of system provides a high standard to aim for, and a prestigious reward for those who achieve that standard, yet avoids denying diplomas to large numbers of students who cannot achieve that standard but are able to reach the minimum competency standard.[2]

Bishop (1998) and Bishop, Mane, Bishop, and Moriarty (2001) analyzed the effects of curriculum-based external exit examination systems, which are exit exam systems that signal multiple levels of achievement. Bishop and his colleagues concluded that this feature significantly changes the incentive effects of exit exams. Minimum competency exams only motivate low-achieving students to work harder, since higher-achieving students pass easily. In contrast, exit exam systems that reward students at every level of achievement potentially motivate all students to work harder. After analyzing data from the Third International Math and Science Study (TIMSS), the International Assessment of Educational Progress, and New York's Regents examination system, Bishop concluded that this type of examination system significantly improves student achievement and has positive effects on curriculum and instruction.

More recently, after reviewing the effects of alternative testing policies, Bishop et al. (2001) concluded that "The policy that clearly has the biggest effects on test scores is the hybrid end-of-course/minimum competency exam system that has been in place in New York state since the early 1980s and in North Carolina since about 1991" (p. 310). Bishop et al. explicitly describe New York's system of multiple diplomas as a curriculum-based external exit examination system: "This policy package is also often referred to as a curriculum-based external exit exam system" (p. 310), suggesting that research findings regarding these types of systems generalize to multiple diploma systems that are similar to those used by New York.

CONCLUSION

The effects of Minnesota's testing system on curriculum and instruction are addressed in chapter 4. These results suggest that Minnesota may benefit from a multiple diploma system. However, despite the use of a single minimum competency test as an exit exam, the results reported here suggest that Minnesota was able to obtain much of the presumed benefits of high-stakes testing with regard to improved student motivation, while minimizing the educational costs of exam failure and discouraged students. Thus, Minnesota's design may serve as a model for other states such as Arizona, where alarmingly high failure rates suggest that high-stakes tests are doing more harm than good. The current study suggests areas where sound choices about test design and implementation policy could dramatically reduce unintended negative consequences of testing. Attention to these choices can help to ensure that high-stakes testing provides a kind rather than wicked learning environment.

The results of the current study are significant because they modify current views about the features of effective accountability systems. For example, Porter, Chester, and Schlesinger (2004) suggest that effective accountability systems should be symmetrical, incorporating stakes for teachers as well as students. Minnesota contradicts this dictum: by all accounts, it appears to be effective, yet it does not include stakes for teachers. In fact, the relatively benign effect of Minnesota's system on the curriculum (chapter 4) suggests that there may be benefits when overt pressure on teachers is minimized.

The view that high-stakes testing may benefit students by compelling them to take advantage of existing educational opportunities to learn has not received attention by researchers concerned that students lack adequate opportunities (Baker & Linn, 2004; Elmore, 2004; Fuhrman, 2001; Kornhaber, 2004; Linn, 2004; McNeil, 2000; O'Day, 2004; Porter et al., 2004; Smith et al., 1999). As noted above, many schools do not provide summer school or after-school tutoring programs. However, federal resources for tutoring often go unused (Saulny, 2006). To the extent that programs are available and are underutilized, interview respondents suggested that high-stakes testing can play an important role in compelling students and parents to take advantage of those opportunities.

A related implication is that high-stakes testing programs should switch from retention to referrals: instead of retaining students in grade, the focus should be on using test results to refer students to summer school, tutoring, and other programs designed to improve performance, long before students reach the exit level. Retention should only be used when necessary to enforce attendance at these programs. Retention policies assume that the threat of retention is what improves performance, but the operative factor may instead be the degree to which students utilize after-school programs. After Chicago ended social promotion, attendance at after-school programs doubled, which may explain why student achievement improved (Jacob & Stone, 2005; Jacob et al., 2004). Mandatory referrals to after-school programs may require implementation of new programs, expansion of existing programs, and funds to ensure that transportation is available. However, this approach may maximize the benefits of high-stakes testing while minimizing the frequency and educational costs of retention.

The current study also suggests that existing literature (Baker & Linn, 2004; Elmore, 2004; Fuhrman, 2001; Kornhaber, 2004; Linn, 2004; McNeil, 2000; O'Day, 2004; Porter et al., 2004; Smith et al., 1999) overlooks the importance of multiple diploma options. If minimum competency tests cause teachers to dumb down the curriculum, while high-standards exit exams such as AIMS result in high failure rates and negate any benefits from high-stakes testing, there is a need for exit exam systems that reward high levels of performance without causing massive failures. Single-level exit exam systems are inherently unable to fulfill this role. There is a need for multiple-level tests and multiple diploma options so that students who pass a minimum competency exam may obtain a regular diploma, yet all students strive to reach the higher standards signaled by more prestigious diplomas. This type of system would provide the motivational incentives that are desired, while minimizing the harm of single-level high-standards exams.

Multiple diploma options, in combination with minimum competency exams, offer a potential solution to the dilemma faced by states attempting to implement high educational standards without subjecting large numbers of schools to federal No Child Left Behind (NCLB) sanctions that are the consequence of failure to make "adequate yearly progress." The use of a minimum competency exit standard would reduce the likelihood of sanctions, since more students will pass this type of exam than a high-standards exit exam. However, without multiple diploma options, this approach is inconsistent with the goal of raising educational standards—which is the goal of NCLB, and also the reason why many states shifted from basic skills graduation tests to high-standards graduation tests in the 1980s and 1990s. On the other hand, a minimum competency standard, coupled with multiple diploma options that reward students with increasingly prestigious diplomas depending on the level of student performance, would provide the incentives necessary to raise achievement and, thus, would effectively raise standards without subjecting large numbers of schools serving disadvantaged students to federal sanctions—which is the inevitable consequence of using a high-standards exit exam.

Alternatives to a multiple diploma system include setting a low initial passing score that is raised over time, or putting off the effective date of an exit exam until more students achieve at a high level. However, neither of these alternatives will avoid situations where students who possess basic competencies and are equipped for a wide range of occupations are denied diplomas because they do not meet the higher standard. These alternatives fail to address the fundamental inequity involved in denying a diploma to students who may otherwise be equipped with the skills needed for their chosen occupations.

Economic research suggests that earnings depend strongly on receipt of a diploma (Cameron & Heckman, 1993; Murnane, Willett, & Tyler, 2000). Therefore, it is critical to determine whether an exit exam contains any items that are not valid for the purpose of predicting occupational success in a majority of occupations. If—as in the case of Arizona—there are items on the exit exam that require skills that are unnecessary for occupational success, these items are by definition invalid for the purpose of predicting occupational success and should be removed from the exam. For example, if professors of education do not need to know algebra and geometry in order to be successful, it would not be valid to deny diplomas to students who do not have algebra and geometry skills. Note that this issue is entirely separate from the desirability of promoting student achievement beyond the exit level. For example, it may be desirable for students to have the analytical abilities required to solve calculus problems, but it is not an appropriate use of exit exams to deny diplomas to students who lack those skills. Instead, other strategies such as multiple diplomas should be used to provide the necessary incentives.

If the primary rationale for the implementation of an exit exam is to motivate low-achieving students to work harder, the research findings presented here suggest that a minimum competency test (MCT) is more likely to motivate—and avoid discouraging—low-achieving students, compared to a high-standards exit exam. These are the students who are most in need of motivation. The research by Bishop and his colleagues, using data from the Third International Math and Science Study (TIMSS), the International Assessment of Educational Progress, and NAEP, confirms that an MCT/multiple diploma system improves student achievement.

The evidence presented in this chapter suggests that Minnesota's system, in combination with a multiple diploma system, would provide appropriate incentives for all students and teachers to aim for high standards—without denying diplomas to students who are trying hard but are only able to achieve the minimum competencies needed for a wide variety of occupations. This relatively simple change in policy addresses problems with the use of basic skills tests and could help to restore the balance between equity and accountability in high-stakes testing.

6

The Future of Testing

The evidence presented in the previous chapters suggests that high-quality instruction is possible in a high-stakes testing environment and can be achieved with state tests that rely primarily on a multiple-choice format. However, advances in testing may soon allow school districts to purchase a completely new type of test, one that uses computer technology to simulate real-life critical thinking tasks and asks students to develop an evidence-based argument supporting the most logical conclusion. Arguably, this type of test represents the "holy grail" of testing: a performance-like critical thinking test that answers the critics of multiple-choice testing.

These critics worry that state-mandated multiple-choice tests focus narrowly on factual recall and basic skills, and are inherently unable to test critical thinking. They worry that teachers who feel pressure to prepare students for those tests will be driven to emphasize the types of basic skills that are key to successful performance on those tests, instead of critical thinking.

However, it may be possible to use computer technology to design state-mandated tests that emphasize critical thinking and thereby encourage teachers to focus on instruction in critical thinking. Researchers are now attempting to translate this notion into reality.

DEFINING CRITICAL THINKING

The starting point is to define what is meant by "critical thinking." In a previous article, I explained that critical thinking skills may be defined as argumentation skills, particularly in the presence of confusing evidence or when an alternative view is defensible (Yeh, 2001). For example, synthesis is an argument that "A," "B," and "C" are related. Analysis is an argument that "X" can be broken down into "A," "B," and "C." Interpretation is an argument that "X" means "Y," and so on. In these arguments, the synthesis, analysis, or interpretation involves a claim backed by reasons. The reasons may be implicit—that is, not formally stated (see Toulmin, 1958, 1988). If the reasons are sound, then the argument is strong; otherwise, it is weak. According to this definition, an effective way to teach critical thinking is to teach students to build arguments, and an effective way to assess critical thinking is to assess the ability to build arguments. While many researchers agree that critical thinking may be conceptualized at an advanced level as argumentation, what is unusual is the proposal that the two concepts may be equated. The implications—if this view is correct—are profound, both for assessment and pedagogy.

In contrast to this view, psychometricians traditionally break down all of the component skills that are required to demonstrate critical thinking with regard to a particular task, for example, diagnosing anemia in a patient. Some of the component skills would involve interpreting lab results and information gathered from an interview with the patient. The assessment of critical thinking ability then requires assessment of each of the component skills. Pedagogically, this approach suggests the importance of teaching each component skill.

It is true that deficiencies in any of the component skills will undermine overall performance of the critical thinking task. Thus, there is a need to assess and teach the component skills. However, in practice, the component skills are generally conceptualized and operationalized in a way that strips those skills of much of the need for a student to weigh confusing evidence and develop an argument. For example, the component skill of interpreting lab results is frequently assessed by presenting lab results, then asking a student to correctly select an answer choice, or supply the correct answer. This type of task is no different than a typical item from a typical norm-referenced standardized test. In general, this type of assessment would not present confusing lab results and ask the student to formulate an argument about the interpretation of the results, which would constitute a true critical thinking task, according to the definition presented above. The difference is that the former task can be practiced to the point where it becomes an automated subroutine, a recall task, for example, of recalling that a low iron level is a symptom of anemia.

If, instead, every critical thinking task is conceptualized as argumentation, and each assessment of a critical thinking task is designed in a way that requires a student to weigh confusing evidence, formulate a claim, and support it with relevant evidence, then assessment would truly be aligned with the pedagogical goal of teaching critical thinking. The danger of forgetting this is that the enormous efforts now being expended to reform assessment through the use of goal-based scenarios will result in watered-down end products that are basically fancy, computerized versions of current norm-referenced tests. If goal-based assessments primarily give students credit for performing well on routine component skills, teachers will emphasize the component skills. If the component skills are stripped of critical thinking, there will be no need to change instruction and it will continue to resemble the type of traditional skill and drill instruction that the new assessments aim to deter.

In short, there is a need to focus assessment on true critical thinking tasks where students are required to weigh confusing evidence. In practice, this means that critical thinking assessments should, in general, supply the evidence needed to develop a defensible argument. We wish to assess critical thinking, not the ability to recall information. This view must be modified, of course, if instruction aims to develop content matter expertise as well as critical thinking skills, in which case it is desirable for students to develop their recall knowledge of particular facts so that they are less dependent on reference materials. However, if the emphasis is on driving pedagogy to focus on critical thinking instruction, the assessment tasks must emphasize items requiring students to weigh confusing evidence, rather than recalling key facts.

In addition, while a critical thinking task is more difficult if a student must supply the correct claim and evidence, rather than selecting a claim and evidence from lists, the desire to emphasize critical thinking rather than recall ability suggests that it is more important to manipulate the degree to which confusing evidence is presented to the student. This latter dimension ought to be the focus of assessment design. For the purpose of large-scale assessment, it may be desirable to constrain assessment tasks to those in which students select a claim and appropriate evidence from suitable sources, and to focus instead on varying the amount of confusing information presented to each student.

The approach presented in this chapter emphasizes a view of critical thinking as argumentation, and a view of critical thinking assessment that focuses on the ability of students to construct and evaluate arguments. This view privileges argumentation skill primarily because students who lack this skill are typically classified as lacking critical thinking ability. In addition, the development of argumentation skill is viewed as an excellent way to motivate the learning of the factual content information that is needed to reason in a given content area, and it encourages students and teachers to focus on the orchestration of component skills in a way that results in critical thinking. In contrast, excessive focus on the separate component skills may obscure the metatask of orchestrating the component skills to arrive at a defensible conclusion (a correct diagnosis, in the example of an anemic patient).

The view of critical thinking as argumentation suggests a useful model for assessing critical thinking with large-scale standardized tests. In the spring of 2001, I met with a group of researchers from Harvard University and Boston College to discuss the future of educational testing. Dr. Alan Collins demonstrated a software program called Nutrition Clinician, designed to teach skills in recognizing and ameliorating nutritional deficiencies to nursing and medical students enrolled at Northwestern University's medical school. I immediately recognized that the program taught critical thinking by teaching argumentation.

The simplest form of an argument is a claim supported by reasons or evidence. Nutrition Clinician asked students to diagnose a "patient" based on her symptoms and lab results. Students selected claims and supporting evidence from appropriate lists. The software then provided "expert" feedback regarding the validity of the resulting argument, prompting students to revise their claims and evidence as necessary. This approach can be adapted for the purpose of standardized testing and could solve the problem of how to test critical thinking in a way that is practical when testing thousands of students at a time.

The type of goal-based scenario illustrated by Nutrition Clinician could be used to test critical thinking, utilizing multidimensional partial credit measurement models developed specifically for this type of open-ended problem (Kennedy, 2005). Presumably, if state-mandated standardized tests incorporated goal-based scenarios, teachers would be encouraged to emphasize this type of critical thinking instruction in order to prepare students for the state-mandated test. Testing would then be aligned with critical thinking instruction. Furthermore, these scenarios could be used to simulate a wide range of situations requiring critical thinking, such as diagnosing problems with an automobile engine or building arguments about the causes of World War II. This would permit state-mandated tests to broaden their emphasis away from a narrow focus on basic math and reading skills.

THE TASK

The task of developing even a small bank of 100 to 200 scenarios for testing purposes posed seemingly insuperable challenges. Other researchers have created goal-based scenarios and are working to adapt these scenarios to demonstrate how they might be used to assess critical thinking (see, for example, DeBarger, Yumoto, & Quellmalz, no date; Gotwals & Songer, 2006; Lajoie, 2000; Mislevy et al., 2003). However, these efforts have been stymied by barriers presented by the conventional mode of test production: the tremendous cost of hiring computer programmers and content specialists, and the lengthy development period that is normally required to write, field-test, and revise each scenario. With current approaches, it is financially prohibitive to develop standardized tests incorporating goal-based scenarios. Furthermore, the necessary development period could easily stretch into the next decade. These barriers currently prevent large-scale production of goal-based scenarios and prevent their incorporation into state-mandated tests. The lack of a solution to this problem has prevented states from switching from multiple-choice tests to tests featuring scenario-based critical thinking tasks.

However, Dr. Christopher Riesbeck and Wolff Dobson, the computer scientists behind the development of Nutrition Clinician, had developed authoring software called "Indie" (for "investigate and decide") that allows individuals with no training in computer programming to develop goal-based scenarios (Qiu, 2005; Qiu, Riesbeck, & Parsek, 2003). This software would allow teachers with access to Indie to create goal-based scenarios. The capacity to field computer-based tests nationwide is already available through the nonprofit Northwest Evaluation Association (NWEA), whose tests are currently used in over 1,800 schools and districts across the United States.

I envisioned a plan to adapt and use Indie to permit regular classroom teachers to write goal-based scenarios that would then be edited, field-tested, and added to NWEA's banks of computer-based test items. This would allow district administrators to incorporate the scenarios into district-administered standardized tests on a field test basis, potentially within the next year, instead of the distant future.

The implications of this development are potentially revolutionary. While multiple-choice items are not likely to disappear from standardized tests, it may be feasible in the near future to emphasize critical thinking through engaging, lifelike simulations of real problem scenarios. Teachers would no longer be asked to teach critical thinking skills, yet have their students assessed primarily on recall of factual knowledge. In fact, teachers might decide to prepare students for tests that incorporate goal-based scenarios by using similar scenarios as instructional units. Thus, instruction could be aligned with assessment, but in a way that fosters development of broadly applicable critical reasoning skills. The scenarios would teach students how to rapidly sift through mounds of information to identify key facts, form conclusions, and build strong arguments—skills useful in whatever occupation a student might choose to pursue.

NUTRITION CLINICIAN

Let's examine Nutrition Clinician more closely, to understand what a goal-based scenario test item might look like. First, students click on a button to hear an introduction and explanation of the scenario (Figure 6.1).

Figure 6.1. Students hear an explanation of the scenario.

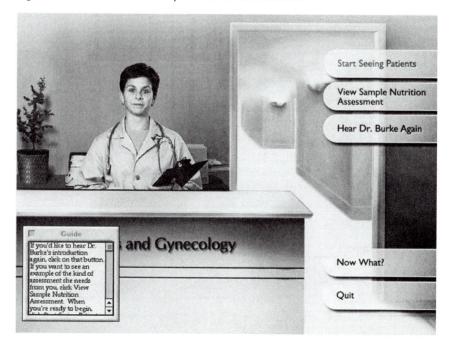

Students are told that they must diagnose a patient's illness, based on information about her symptoms and lab results. Students begin by interviewing the patient, clicking on questions to which the patient replies. As the patient replies, the information appears on the patient's chart, on the left side of the screen (Figure 6.2).

Students can "order" tests by clicking on appropriate buttons. The results then appear on the patient's chart (Figure 6.3).

By clicking the appropriate buttons, students can consult "experts" to gather information that may assist in diagnosing the patient. The expert responds verbally, and the text of the expert's response is displayed (Figure 6.4).

Figure 6.2. Students "interview" the patient and the information appears in the "Interview Notes."

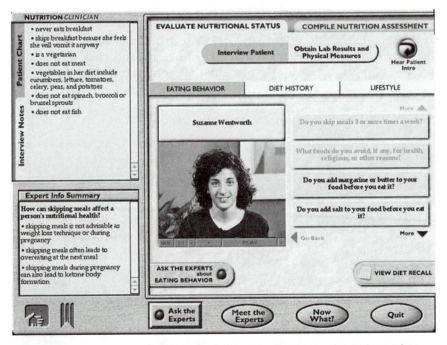

Figure 6.3. Students order tests and the information appears in the "Lab Results."

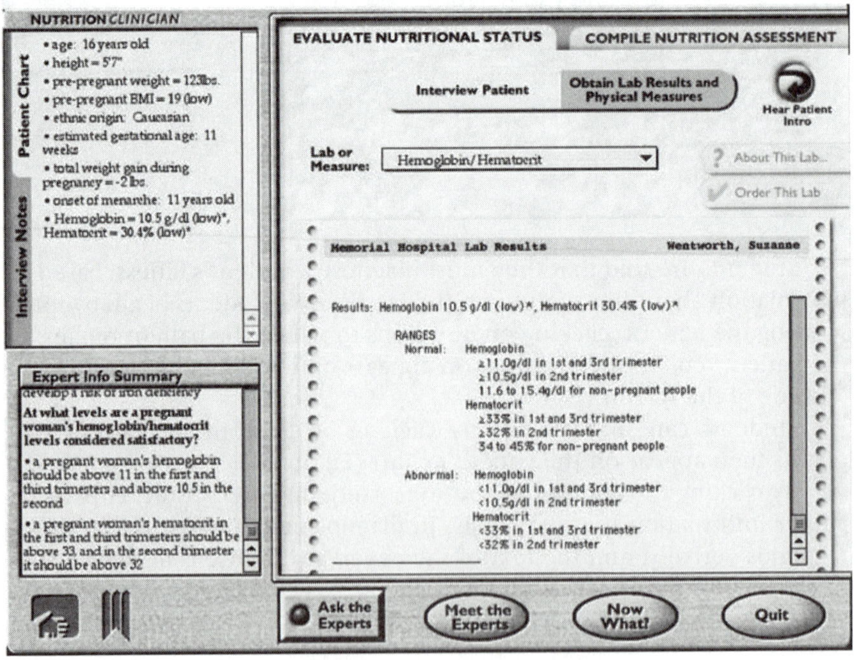

Figure 6.4. Students consult experts and their responses appear in the "Expert Info Summary."

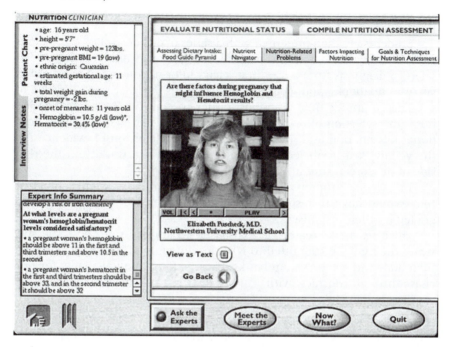

Figure 6.5. Students click on the appropriate buttons to gather information.

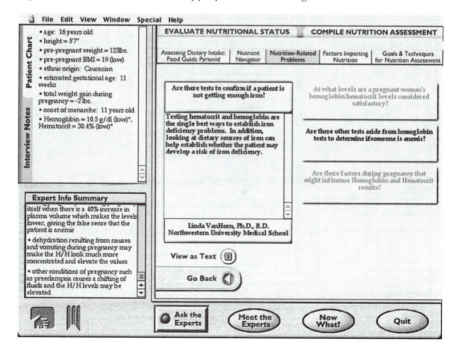

Students gather information by clicking on the appropriate buttons (Figure 6.5).

Students are then presented with a series of diagnostic tasks. For example, one task is to determine whether the patient is anemic. The student selects a diagnosis from a list, then selects information from the interview, lab tests, textbooks, and specialists that supports that diagnosis (Figure 6.6).

The computer then responds, either to confirm the student's diagnosis and selection of evidence, or to prompt the student to gather additional information and revise the diagnosis or selection of evidence (see the yellow Post-It labeled "R_x From the Desk of Dr. Burke" on the right side of the screen shot in Figure 6.7).

In essence, students must respond to counterarguments, much as they would have to respond to counterarguments in a debate, and are graded on their responses.

Once teachers create the goal-based scenarios using the Indie software, they will be submitted to NWEA, edited, field-tested, revised, and then added to NWEA's item banks, thus making them available for purchase through contracts with schools, districts, and states (Figure 6.8).

Figure 6.6. Students select a diagnosis along with information that supports the diagnosis.

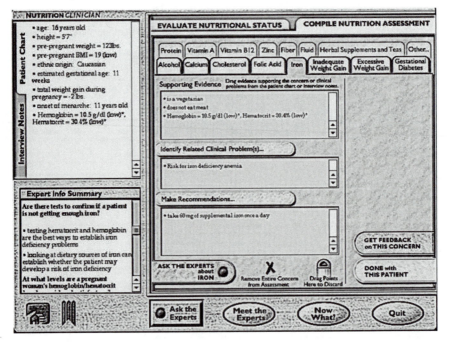

Figure 6.7. The computer responds with feedback (e.g., "R$_x$ From the Desk of Doctor Burke").

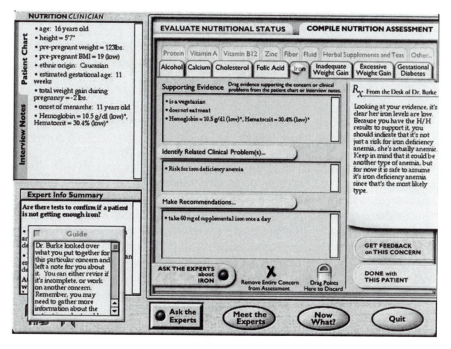

Figure 6.8. The creation of goal-based scenarios could help to align testing and critical thinking instruction.

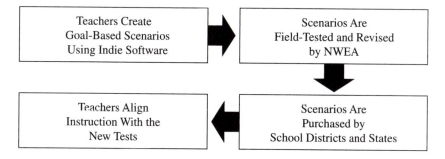

The development of Indie, the ability of NWEA to field computer-based tests, and an innovative scheme to streamline the conventional mode of test production may give states the opportunity in the near future to implement state-mandated tests that compel students to reason critically and encourage teachers to teach critical thinking.

7

The Policy Context

The evidence presented in the previous chapters suggests that feedback is a key factor in the learning process, and the implementation of rapid assessment systems is a promising way of improving student achievement. The evidence suggests that rapid feedback immediately reinforces student and teacher actions that improve student achievement. Without this corrective feedback, it appears less likely that students and teachers will address learning difficulties, and an important source of reinforcement that encourages and motivates increased effort appears to be missing. If rapid feedback is necessary for optimal learning, and if it is currently missing in most schools, the implementation of rapid assessment systems may be more effective in improving student achievement than other changes, such as increased spending, reduced class size, improved teacher quality, educational choice and competition, and increased accountability. If feedback is not adequate, the effectiveness of policies that do not influence the feedback loop may be minimal. This chapter reviews the evidence.

SPENDING AND ACHIEVEMENT

Per pupil spending on America's elementary and secondary schools more than doubled from $4,505 to $9,614 (in constant dollars) between 1970 and 2002, yet student achievement, measured by NAEP test scores, remains low (National Center for Education Statistics, 2004). As described in chapter 1, substantial percentages of 12th-grade students, especially African-American and Hispanic students, continue to fall into the lowest performance category, where students cannot even perform at a "basic" level.

Some researchers suggest that overall spending figures are misleading because much of the new spending has been allocated for students with learning disabilities and thus cannot be expected to improve the achievement of the vast majority of students who do not receive special education services. However, it is estimated that special education spending accounts for less than 20% of the growth in per pupil expenditures (Hanushek, 2001b).

Hanushek (1986, 1989) reviewed the research evidence and concluded that there is only a weak relationship between educational spending and student achievement:

> The results are startlingly consistent in finding no strong evidence that teacher-student ratios, teacher education, or teacher experience have an expected positive effect on student achievement. According to the available evidence one cannot be confident that hiring more educated teachers or having smaller classes will improve student performance. Teacher experience appears only marginally stronger . . . There appears to be no strong or systematic relationship between school expenditures and student performance. (Hanushek, 1986, p. 1162)

A second review, however, appeared to contradict this conclusion. Based on a more narrow selection and meta-analysis of 60 studies, Greenwald, Hedges, and Laine (1996) concluded that "moderate increases in spending may be associated with significant increases in achievement" (p. 361). Based on their results, Greenwald et al. estimated that a 10% increase in per pupil expenditure could result in an increase in student achievement of .083 standard deviations (SD) per year. But recall from chapter 1 that providing feedback to students two to five times weekly can improve student achievement by 0.7 SD (Fuchs & Fuchs, 1986), in other words, over *eight times* as much as increasing per pupil expenditure by 10%. This comparison is probably conservative. Hanushek (1996) argued that Greenwald et al. systematically excluded studies in a way that biased their conclusions, suggesting that the .083 SD figure may be overstated. In any case, it is estimated that it would cost an enormous $43 billion to increase per pupil expenditure sufficiently to increase NAEP test scores by 2% (Hanushek, 2001a).

The limitations of increasing spending to improve student achievement are graphically illustrated by the experience of Kansas City, Missouri. In 1985, in response to a desegregation suit, federal district judge Russell Clark ordered the state and district to increase spending on Kansas City schools by a prodigious $2 billion (Churcher & George, 2002; Ciotti, 1998; Simon, 2001). This increased per pupil expenditures to $11,700—more money per pupil, on a cost-of-living–adjusted basis, than any of the other 280 largest districts in the country (Ciotti, 1998). Despite new facilities, a highly paid teaching staff, and a reduction in student-teacher ratio to 12 to 1, student achievement remained low, and Clark labeled the entire experiment a "debacle" (Churcher & George, 2002; Ciotti, 1998; Simon, 2001). This example illustrates that there is no guarantee that student achievement will improve if educational expenditures are increased.

It seems obvious that money must be spent wisely in order to improve student achievement. Perhaps there was some flaw, unique to Kansas City, in the way the funds were spent. However, the available research evidence suggests that the most popular proposals—reducing class size (reducing student-teacher ratios), raising salaries to recruit better teachers, and increasing spending on teacher professional development—are unlikely to achieve the desired results.

California implemented a $4 billion program to reduce class sizes in grades K–3, starting in 1996. By the 1999–2000 school year, average class size in those grades had dropped from 29 to 19 students. Yet two studies suggest that the overall improvement in student achievement has been small (Jepson & Rivkin, 2002; Stecher & Bohrnstedt, 2000). Furthermore, it appears that rapid implementation may have increased underlying inequities in the state's education system (Stecher & Bohrnstedt, 2000). While reading scores rose slightly, math scores declined in schools with the highest proportions of Black students (Jepson & Rivkin, 2002). The problem was that class size reduction required California to hire 25,000 new teachers—21,000 more than normal. Many were inexperienced and underqualified, and were ill-prepared to handle the needs of low-income Black and Hispanic students. Stanford University economist Edward P. Lazear constructed a statistical model and found that reducing class size to 20 students increased educational achievement by 4% while increasing costs by 30% (Lazear, 1999). Furthermore, he found that student achievement of African-American students in largely minority schools declined.

Perhaps the strongest evidence supporting the effectiveness of class size reduction is Tennessee's class size experiment (Finn & Achilles, 1999). This randomized study suggested that reduction of class sizes to the range of 13 to 17 students can be effective in improving student achievement, under the condition that students are not taught by inexperienced and underqualified teachers. However, California was unable to duplicate these conditions: class sizes could only be reduced to 19 students, and the demand for experienced, fully qualified teachers exceeded supply. The Tennessee experiment involved hiring a much smaller number of teachers, so demand for experienced teachers did not exceed supply. One could fault California for "poor implementation," but perhaps the lesson is that the type of class size reduction achieved in the Tennessee experiment is unrealistic to implement on a large scale, under prevailing fiscal and labor market constraints. The results from California are the best available evidence of what happens under these conditions and suggest that class size reduction is not a panacea.

What about raising salaries to recruit better teachers? A widely cited meta-analysis asserted that there is a positive correlation between teacher quality and student achievement but the authors conceded that the research evidence relating teacher ability and student achievement was "too limited to draw conclusions" (Greenwald, Hedges, & Laine, 1996, p. 375). Without random assignment of teachers and students to classrooms, it is difficult to disentangle the contribution of teacher quality. Thus, it is significant that the only study of teacher quality using random assignment concluded that the main observable characteristics of teachers—years of experience and level of education—are essentially uncorrelated with gains in student achievement: "Neither teacher experience, nor teacher education explained much variance in teacher effects (never more than 5%)" (Nye, Konstantopoulos, & Hedges, 2004, p. 249).

While few would disagree with the claim that better teachers would improve the quality of education and student achievement, the task of identifying and hiring effective teachers is not simple. For example, one study found that only 3% of the contribution teachers made to student learning was associated with teacher experience, degrees attained, and other readily observable characteristics (Goldhaber, 2002). In other words, years of experience and graduate degrees do not have a strong impact on student achievement. Students whose teachers have master's degrees do not outperform students whose teachers have only a bachelor's degree (Grissmer, Flanagan, Kawata, & Williamson, 2000; Wenglinsky, 2000). Meta-analyses and reviews of research suggest that there is no clear relationship (Greenwald et al., 1996; Hanushek, 1989; Wilson & Floden, 2003) or close to zero relationship (Hanushek, 1996; Hedges, Laine, & Greenwald, 1994) between teachers' level of educational attainment and student achievement. The relationship between teacher experience and student achievement is also inconsistent (Wilson & Floden, 2003). First- and second-year teachers are less effective, on average, than more experienced teachers, but after this period, experience has little effect (Grissmer et al., 2000; Wenglinsky, 2000). Therefore, if readily observable characteristics such as graduate credentials and years of experience are weakly related to teacher quality, it may be extremely difficult for a school principal to identify and hire good teachers.

What about increasing spending on teacher professional development? This policy was tried in San Diego. When Alan Bersin became superintendent in 1998, he made the improvement of instructional quality the district's top priority. The district's annual budget for the professional development of teachers was increased dramatically, from just over $1 million to almost $70 million in the 2002–2003 school year (Hightower & McLaughlin, 2004). This amounted to an extraordinary $7,000 per teacher (Thernstrom & Thernstrom, 2004).

Researchers suggested that the money was well spent. "The reform emphasizes literacy as the primary focus of elementary schooling, especially in the elementary grades" (Darling-Hammond, Hightower, Husbands, LaFors, & Young, 2002, p. 23). "By the start of the second year of reform, nearly 100 certified and trained literacy peer coaches blanketed two-thirds of district schools" (Hightower, 2002, p. 13). "The approach to balanced literacy in San Diego, as embodied in its Literacy Framework . . . is founded on leading edge research on teaching and learning and encompasses a varied array of pedagogical techniques and expected outcomes from students, including extensive, high level strategic reading and writing, as well as evidence- and reason-based discussion and other forms of oral discourse" (Darling-Hammond et al., 2002, p. 28). This emphasis on literacy in the elementary grades suggests that the relevant measure of success is test scores in reading.

At first glance, the results seemed encouraging. In reading, the percentage of San Diego's 3rd-grade students who scored at or above the 50th percentile on standardized tests surged from 41% in 1998, before funding was increased, to 47% in 2002 (California State Department of Education, 2005). However, this gain was exceeded by the gains of students statewide, from 38% to 47%. Most disappointing of all, the figure for San Diego's students fell to 41% by 2005—no higher than in 1998.[1] In math, the percentage of San Diego's 3rd-graders exceeding the 50th percentile surged from 46% in 1998 to 60% in 2005. However, this 14-point gain was matched by students across the state. The fact that reading and math gains in San Diego were no better than gains in the statewide averages strongly suggests that San Diego's massive investment in teacher professional development had no effect on student achievement. Students in schools that did not have the benefit of extra spending on teacher development fared just as well as San Diego's students, that is, there was no "value-added" of the extra spending.

Hanushek (1997) reviewed the evidence once again and concluded: "The close to 400 studies of student achievement demonstrate that there is not a strong or consistent relationship between student performance and school resources, at least after variations in family inputs are taken into account" (p. 141). Furthermore, "There is little reason to be confident that simply adding more resources to schools as currently constituted will yield performance gains among students" (p. 148). This does not mean that money cannot make a difference. It means that we cannot be confident that more spending, *per se*, will lead to improved student achievement. In some instances more spending will be helpful; in other instances it will not. In general, educational researchers have not been able to say precisely how money should be spent in order to *reliably* improve achievement. However, the studies reviewed previously suggest that increased expenditure on rapid assessment could be effective.

EDUCATIONAL CHOICE AND COMPETITION

What about vouchers: is educational choice the answer? According to Paul Peterson, a professor at Harvard University, "The New York evaluation provides the best evidence we now have on voucher impacts" (Myers, Pfleiderer, & Peterson, 2002). However, when all students were considered, the randomized field trial indicated that after 3 years there was no impact on reading and math achievement (Mayer, Peterson, Myers, Tuttle, & Howell, 2002). While Peterson and Howell (2004) argue that there were significant impacts for African-American students, these impacts were "trivial," according to Krueger and Zhu (2003), who used a different set of assumptions. Two authors of the study cautioned against placing too much emphasis on the impacts for African-American students (Myers & Mayer, 2003). But when the results are considered together with 2 additional randomized field trials, it appears that vouchers may indeed boost achievement for African-American students. Howell, Wolf, Campbell and Peterson (2002) estimated that African-American students gained an average of 6.3 National Percentile Rank (NPR) points in "total achievement" (math and reading) over two years [3.15 NPR points or 2.2 normal curve equivalent (NCE) points per year, equal to an effect size of 0.10 SD][2] in New York City, Dayton, Ohio, and Washington D.C. on the Iowa Tests of Basic Skills (ITBS). This effect is one-seventh of the 0.7 SD effect for rapid assessment.

In Milwaukee, the use of a lottery system to allocate vouchers approximated a random-assignment design, but only 50% of students who were selected to receive vouchers were still attending their choice schools 2 years later (Rouse, 1998). In any case, Rouse (1998) estimated that "students selected for the Milwaukee Parental Choice Program . . . likely scored 1.5–2.3 (NCE) percentile points per year in math more than students in the comparison groups. On the other hand, the results for reading scores were quite mixed with both positive and negative coefficient estimates" (p. 593). The average math gain (1.9 NCE points) equals an effect size of 0.09 SD. Greene, Peterson, and Du (1999) conducted numerous analyses, but their "best estimate" is that after 4 years, math scores were 10.65 NCE points higher (an annual gain of 2.7 NCE points or an effect size of 0.13 SD), while reading scores were 5.84 NCE points higher (an annual gain of 1.5 NCE points or an effect size of 0.07 SD) (pp. 200–201). These estimates suggest gains that are less than one-fifth the size of the 0.7 SD effect associated with the implementation of rapid assessment systems.

What about charter schools? The only national comparison casts doubt on this approach. The study, involving a nationally representative sample of 4th- and 8th-grade students, suggests that students in traditional public schools outperformed students in charter schools (Nelson, Rosenberg, & Van Meter, 2004). The study showed students in traditional schools outperforming the charter school students in every racial category (White, Black, and Hispanic). The results were consistent whether or not students were eligible for subsidized lunches, and whether or not students attended urban or suburban schools. Only charter school students in rural towns outperformed their traditional school peers.

The scores of students who were eligible for free or reduced-price lunch, as well as the scores of students who were not, were lower in charter schools than in regular public schools in grades 4 and 8, in math as well as reading. Among lunch-eligible students in grade 4, the statistically significant difference was nearly six scale points in math and seven points in reading. These differences translate into a little more than a half-year of schooling. In grade 8, the difference between charter and regular public schools was nearly seven scale points in math and four points in reading, but only the math result was statistically significant. These results are consistent with a study of 569 charter schools in 10 states that found that charter school students typically score lower on state tests (Loveless, 2002). Neither study suggests that charter schools are a panacea.

Howell and West (2005) criticized the methodology used by Nelson et al. and argued that charter school students are likely to be more disadvantaged than lunch-eligible students who remain in traditional schools. However, a rigorous analysis conducted specifically in response to this claim found that charter school students are no harder to educate than similar students enrolled in traditional public schools (Buckley & Schneider, 2005).

Perhaps the most rigorous methodology for evaluating the effects of charter schools involves random assignment of students to charter schools or traditional schools. Hoxby and Rockoff (2005) conducted the only evaluation of charter school effects that approximated random assignment. The study compared the performance of students who were randomly accepted into three charter schools with the performance of students who were randomly rejected and attended traditional schools. This study concluded that charter school students gained 6.4 NPR points in math and 5.6 NPR points in reading on the ITBS over a 4-year period, or annual gains of 1.6 NPR (0.9 NCE) points in math (an effect size of 0.04 SD) and 1.4 NPR (0.8 NCE) points in reading (an effect size of 0.04)[3]—less than one-seventeenth of the 0.7 SD effect associated with the implementation of rapid assessment.

There is, however, another way of analyzing the effect of increased choice and competition: examine the effect of vouchers or charter schools on the performance of students in schools that face increased competition. The question is whether increased competition causes student achievement to increase in the regular public schools. The focus here is not on the achievement of students who used vouchers or attended charter schools. Instead, the focus is on the achievement of students who remained in the regular public schools. Does competitive pressure cause those schools to improve their performance?

In Florida, students in schools that receive a grade of F twice during any 4-year period are eligible to receive vouchers to attend another public school or a private school. Students eligible for vouchers gained 5.9 NPR (3.3 NCE)[4] points in math (an effect size of 0.16 SD, or less than one-fourth of the 0.7 SD effect of rapid assessment) on the Stanford Achievement Test, compared to students in all other Florida public schools (Greene & Winters, 2004b).

Hoxby (2002) analyzed three choice reforms selected "because they are the only ones in which the choice schools can, legally, garner a large enough share of enrollment to provide a nonnegligible amount of competition for the regular public schools" (p. 142). In Milwaukee, where parents could use vouchers to choose their children's schools, elementary schools facing the most competition for their students showed greater improvements on 4th-grade test scores. Reading scores increased by an average of 0.8 NPR points per year in the 3 years after the voucher program was expanded, compared to a negative 1.3 NPR points per year for the control schools. The difference represents a gain of 2.1 NPR points. Math scores increased by an average of 6.3 NPR points per year, compared to only 3.5 NPR points per year for the control schools. The difference represents a gain of 2.8 NPR points. These results suggest small gains in student achievement from increased competition associated with vouchers.

In Michigan and Arizona, sufficient students in each state were enrolled in charter schools to provide competitive pressure on regular schools. The net increase in the achievement of schools that faced competition, beyond the increase achieved by schools that did not face competition, ranged from 1.11 NPR points to 2.68 NPR points for 4th- and 7th-grade students in reading and math over a 7-year period (the annual gains were much smaller) (Hoxby, 2002). These results suggest small gains in student achievement in each state from increased competition associated with charter schools.

Of the gains reported by Hoxby, the largest annual gains were achieved in Milwaukee—2.1 NPR (1.2 NCE) points per year in reading (an effect size of 0.06 SD) and 2.8 NPR (1.6 NCE) points per year in math (an effect size of 0.08 SD).[5] These gains are less than one-ninth of the 0.7 SD gain associated with the implementation of rapid assessment systems.

In both reading and math, the gains associated with rapid assessment were achieved over time periods much shorter than the annual rates of gain associated with studies of educational choice. Over a comparable time period, the gains associated with rapid assessment would likely be even greater. Thus, the estimates of relative effects are probably conservative.

A recent, rigorous study of the effects of charter school competition on the achievement of students in public schools concluded that the presence of charter school competition increases traditional school performance by about 1% (Holmes, Desimone, & Rupp, 2003, 2006). The authors do not report the information needed to caluculate effect sizes, so it is difficult to compare the magnitude of this gain with the size of gains associated with the implementation of rapid assessment systems. However, a 1% gain does not appear to be large. Furthermore, a second recent, rigorous study of North Carolina found a *negative* effect of charter schools on student performance—an effect that is not offset by positive effects due to increased competition:

> Our results can only be described as discouraging for charter school supporters. Students in these grades make considerably smaller achievement gains in charter schools than they would have in traditional public schools, and the negative effects are not limited to schools in their first year of operation. Nor are the negative effects of attending a charter school substantially offset by positive effects of charter schools on traditional public schools, a finding that may reflect the fact that North Carolina charter schools provide only a limited amount of competition. (Bifulco & Ladd, 2005, p. 66)

Nor are negative effects explained by observable or unobservable differences in the students who attend charter schools. The pattern of the data "provides strong evidence that the smaller gains made by these charter school students are indeed due to the quality of the schools they attend rather than to any unobserved differences between charter school students and students in traditional public schools" (Bifulco & Ladd, 2005, p. 62).

In summary, the results reviewed above suggest that there is at best a small positive impact on student achievement in public schools due to increased competition from voucher programs and charter schools. Even if negative studies (Loveless, 2002; Mayer et al., 2002; Nelson et al., 2004) and cautionary views (Krueger & Zhu, 2003; Myers & Mayer, 2003) are excluded, the average impact of the most positive studies of choice and competition is only 0.07 SD in reading (one-tenth the impact of the 0.7 SD impact of rapid assessment) and 0.10 SD in math (one-seventh the impact of rapid assessment) (Table 7.1).

Table 7.1. Effect sizes for key studies of choice and competition.

Study	Effect Size (Standard Deviation)	
	Reading	Math
Howell et al., 2002	.10	.10
Rouse, 1998	?	.09
Greene et al., 1999	.07	.13
Hoxby & Rockoff, 2005	.04	.04
Greene & Winters, 2004b	—	.16
Hoxby, 2002	<.06	<.08
AVERAGE OF ALL STUDIES	0.07	0.10

INCREASED ACCOUNTABILITY

What about the push for increased accountability that is embodied in the No Child Left Behind Act? What is the likely impact of this approach on student achievement? Studies by Amrein and Berliner (2002a; 2002b) concluded that there is no evidence that states that implemented high-stakes tests demonstrated improved student achievement on various measures such as the Scholastic Achievement Test (SAT), American College Test (ACT), Advanced Placement (AP) exams, or NAEP. However, both their methodology and their findings have been challenged (Braun, 2004; Rosenshine, 2003).

Among the most rigorous studies is Carnoy and Loeb's (2002) statistical model that relates gains in student achievement to changes in degree of accountability pressure. Carnoy and Loeb constructed a 5-point index of accountability pressure and found that significantly stronger accountability was associated with modest increases in student achievement at the 8th-grade level. For example, a two-step increase in accountability was associated with a 4.8-percentage-point gain in the percentage of 8th-graders scoring at the "basic" skill level or higher. However, the effects of increased accountability on 4th-grade scores were not significant. There was no impact for the average 4th-grade student, or for students disaggregated according to race (White, Black, or Hispanic). In contrast, the findings regarding the effect of rapid assessment programs suggest that rapid assessment is much more effective than increased accountability pressure for improving student achievement at the elementary school level.

Perhaps the best evidence for the impact of accountability policies is a recent study that employed a sophisticated design to control for numerous factors that would otherwise confound the findings (Hanushek & Raymond, 2005). This study found that high-stakes testing leads to larger growth in student achievement than would have occurred in the absence of such tests. To account for differences among states that would otherwise confound the results, the study examined growth in student NAEP scores between 4th and 8th grades, controlling for measures of parental education, school spending, race, and fixed state effects. The study found minimal impacts from merely reporting test results—performance improvements depended on linking consequences to student achievement. However, the introduction of accountability systems was only associated with small gains in achievement on the order of 0.2 SD over 4 years, or 0.05 SD per year (Hanushek & Raymond, 2005), one-fourteenth of the 0.7 SD gains in achievement associated with rapid assessment.

Conclusion and Recommendations

The research findings presented in chapter 7 suggest that rapid assessment is 8 times as effective as a 10% increase in per pupil expenditure, at least 7 times as effective as charter schools or vouchers, and 14 times as effective as accountability alone. These comparisons are conservative because they are based on chapter 7's upper bound estimates of the effects of increased spending, charter schools, vouchers, and accountability, derived from the most optimistic assessments by researchers who argue that these policies do indeed have positive effects on student achievement. The comparisons would be even more dramatic had I used chapter 7's lower bound estimates by those researchers who are most pessimistic about the effects of those policies.

Why would rapid assessment be more effective than the alternatives—increased spending, reduced class size, more educated and experienced teachers, more professional development, increased competition, and increased accountability? The research evidence presented in this book suggests that rapid feedback is essential for student motivation, learning, and instructional improvement. According to this evidence, feedback builds students' intrinsic interest and engagement, and fosters continuous improvement in teaching. The evidence suggests that rapid feedback regarding student progress could improve student achievement—perhaps dramatically.

The implementation of rapid assessment responds directly and precisely to the human need for feedback. In contrast, the broad policy alternatives reviewed in chapter 7 are indirect and imprecise. They are blunt instruments. If the problem is lack of feedback, these instruments are unsuited for the task.

A precise response that directly addresses the source of a problem can be dramatically more effective than imprecise approaches. The story of John Snow demonstrated how precise knowledge that cholera can be transmitted through contaminated water could have been used to prevent further outbreaks. This insight could have ended the death toll. Unfortunately, leading physicians of his day remained unconvinced. They believed that the problem could not possibly be so simple. The handle of the Broad Street pump was replaced, residents continued to draw water from the well, and cholera continued to plague Europe's cities until the advent of modern sewage systems.

While many readers will argue that the challenge of educational reform is far more complex than the transmission of disease, the solution to the problem of cholera was only simple in hindsight. The problem had defeated England's best scientists, including William Farr, who argued that, while contaminated water might explain some cases, Snow's theory ignored the bulk of previous research, which implicated miasma and suggested the need for complex, multifactor explanations. Indeed, the transmission of cholera involves a complex interaction of human behavior with urban environments. Farr demonstrated a relation between elevation and morbidity that seemed to support the notion of miasma—bad air that was concentrated and killed disproportionately at low elevations (Eyler, 2001). In addition, many documented cases seemed to demonstrate that individuals who had ingested cholera evacuations suffered no ill effects (Eyler, 2001). Finally, it was believed that, in India, pariahs who regularly cleaned up the excreta of cholera victims were no more likely to suffer ill effects (Eyler, 2001). The germ theory seemed far too simplistic. But what is simplistic is the notion that the complexity of teaching and learning is beyond the reach of science.

If meta-analyses of controlled research studies suggest that rapid assessment produces some of the largest effect sizes ever observed for an intervention, we should ask about the mechanism. If teachers observe that students who receive rapid feedback demonstrate enthusiasm for learning, feelings of control over their progress, and improved academic achievement, we should inquire about the scientific principles underlying this phenomenon. If there is a series of research studies demonstrating that feelings of control are related to academic achievement, and early academic achievement fosters feelings of control over future achievement, we should inquire about the long-term effects. And if research demonstrates that early academic achievement is strongly related to later academic achievement, and this relationship is mediated by a student's sense of control over his or her academic achievement, we should inquire about methods of improving student feelings of control over academic achievement.

There are many ways to increase students' feelings of control over their academic achievement. Encouragement is one. Tutoring is another. Excellent instruction is a third. Rapid assessment is a fourth. So, why privilege rapid assessment? Why not simply say that rapid assessment and feedback are among many excellent ways of improving student engagement and achievement?

To borrow a concept from learning theory, rapid assessment is an affordance—a way of structuring the learning situation to promote learning. It is a special type of affordance in that it is an intervention that can be readily implemented on a large scale through state or federal policies, or on a small scale through policies at the local district-, school-, classroom-, or individual-student level. It can be implemented independently of other actors. An individual building principal can choose to implement this intervention without a need to change existing district or state or federal policies, and without the formal concurrence of teacher unions, school boards, parents, or the political party that happens to control the state legislature. It can be implemented with whole classrooms or targeted to specific groups of students, during the regular school day or after school. Although additional federal or state funding would be helpful, over 60,000 schools have implemented rapid assessment with their own funds—demonstrating its economic feasibility (Nunnery, Ross, & Goldfeder, 2003). The large number of schools that have adopted rapid assessment suggests that it fits within current operating routines, without requiring whole school reform or other disruptive changes. Perhaps no other educational intervention can claim this combination of large effect size, flexibility, affordability, ease of implementation, and ability to scale-up (as evidenced by Idaho's statewide implementation; see Renaissance Learning, 2002).

The following are steps that can be taken at different government and administrative levels.

THE FEDERAL GOVERNMENT SHOULD:

1. Provide sufficient funding for a 3-year, five-state demonstration and evaluation of rapid assessment technology, providing computers, software, and training necessary to implement classroom-based rapid assessment and quarterly district assessments aligned with the state-mandated assessment in districts that otherwise cannot afford it.

2. Allow schools that are classified as "in need of improvement" to fulfill the supplemental services requirement of NCLB by implementing classroom-based rapid assessment technology and quarterly district assessments for all students who are below grade-level in math or reading.

3. Require that each state provide a summary of research regarding the effectiveness of rapid assessment technology to every principal, superintendent, director of testing, and state school officer by January 1, 2008.

4. Change federal policy to allow states to use fully computer-adaptive tests for NCLB testing purposes.

5.   Provide sufficient funding for a 3-year, five-state demonstration and evaluation of computer-adaptive testing for NCLB purposes, providing computers, software, and training necessary to implement a computer-adaptive state-mandated test that would provide growth information for individual students as well as accountability information on a constant scale that can be used to judge school effectiveness.

6.   Provide supplemental funding for transportation, teachers, and associated costs of summer school and after-school tutoring programs for any district where more than 15% of students are eligible for free or reduced-price lunch.

STATE GOVERNMENTS SHOULD:

1.   Provide state funding for computers, software, and training necessary to implement classroom-based rapid assessment in any district where more than 15% of students are eligible for free or reduced-price lunch, and direct district staff to existing sources of funding.

2.   Provide a summary of research regarding the effectiveness of rapid assessment technology to every principal, superintendent, director of testing, and state school officer by January 1, 2008.

3.   Provide financial incentives for schools to implement rapid assessment technology.

4.   Establish institutes to provide professional development to aspiring and experienced principals and instructional leaders regarding effective instructional strategies and effective use of assessment data for instructional improvement.

5.   Ensure that the content of state-mandated tests is properly aligned with the skills and knowledge that students may be expected to know outside school.

6.   If using a high school exit exam, use a minimum-competency, rather than a high-standards, exam.

7.   Use multiple diploma options that signal multiple levels of achievement and encourage all students to achieve at high levels.

8.   Implement high-standards grade-level exams (in addition to minimum competency exit exams) that encourage all students and teachers to strive for high standards.

9.   Use grade-level exams for mandatory referrals to summer school and after-school tutoring programs, enforced by grade retention for students who do not attend those programs.

10.   Provide funding as needed for transportation, teachers, and associated costs of summer school and after-school tutoring programs.

11.   Avoid excessively fact-oriented curriculum standards that may inadvertently cause teachers to drill students on large numbers of facts.

12. Avoid compensating, rewarding, or punishing teachers based on test results, which may create pressure to narrow the curriculum to material that is tested.

13. Consider segmenting state-mandated tests into a number of short tests administered over the course of the school year, rather than one lengthy test at the end of the year.

14. If using a high school exit exam, allow the passing score to be adjusted for students with disabilities (acknowledging the need for flexibility with disabled students to avoid discouraging them, as well as acknowledging that exams are imprecise measures of competency and predictors of future success).

15. If using a high school exit exam, require schools to write a remediation plan and provide remediation services for all students who fail the exit exam the first time they encounter it, ensuring that students receive the help they need in order to improve their performance.

16. Give students as many as 11 opportunities to pass an exit exam.

DISTRICTS AND SCHOOLS SHOULD:

1. Provide a summary of research regarding the effectiveness of rapid assessment technology to every principal and instructional leader by January 1, 2008.

2. Provide computers, software, and training necessary to implement classroom-based rapid assessment and quarterly district assessments for all students who are below grade level in math or reading by January 1, 2009.

3. Use grade-level exam results for mandatory referrals to summer school and after-school tutoring programs, enforced by grade retention for students who do not attend those programs.

4. Implement summer school and after-school tutoring programs and provide transportation and teachers as necessary.

5. If using an exit exam, write a remediation plan and provide remediation services for all students who fail the exam the first time they encounter it, ensuring that students receive the help they need in order to improve their performance.

6. Avoid excessively fact-oriented curriculum standards that may inadvertently cause teachers to drill students on large numbers of facts.

7. Avoid compensating, rewarding, or punishing teachers based on test results, which may create pressure to narrow the curriculum to material that is tested.

Appendix

Interview Questions

I. Overall, is your opinion about the impact of the state testing program positive or negative? Why?

II. Does the state testing program influence the type of skills and knowledge that you focus on?

- Are these skills and knowledge important?
- Is the test designed so you feel a need to drill students on factual material?

III. How does the state test affect low-functioning students?

IV. What are the strengths and weaknesses of the computer-adaptive test, compared to the state-mandated test?

V. Recommendations.

A. To guide instruction, would you favor redesigning the state test to provide more detailed diagnostic information about student strengths and weaknesses?
B. Would you favor consolidation of all of the state and district tests into one test?
C. Suppose this was done and suppose that you could receive scores within 7 days. Would you favor, at every grade level, giving the test before the school year, as a pretest to diagnose students, and at the end of the school year, as a posttest to determine how much students improved during the year?
D. Would you favor using the test to determine which students should receive after-school tutoring?
E. Should students who fail the end-of-the-year test be required to attend summer school as a condition of promotion to the next grade?

F. Would you favor the use of a computer-adaptive test that adapts the difficulty of the questions to the student's level?

G. Would you favor the use of a test that provided the option of performance assessments for low-functioning students, vocational education students, bilingual students, and special education students, even if it meant that regular education teachers might have to share the responsibility of administering and scoring the performance assessments? [Perhaps 2 days of work per teacher.]

H. Would you favor state tests that focus on critical thinking rather than recall of facts?

I. Until these changes are made, would you favor delaying the requirement that students pass the state test in order to graduate from high school?

J. Are there other suggestions that you would make regarding the design or implementation of the state testing program?

Notes

Chapter 1

1. All of the NAEP results reported here were obtained by using the NAEP Data Explorer (see http://nces.ed.gov/nationsreportcard/nde/). The 2005 NAEP 12th-grade assessments will become available in Spring, 2006, and will provide updated percentages of students scoring Below Basic, but these results were not available as this book went to press. However, 2004 NAEP results show that scale scores in math and reading for White, Black and Hispanic 17-year-old students were either flat or declined between 1999 and 2004 (Perie, Moran, Lutkus, & Tirre, 2005), suggesting that the percentages of students scoring Below Basic have not changed significantly in recent years.

2. News of the outbreak caused residents to flee, sharply reducing the death toll. However, Snow's study clearly points to contaminated water as the main source of transmission of cholera.

3. "On the Mode of Communication of Cholera" by John Snow, M.D. London: John Churchill, New Burlington Street, England, 1855. The full text of Snow's study, his maps, and commentary on the significance of his work are available at http://www.ph.ucla.edu/epi/snow.html. See also http://www.sph.unc.edu/courses/john_snow/prologue.htm, as well as Judith Summers's description of the Broad Street Pump Outbreak in *Soho— A History of London's Most Colourful Neighborhood*, (London: Bloomsbury, 1989, pp. 113–117).

4. Cholera is also transmitted when caretakers of the victims handle soiled bedsheets and do not wash their hands thoroughly before preparing food. Thus, a small number of new cases appeared after the pump handle was removed.

5. Participants included 49 randomly selected teachers and school administrators in McKinney. McKinney was selected because it is one of the first districts in the United States that has implemented District Assessment, Reading Assessment, and Math Assessment districtwide. One-third of students enrolled in McKinney were minorities; 20% received free or reduced-price lunches.

Interviewees were asked for detailed explanations of their school's implementation of District Assessment, Reading Assessment, and Math Assessment, as well as their views of the consequences, including possible unintended consequences, of testing and the use of the rapid assessment programs. Each interviewer asked follow-up questions to make certain that the meanings respondents intended were understood. As interviews were conducted, emergent findings were checked through follow-up questions with subsequent interviewees. Interviews were transcribed and coded to identify primary themes. The themes were identified jointly by two raters and cross-checked by a third researcher. Discrepancies were resolved through discussion. Interview excerpts were selected that illustrated and elaborated on the range of views expressed by participants. Classrooms were observed to assess the implementation of the Reading and Math Assessment programs and to assess student engagement and behavior.

6. A rigorous matched treatment-control pretest-posttest evaluation in the McKinney, Texas, school district (the same district investigated in the current report) found that a sample of 891 students demonstrated significantly higher reading achievement over a 3-year period than 911 students in matched control schools, with effect sizes ranging from .17 to .22 SD in grade 5 on the state-mandated test (effects for 8th-grade students were not statistically significant) (Nunnery et al., 2003). A sample of 898 students demonstrated significantly higher math achievement over a 3-year period than 959 students in matched control schools, with an average effect size of .20 SD in grade 5 and .17 SD in grade 8 on the state-mandated test (Nunnery et al., 2003).

A previous evaluation during the 1999–2000 school year found that 3,649 McKinney students in grades 1 through 5 improved by 7 normal curve equivalent (NCE) points [approximately 0.9 grade equivalent (GE) points above a national sample of students] on the STAR Reading test (Smith & Clark, 2001).

7. Pseudonyms are used to avoid the appearance that the author endorses the assessment products and the company that produces them. The author has no affiliation with the Rapid Assessment Corporation and has received no funding from the corporation.

8. Reading Assessment was implemented districtwide in McKinney, Texas— the district that is the focus of this chapter—starting in 1999. An evaluation during the 1999–2000 school year found that 3,649 students in grades 1 through 5 improved by 7 NCE points (approximately 0.9 GE above a stratified, nationally representative sample of students) on the STAR reading test (Smith & Clark, 2001).

A second evaluation using a rigorous matched treatment-control pretest-posttest design, involving 891 students in the McKinney school district, found that two cohorts of Reading Assessment students demonstrated significantly higher achievement over a 3-year period than 911 controls in matched schools who did not participate in Reading Assessment, with effect sizes ranging from .17 SD to .22 SD in grade 5 on the state-mandated Texas Assessment of Academic Skills (TAAS) test (effects for two 8th-grade cohorts were not statistically significant) (Nunnery et al., 2003).

Reading Assessment was implemented statewide in Idaho, starting in 1998. An evaluation during the 2000–2001 school year found that 10,381 students in grades 1 through 4 gained 4.5 NCE points on the STAR reading test, a computer-adaptive norm-referenced test (approximately half of a grade equivalent above the performance of a stratified, nationally representative sample of students over the equivalent time period), with the bulk of the improvement in 1st grade (Renaissance Learning, 2002). On average, each student reportedly read over 40 books during the 7-month period of the evaluation.

9.   In a rigorous matched treatment-control pretest-posttest evaluation involving 898 students in the McKinney, Texas, school district (the same district that is the focus of this chapter), Math Assessment students demonstrated significantly higher achievement than 959 controls in matched schools who did not participate in Math Assessment, with an average effect size of .20 SD in grade 5 and .17 in grade 8 on the state-mandated test (Nunnery et al., 2003).

In a second quasi-experimental evaluation involving 495 4th- and 5th-grade students in a large urban school district, Math Assessment students demonstrated significantly greater growth in achievement relative to comparable students in the same schools, and students in the same district who did not participate in Math Assessment, although the program was implemented for only half of a school year (Spicuzza et al., 2001).

In a third quasi-experimental evaluation of Math Assessment involving 111 3rd- and 4th-grade students in a large urban school district who had failed state or district tests, students gained 2.7 NCE points in the 9 months prior to receiving Math Assessment, 5.5 NCEs after receiving Math Assessment for 16 days, and only 1.7 NCEs in the 9 months thereafter (Spicuzza & Ysseldyke, 1999). In other words, student gains doubled during the short duration of the program, then leveled off after the program was discontinued, suggesting that the program caused the improvement in outcomes.

In a fourth quasi-experimental evaluation involving 201 4th- and 5th-grade English Language Learner (ELL) students in a large urban school district, participants in Math Assessment gained 6.7 NCEs, significantly greater than the 3.9 NCEs gained by comparable ELL students who did not participate in the program (Teelucksingh, Ysseldyke, Spicuzza, & Ginsburg-Block, 2001).

In a large quasi-experimental evaluation involving a nationwide sample of 2,201 students in grades 3 through 10, participants in Math Assessment gained 1 to 1.4 grade equivalents (GE) during the 5 months of intervention. The gains by participants exceeded the gains of the comparison group by a margin ranging from 0.3 GE in 6th grade to 0.7 GE in 5th grade over one semester (Ysseldyke & Tardrew, 2002).

In a sixth quasi-experimental evaluation involving 711 students in grades 4–5 in a large urban school district, participants in Math Assessment gained 6.7 NCEs, more than double the 2.7 NCEs for comparable students not participating in the program (Ysseldyke et al., 2000).

10.   Using a fully crossed Latin square design [4 classrooms × 2 self-initiated feedback conditions (yes/no) × 2 external feedback conditions (yes/no)], Kahn (1989) randomly assigned 32 6th-grade students to four conditions: 1) self-initiated feedback paired with external feedback, 2) self-initiated feedback only, 3) external feedback from the experimenter only, and 4) training only (control).

11.   In addition to the reviews of feedback studies previously cited (Black & Wiliam, 1998a; Fuchs & Fuchs, 1986; Kluger & DeNisi, 1996), highly controlled individual studies have consistently found positive effects of performance feed-

back on measures of persistence and attitudes toward math and reading as well as student achievement. Using a within-subject A-BC-D-BC withdrawal of treatment design, Ninness et al. (1998) found that 5th- and 6th-grade students trained to self-assess themselves through computerized tests exhibited high rates and long durations of mathematics problem-solving when given feedback regarding accuracy, compared to periods when they were not given feedback.

Using a within-subject treatment design, Robinson et al. (1989) found that immediate, item-by-item computerized feedback significantly improved the performance of 15 learning-disabled (LD) elementary students (aged 10–13 years) working on long division mathematics problems. When feedback was in force, the students completed significantly more problems and more correct problems, and the level of accuracy increased from 73% without feedback to 94% with feedback.

Using a factorial experimental design, Elawar and Corno (1985) found that 6th-grade students who received feedback three times per week for 10 weeks on their mathematics homework demonstrated significantly higher math achievement and significantly more positive attitudes toward math compared to students who did not receive feedback. Students in the experimental group demonstrated over 100% improvement on measures of math "enjoyment," "value," and "self-concept." The feedback had positive effects on student learning regardless of ability levels.

Using a within-subjects multiple baseline design, McLaughlin (1992) evaluated the effects of written feedback on accuracy in reading with "behaviorally-disordered" students aged 10–11. The outcomes indicated improved accuracy in reading when written feedback was provided by the teacher. The students rated the written feedback procedure favorably.

In six experiments, Smith et al. (1969) found that elementary grade students produced significantly higher output on language arts tasks when provided with performance feedback under conditions of self-selection and pacing, compared to students who did not receive such feedback (see Figures 1.1 and 1.2).

Chapter 2

1. The author has no affiliation with Renaissance Learning and has received no funding from the corporation.

2. Beginning in 1999, the McKinney, Texas, school district implemented the StandardsMaster program, designed to provide teachers with rapid assessments of student progress. The selection of McKinney was based on two factors: 1) relatively mature implementation of StandardsMaster provided a suitable site to investigate the effects of rapid assessment, and 2) the opportunity to investigate the research questions in a state whose system of high-stakes testing is often viewed as a forerunner of the changes that are in store when the No Child Left Behind Act is fully implemented. Demographically, one-third of students enrolled in McKinney are minority; 20% receive free or reduced-price lunches. The participants in this study included 37 teachers, 5 principals, 6 assistant principals, and 1 librarian in 2 high schools, 2 junior high schools, and 4 elementary schools. Teachers and

administrators were randomly selected to represent the entire range from grades 2–12. All participants had bachelor's degrees and approximately one-third also held master's degrees. Years of experience in the classroom ranged from 1 to 29. Approximately 60% of the participants were female, and 40% were male.

Each participant was interviewed individually for 50 minutes using a semistructured interview protocol. Interviews were audio-recorded. Interviewees were asked about their views of Texas's state-mandated testing program, whether test results were used, how they were used, and possible unintended consequences on the quality of curriculum and instruction. Development of the interview protocol was informed by four rounds of previous interviews with approximately 160 teachers and principals in four states regarding the effects of state-mandated testing.

Multiple methods were used to triangulate findings from the interviews. Observations were conducted in 10 randomly selected classrooms to assess the quality of instruction. In each of these classrooms, three to five randomly selected students were interviewed regarding their views of the quality of instruction. Documents were reviewed, including assessment reports and curriculum and instruction materials.

In keeping with established methods of qualitative research (Bogdan & Biklen, 1992; Glaser & Strauss, 1967; Miles & Huberman, 1994; Strauss, 1987), data analysis followed the three-part modified constant comparative method. Each interviewer asked follow-up questions to make certain that the meanings respondents intended were understood. As interviews were conducted, emergent findings were checked through follow-up questions with subsequent interviewees. Interviews were transcribed and coded to identify primary themes. The themes were identified jointly by two raters and cross-checked by a third researcher. Discrepancies were resolved through discussion. Interview excerpts were selected that illustrated and elaborated on the range of views expressed by participants.

Chapter 3

1. The current study examines the responses of teachers and administrators who have used computer-adaptive tests developed by the Northwest Evaluation Association (NWEA). The researcher is not affiliated with NWEA and has not received funding from NWEA. The study was prepared independently of NWEA and was not reviewed by NWEA prior to publication.

2. The NWEA tests were designed using a Rasch model. Some measurement specialists caution against using this model with multiple-choice tests; at the same time, the choice of an IRT model is not really a "make-or-break" issue—the quality of the tests is what matters, and at least one expert regards the quality of NWEA tests as relatively high (E. H. Haertel, personal communications, October 30, 2001, and December 8, 2005). Also, alternative measurement approaches that function properly with multiple-choice items have been successfully used with computer-adaptive tests (D. J. Weiss, personal communication, April 7, 2003). A second concern is that the Rasch model assumes unidimensionality of the pool of test items, whereas achievement tests cover multiple learning objectives, different objectives are covered in different grade levels, and departures from unidi-

mensionality may be expected (Ackerman, 1987; Folk & Green, 1989). Although achievement domains have different content, all item response theory (IRT) models in use assume unidimensionality and work with a single dimension in the data. The issue of content coverage is best addressed directly in computer-adaptive testing through content balancing across tests so that each student will receive similar numbers of items from specified content areas. As long as all the items are calibrated together on (or linked onto) a common dimension, content balancing can still be achieved within a computer-adaptive test to ensure adequate coverage at the student level (D. J. Weiss, personal communication, April 7, 2003). In the upper grades, when departures from unidimensionality are expected to be greatest, it may be possible to calculate growth based on topical subscores (this may require increasing the number of items included on the test) (Linn, 1990). In any case, Linn (1990) and Traub and Wolfe (1981) caution against limiting the definition of achievement to items that fit a unidimensional IRT model, suggesting that it may be better to live with violations of IRT assumptions rather than to artificially restrict the types of items that are included on tests. A third concern is that the assumption that abilities can be measured on an equal-interval scale may be unfounded. NWEA, however, asserts that test scores track student development as predicted and therefore are valid indicators of growth.

3. A district study of the adaptive test found that spring test scores correlated highly with scores from the test administered at the beginning of the following school year, suggesting that scores from spring administrations can serve both as pretest scores for the following school year as well as posttest scores for students in the previous year.

4. The MBST is being replaced by the MCA-II high standards graduation test starting with the class of 2010.

5. The Department of Education has allowed Idaho to implement a hybrid computerized test developed by NWEA. The first part of the test contains fixed items administered to all students in a given grade level; the second part of the test is adaptive. However, this design negates many of the advantages of a fully adaptive test since all of the criticisms that apply to nonadaptive tests apply to the first part of the hybrid test. In addition to Idaho, states that use computer-adaptive testing to supplement NCLB-approved tests include: the District of Columbia, Maryland, Oregon, and South Dakota.

6. The author thanks an anonymous reviewer for this point.

Chapter 5

1. Ironically, Minnesota has joined the nationwide shift away from basic skills exams and is currently in the process of switching to a high-standards exit exam. It will be interesting to see the impact of this change.

2. New York has also joined the nationwide shift away from basic skills exams. Thus, the current approach is actually less two-tiered than New York's previous approach, where students could obtain a regular diploma by passing the easier Regents Competency Tests, but needed to pass the more difficult Regents Examinations to obtain the more prestigious Regents Diploma.

Chapter 7

1. "Standardized Testing and Reporting (STAR) Results" available at http://star.cde.ca.gov/. Note that all districts in California switched from the SAT9 to the CAT6 in 2003. ETS conducted a linking study in 2003 (California Department of Education, 2003). For most grades and content areas, the NPRs based on the CAT6 were lower than the NPRs for the SAT9. Thus, the percentage of students scoring above the 50th national percentile is not strictly comparable across both exams (some of the drop in performance in 2003—in San Diego as well as statewide—can be attributed to the change in exams). For this reason, it is best to compare San Diego's performance against the performance of students statewide.

2. Average baseline scores of African-American students in the three studies ranged from the 17th to the 30th national percentile on the ITBS (Howell et al., 2002, Table 3, p. 199). In this range on the ITBS, each NPR point is equal to 0.7 NCE points; thus, 6.3 NPR points equal 4.4 NCE points (see www.usoe.k12.ut.us/eval/DOCUMENTS/IOWA_FAQ.pdf).

3. Average initial test scores on the ITBS ranged between the 36th and 47th percentiles (Hoxby & Rockoff, 2005, p. 55, Figure 1d). In this range on the ITBS, each NPR point is equivalent to 0.55 NCE points. Thus, annual math gains were equivalent to 0.9 NCE points, while annual reading gains were equivalent to 0.8 NCE points.

4. This calculation is based on data from the Stanford Achievement Test, 9th Edition, Technical Data Report, Table 3 (Harcourt-Brace Educational Measurement, 1997, p. 21), which translates NPR scores into NCE scores. The rate of change in NCE scores was calculated for the 25th through the 50th percentile range, where the majority of Florida students in "F" schools would be expected to score. In this range, NCE scores for math increased from 36 to 50 points, or 0.56 NCE points per percentile point. Thus, an increase of 5.9 NPR points is equivalent to 3.3 NCE points.

5. This calculation is based on data from the Wisconsin Department of Public Instruction, Office of Educational Accountability, "Changing the Wisconsin Knowledge and Concept Examinations Norms from 1996 to 2000," Table 3, available at http://www.dpi.state.wi.us/oea/kcnorms02.html. Using the 1996 norm data, the rate of change in NCE scores was calculated for the 25th through the 50th percentile range, where the majority of Milwaukee students would be expected to score. In this range, NCE scores for reading (as well as math) increased from 36 to 50 points, or 0.56 NCE points per percentile point. Thus, an increase of 2.8 NPR points is equivalent to 1.6 NCE points, while an increase of 2.1 NPR points is equivalent to 1.2 NCE points. Note that direct comparisons across tests are complicated by differences in norm samples, test difficulty, and test content. However, the magnitude of the difference in student achievement suggests that rapid assessment was more effective than increased competition due to vouchers or charter schools.

References

Abrahams, S. (1987, August 31). *Focus-of-evaluation and intrinsic motivation.* Paper presented at the Annual Convention of the American Psychological Association, New York, NY.

Ackerman, T. (1987). *The use of unidimensional item parameter estimates of multidimensional items in adaptive testing* (ACT Research Report Series No. 87-13). Iowa City, IA: American College Testing Program.

Allensworth, E. (2004). *Ending social promotion: Dropout rates in Chicago after implementation of the eighth-grade promotion gate.* Chicago: Consortium on Chicago School Research.

Allensworth, E. (2005). Dropout rates after high-stakes testing in elementary school: A study of the contradictory effects of Chicago's efforts to end social promotion. *Educational Evaluation and Policy Analysis, 27*(4), 341–364.

Allinder, R. M., & Oats, R. G. (1997). Effects of acceptability on teachers' implementation of curriculum-based measurement and student achievement in mathematics computation. *Remedial and Special Education, 18*(2), 113–120.

Amrein, A. L., & Berliner, D. C. (2002a). High-stakes testing, uncertainty, and student learning. *Education Policy Analysis Archives, 10*(18). Retrieved April 4, 2006 from http://epaa.asu.edu/epaa/v10n18/.

Amrein, A. L., & Berliner, D. C. (2002b, December). *The impact of high-stakes tests on student academic performance: An analysis of NAEP results in states with high-stakes tests and ACT, SAT, and AP test results in states with high school graduation exams.* Retrieved June 5, 2004, from http://www.asu.edu/educ/epsl/EPRU/documents/EPSL-0211-126-EPRU.pdf

Amrein, A. L., & Berliner, D. C. (2003). The testing divide: New research on the intended and unintended impact of high-stakes testing. *Peer Review, 5*(2), 31–32.

Amrein-Beardsley, A., & Berliner, D. C. (2003). Re-analysis of NAEP math and reading scores in states with and without high-stakes tests: Response to Rosenshine. *Education Policy Analysis Archives, 11*(25). Retrieved April 4, 2006 from http://epaa.asu.edu/epaa/v11n25/.

Arizona Education Association. (2003). *Arizona academic standards and assessment: Position paper.* Phoenix, AZ: Quality Teaching and Learning Center.

Baker, E. L., & Linn, R. L. (2004). Validity issues for accountability systems. In

S. H. Fuhrman & R. F. Elmore (Eds.), *Redesigning accountability systems for education* (pp. 47–72). New York: Teachers College Press.

Bangert-Drowns, R. L., Kulik, C. C., Kulik, J. A., & Morgan, M. (1991). The instructional effect of feedback in test-like events. *Review of Educational Research, 61*(2), 213–238.

Baron, J. B., & Wolf, D. P. (1996). *Performance-based student assessment: Challenges and possibilities.* Chicago: University of Chicago.

Bifulco, R., & Ladd, H. F. (2005). Results from the Tar Heel state. *Education Next, 5*(4), 60–66.

Bishop, J. (1990). Incentives for learning: Why American high school students compare so poorly to their counterparts overseas. *Research in Labor Economics, 11*, 17–51.

Bishop, J. (1998). *Do curriculum-based external exit exam systems enhance student achievement?* (CPRE Research Report Series RR-40). Philadelphia: Consortium for Policy Research in Education, University of Pennsylvania, Graduate School of Education.

Bishop, J. H., Mane, F., Bishop, M., & Moriarty, J. (2001). The role of end-of-course exams and minimum competency exams in standards-based reforms. In D. Ravitch (Ed.), *Brookings papers on education policy* (pp. 267–345). Washington, DC: Brookings Institution Press.

Black, P., & Wiliam, D. (1998a). Assessment and classroom learning. *Assessment in Education, 5*(1), 7–74.

Black, P., & Wiliam, D. (1998b). Inside the black box: Raising standards through classroom assessment. *Phi Delta Kappan, 80*(2), 139–148.

Bogdan, R., & Biklen, S. (1992). Qualitative research for education: An introduction to theory and methods. Boston: Allyn & Bacon.

Boggiano, A. K., Main, D. S., & Katz, P. A. (1988). Children's preference for challenge: The role of perceived competence and control. *Journal of Personality & Social Psychology, 54*(1), 134–141.

Bracey, G. W. (2002). The 12th Bracey report on the condition of public education. *Phi Delta Kappan, 84*(2), 135–150.

Braun, H. (2004). Reconsidering the impact of high-stakes testing. *Education Policy Analysis Archives, 12*(1). Retrieved April 4, 2006 from http://epaa.asu.edu/epaa/v12n1/.

Brookover, W. B., Beady, C. H., Flood, P. K., Schweitzer, J. G., & Wisenbaker, J. M. (1979). *Schools, social systems and student achievement: Schools can make a difference.* New York: Praeger.

Brookover, W. B., Schweitzer, J. G., Schneider, J. M., Beady, C. H., Flood, P. K., & Wisenbaker, J. M. (1978). Elementary school social climate and school achievement. *American Educational Research Journal, 15*, 301–318.

Buckley, J., & Schneider, M. (2005). Are charter school students harder to educate? Evidence from Washington, DC *Educational Evaluation and Policy Analysis, 27*(4), 365–380.

California Department of Education. (2003). *2003 California Standardized Testing and Reporting Stanford 9–CAT/6 Linking Study.* [No city]: Author.

California State Department of Education. (2005). *Standardized testing and reporting*

(STAR) results. Retrieved December 12, 2005, from http://star.cde.ca.gov/

Cameron, S. V., & Heckman, J. J. (1993). *Determinants of young male schooling and training choices* (NBER Working Papers No. 4327). Cambridge, MA: National Bureau of Economic Research.

Carnoy, M., & Loeb, S. (2002). Does external accountability affect student outcomes? A cross-state analysis. *Educational Evaluation and Policy Analysis, 24*(4), 305–331.

Carnoy, M., Loeb, S., & Smith, T. L. (2001). *Do higher state test scores in Texas make for better high school outcomes?* (CPRE Research Report Series No. RR-047) [No city]: Consortium for Policy Research in Education, University of Pennsylvania, Graduate School of Education. Retrieved April 4, 2006, from http://www.cpre.org/Publications/rr47.pdf.

Catterall, J. (1987). *Toward researching the connections between tests required for high school graduation and the inclination to drop out* (Technical Report Grant G00869003). Los Angeles: University of California, Center for Research on Evaluation, Standards, and Student Testing.

Center on Education Policy. (2006). *From the capitol to the classroom: Year 4 of the No Child Left Behind Act.* Retrieved March 28, 2006, from http://www.cep-c.org/nclb/Year4/Press/.

Churcher, S., & George, A. (2002, July 21). In Kansas [City] they spent $2 billion on schools. Now they have Greek statues and the pupils can't read. *Mail on Sunday,* p. 58.

Cimbricz, S. (2002). State-mandated testing and teachers' beliefs and practice. *Education Policy Analysis Archives, 10*(2). Retrieved April 4, 2006 from http://epaa.asu.edu/epaa/v10n2.html.

Ciotti, P. (1998). *Money and school performance: Lessons from the Kansas City desegregation experiment* (No. 298). Washington, DC: Cato Institute.

Clarke, M., Shore, A., Rhoades, K., Abrams, L., Miao, J., & Li, J. (2003). *Perceived effects of state-mandated testing programs on teaching and learning: Findings from interviews with educators in low-, medium-, and high-stakes states.* Chestnut Hill, MA: National Board on Educational Testing and Public Policy, Lynch School of Education, Boston College.

Cohen, P. A., & Kulik, J. A. (1981). Synthesis of research on the effects of tutoring. *Educational Leadership, 39*(3), 227–229.

Coleman, J. S., Campbell, E., Hobson, C., McPartland, J., Mood, A., Weinfeld, R., et al. (1966). *Equality of educational opportunity.* Washington, DC: Government Printing Office.

Committee on Developments in the Science of Learning. (2000). *How people learn: Brain, mind, experience, and school.* Washington, DC: National Academy Press.

Cooper, H. (2001). *Summer school: Research-based recommendations for policymakers* (SERVE Policy Brief). Greensboro, NC: Southeastern Regional Vision for Education.

Corbett, H. D., & Wilson, B. L. (1991). *Testing, reform, and rebellion.* Norwood, NJ: Ablex.

Cotton, K. (2003). *Principals and student achievement: What the research says.* Alexandria, VA: Association for Supervision and Curriculum Development.

Crandall, V. C., Katkovsky, W., & Crandall, V. J. (1965). Children's beliefs in their own control of reinforcements in intellectual-academic situations. *Child Development, 36*, 91–109.

Creswell, J. W. (1998). *Qualitative inquiry and research design: Choosing among five traditions.* Thousand Oaks, CA: Sage.

CTB/McGraw-Hill. (2004). *Overview of the U.S. Department of Education's position on the use of computer-adaptive testing.* Retrieved November 26, 2005, from the World Wide Web: http://www.ctb.com/media/articles/pdfs/AssessmentRelated/Computer_Based_Testing.pdf

Darling-Hammond, L., Hightower, A. M., Husbands, J. L., LaFors, J. R., & Young, V. M. (2002, April 4). *Building instructional quality: Inside-out, bottom-up, and top-down perspectives on San Diego's school reform.* Paper presented at the Annual Meeting of the American Educational Research Association, New Orleans, LA.

Davis, L. B., Fuchs, L. S., Fuchs, D., & Whinnery, K. (1995). "Will CBM help me learn?" Students' perception of the benefits of curriculum-based measurement. *Education and Treatment of Children, 18*(1), 19–32.

DeBard, R., & Kubow, P. K. (2002). From compliance to commitment: The need for constituent discourse in implementing testing policy. *Educational Policy, 16*(3), 387–405.

DeBarger, A. H., Yumoto, F., & Quellmalz, E. (no date). *An illustration of PADI design system capability with GLOBE assessments* (Principled Assessment Designs for Inquiry Technical Report No. 18): SRI International.

Draper, N. (2000, February 3). Poll finds most teachers dislike Profile of Learning; An Education Minnesota survey also found general approval for the state's basic-skills tests. *Star Tribune*, p. 3B.

Edmonds, R. R. (1979). Effective schools for the urban poor. *Educational Leadership, 37*(10), 15–24.

Elawar, M. C., & Corno, L. (1985). A factorial experiment in teachers' written feedback on student homework: Changing teacher behavior a little rather than a lot. *Journal of Educational Psychology, 77*(2), 162–173.

Elmore, R. F. (2004). Conclusion: The problem of stakes in performance-based accountability systems. In S. H. Fuhrman & R. F. Elmore (Eds.), *Redesigning accountability systems for education* (pp. 274–296). New York: Teachers College Press.

Eyewitness News 4. (2005, May 13). *Board of Education lowers score needed to pass high school exit exam.* Retrieved June 9, 2005, from http://www.kvoa.com/global/story.asp?s=3340187&ClientType=Printable

Eyler, J. M. (2001). The changing assessment of John Snow's and William Farr's cholera studies. *Soz Preventiv Med, 46*(4), 225–232.

Finn, J. D., & Achilles, C. M. (1999). Tennessee's class size study: Findings, implications, misconceptions. *Educational Evaluation and Policy Analysis, 21*(2), 97–109.

Finn, J. D., & Rock, D. A. (1997). Academic success among students at risk for school failure. *Journal of Applied Psychology, 82*(2), 221–234.

Firestone, W. A., Mayrowetz, D., & Fairman, J. (1998). Performance-based assessment and instructional change: The effects of testing in Maine and Maryland. *Educational Evaluation and Policy Analysis, 20*(2), 95–113.

Fischer, H. (2005, May 20). Good grades will soften '06, '07 AIMS requirements. *Arizona Daily Star.* Retrieved April 4, 2006, from http://www.azstarnet.com/ sn/hourlyupdate/76098.php

Folk, V. G., & Green, B. F. (1989). Adaptive estimation when the unidimensionality assumption of IRT is violated. *Applied Psychological Measurement, 13*(4), 373–389.

Frederiksen, N. (1994). *The influence of minimum competency tests on teaching and learning.* Princeton, N.J.: Educational Testing Services, Policy Information Center.

Fuchs, L. S., Deno, S. L., & Mirkin, P. K. (1984). The effects of curriculum-based measurement and evaluation on pedagogy, student achievement, and student awareness of learning. *American Educational Research Journal, 21,* 449–460.

Fuchs, L. S., & Fuchs, D. (1986). Effects of systematic formative evaluation: A meta-analysis. *Exceptional Children, 53*(3), 199–208.

Fuchs, L. S., Fuchs, D., & Hamlett, C. L. (1989). Monitoring reading growth using student recalls: Effects of two teacher feedback systems. *Journal of Educational Research, 83,* 103–111.

Fuchs, L. S., Fuchs, D., & Hamlett, C. L. (1994). Strengthening the connection between assessment and instructional planning with expert systems. *Exceptional Children, 61*(2), 138–146.

Fuchs, L. S., Fuchs, D., Hamlett, C. L., & Allinder, R. M. (1991). The contribution of skills analysis to curriculum-based measurement in spelling. *Exceptional Children, 57,* 443–452.

Fuchs, L. S., Fuchs, D., Hamlett, C. L., & Hasselbring, T. S. (1987). Using computers with curriculum-based monitoring: Effects on teacher efficiency and satisfaction. *Journal of Special Education Technology, 8*(4), 14–27.

Fuchs, L. S., Fuchs, D., Hamlett, C. L., & Stecker, P. M. (1990). The role of skills analysis in curriculum-based measurement in math. *School Psychology Review, 19,* 6–22.

Fuchs, L. S., Fuchs, D., Hamlett, C. L., & Stecker, P. M. (1991). Effects of curriculum-based measurement and consultation on teacher planning and student achievement in mathematics operations. *American Educational Research Journal, 28,* 617–641.

Fuchs, L. S., Hamlett, C. L., Fuchs, D., Stecker, P. M., & Ferguson, C. (1988). Conducting curriculum-based measurement with computerized data collection: Effects on efficiency and teacher satisfaction. *Journal of Special Education Technology, 9*(2), 73–86.

Fuhrman, S. H. (Ed.). (2001). *From the Capitol to the classroom: Standards-based reform in the states. One hundredth yearbook of the National Society for the Study of Education, Part II.* New York: The University of Chicago Press.

Fusarelli, L. D. (2004). The potential impact of the No Child Left Behind Act on equity and diversity in American education. *Educational Policy, 18*(1), 71–94.

Gayler, K., Chudowsky, N., Hamilton, M., Kober, N., & Yeager, M. (2004). *State high school exit exams: A maturing reform.* Washington, DC: Center on Education Policy.

Gayler, K., Chudowsky, N., Kober, N., & Hamilton, M. (2003). *High school exit exams: Put to the test.* Washington, DC: Center on Education Policy.

Glaser, B. G., & Strauss, A. L. (1967). *The discovery of grounded theory: Strategies for qualitative research.* New York: Aldine De Gruyter.

Glass, G. V. (2003). *High-stakes AIMS is a brutal test that hurts the students.* Tempe, AZ: Arizona State University, Education Policy Research Unit.

Goldhaber, D. D. (2002). The mystery of good teaching. *Education Next, 2*(1), 50–55.

Gordon, S. P., & Reese, M. (1997). High-stakes testing: Worth the price? *Journal of School Leadership, 7,* 345–368.

Gorin, J. S., & Blanchard, J. (2004, April 12–16). *The effect of curriculum alignment on elementary mathematics and reading achievement.* Paper presented at the Annual Meeting of the American Educational Research Association, San Diego, CA.

Gotwals, A. W., & Songer, N. B. (2006). *Cognitive predictions: BioKids implementation of the PADI assessment system* (PADI Technical Report No. 10). Menlo Park, CA: SRI International, Center for Technology in Learning.

Grant, S. G. (2000). Teachers and tests: Exploring teachers' perceptions of changes in the New York state testing program. *Education Policy Analysis Archives, 8* (14). Retrieved April 4, 2006, from http://epaa.asu.edu/epaa/v8n14

Grant, S. G. (2001). An uncertain lever: Exploring the influence of state-level testing in New York State on teaching social studies. *Teachers College Record, 103*(3), 398–426.

Greene, J. P., Peterson, P. E., & Du, J. (1999). Effectiveness of school choice: The Milwaukee experiment. *Education and Urban Society, 31*(2), 190–213.

Greene, J. P., & Winters, M. A. (2004a). *Pushed out or pulled up: Exit exams and dropout rates in public high schools.* New York: Center for Civic Innovation, Manhattan Institute.

Greene, J. P., & Winters, M. A. (2004b). Competition passes the test: Vouchers improve public schools in Florida. *Education Next, 4*(3), 66–71.

Greene, J. P., & Winters, M. A. (2006). Getting ahead by staying behind: An evaluation of Florida's program to end social promotion. *Education Next, 6*(2), 65–69.

Greenwald, R., Hedges, L. V., & Laine, R. D. (1996). The effect of school resources on student achievement. *Review of Educational Research, 66*(3), 361–396.

Griffin, B. W., & Heidorn, M. H. (1996). An examination of the relationship between minimum competency test performance and dropping out of high school. *Educational Evaluation and Policy Analysis, 18*(3), 243–252.

Grissmer, D., & Flanagan, A. (1998). *Exploring rapid achievement gains in North Carolina and Texas.* Retrieved June 16, 2005, from http://govinfo.library.unt.edu/negp/reports/grissmer.pdf

Grissmer, D. W., Flanagan, A., Kawata, J., & Williamson, S. (2000). *Improving student achievement: What state NAEP test scores tell us (No. MR-924-EDU).* Santa Monica, CA: RAND Corporation.

Haney, W. (2000). The myth of the Texas miracle in education. *Education Policy Analysis Archives, 8*(41). Retrieved April 4, 2006, from http://epaa.asu.edu/epaa/v8n41/

Haney, W., & Madaus, G. (1989). Searching for alternatives to standardized tests. *Phi Delta Kappan, 70*(9), 683–687.

Hanushek, E. A. (1986). The economics of schooling: Production and efficiency in public schools. *Journal of Economic Literature, 24,* 1141–1171.

Hanushek, E. A. (1989). The impact of differential expenditures on school performance. *Educational Researcher, 18*(4), 45–50.

Hanushek, E. A. (1996). A more complete picture of school resource policies. *Review of Educational Research, 66*(3), 397–409.

Hanushek, E. A. (1997). Assessing the effects of school resources on student performance: An update. *Educational Evaluation and Policy Analysis, 19*(2), 141-164.

Hanushek, E. A. (2001a). Deconstructing RAND. *Education Next, 1*(1), 65.

Hanushek, E. A. (2001b). Spending on schools. In T. Moe (Ed.), *A primer on America's schools* (pp. 79–81). Stanford, CA: Hoover Institution Press.

Hanushek, E. A., & Raymond, M. E. (2005). Does school accountability lead to improved student performance? *Journal of Policy Analysis and Management, 24*(2), 297–327.

Harcourt-Brace Educational Measurement. (1997). Technical Data Report, Stanford Achievement Test Series, Ninth Edition (Stanford 9). San Antonio, TX: Author.

Hardwicke, S. B., & Yoes, M. E. (1984). *Attitudes and performance on computerized vs. paper-and-pencil tests.* San Diego, CA: Rehab Group.

Hedges, L. V., Laine, R. D., & Greenwald, R. (1994). Money does matter somewhere: A reply to Hanushek. *Educational Researcher, 23*(4), 9–10.

Heubert, J., & Hauser, R. (Eds.). (1999). *High stakes: Testing for tracking, promotion, and graduation.* Washington, DC: National Academy Press.

Heyneman, S. P. (1990, March). Education on the world market. *American School Board Journal,* 28–30.

Hightower, A. M. (2002). *San Diego's big boom: District bureaucracy supports culture of learning* (No. Document R-02-2). Seattle, WA: University of Washington, Center for the Study of Teaching and Policy.

Hightower, A. M., & McLaughlin, M. W. (2004). *Building and sustaining an infrastructure for learning in San Diego City Schools* (Draft report). American Federation of Teachers, Stanford University.

Hintze, J. M., & Shapiro, E. S. (1997). Curriculum-based measurement and literature-based reading: Is curriculum-based measurement meeting the needs of changing reading curricula? *Journal of School Psychology, 35*(4), 351–375.

Hoffman, J., Pennington, J., Assaf, L., & Paris, S. (1999). High stakes testing in reading and its effects on teachers, teaching, and students: Today in Texas, tomorrow? Unpublished manuscript.

Hogarth, R. M. (2005). Deciding analytically or trusting your intuition? The advantages and disadvantages of analytic and intuitive thought. In T. Betsch & S. Haberstroh (Eds.), *The routines of decision making* (pp. 67–82). Mahwah, NJ: Erlbaum.

Holmes, G. M., Desimone, J., & Rupp, N. G. (2003). *Does school choice increase school quality?* (NBER Working Paper No. 9683). Cambridge, MA: National Bureau of Economic Research.

Holmes, G. M., Desimone, J., & Rupp, N. G. (2006). Friendly competition: Does the presence of charters spur public schools to improve? *Education Next, 6*(1), 67–70.

Hopfenberg, W. S., Levin, H. M., Chase, C., Christensen, S. G., Moore, M., Soler, P., et al. (1993). *The Accelerated Schools resource guide.* San Francisco: Jossey-Bass.

Howell, W. G., & West, M. R. (2005). Grey lady wheezing: The AFT hoodwinks the *Times. Education Next.*

Howell, W. G., & Wolf, P. J., Campbell, D. E., & Peterson, P. E. (2002). School vouchers and academic performance: Results from three randomized field trials. *Journal of Policy Analysis and Management, 21*(2), 191–217.

Hoxby, C. M. (2002). How school choice affects the achievement of public school students. In P. T. Hill (Ed.), *Choice with equity* (pp. 141–177). Stanford, CA: Hoover Institution Press.

Hoxby, C. M., & Rockoff, J. E. (2005). Findings from the city of big shoulders. *Education Next, 5*(4), 52–58.

Jacob, B. A. (2001). Getting tough? The impact of high school graduation exams. *Educational Evaluation and Policy Analysis, 23*(2), 99–121.

Jacob, B. A., & Lefgren, L. (2004). Remedial education and student achievement: A regression-discontinuity analysis. *Review of Economics and Statistics, 86*(1). Retrieved April 4, 2006, from http://papers.nber.org/papers/w8918

Jacob, R. T., & Stone, S. (2005). Educators and students speak. *Education Next, 5*(1), 49–53.

Jacob, R. T., Stone, S., & Roderick, M. (2004). *Ending social promotion: The response of teachers and students.* Chicago: Chicago Consortium on School Research.

Jennings, J. F. (2000). *Why national standards and tests? Politics and the quest for better schools.* Thousand Oaks, CA: Sage.

Jepson, C., & Rivkin, S. (2002). *Class size reduction, teacher quality, and academic achievement in California public schools.* San Francisco: Public Policy Institute of California.

Johnson, D. R., & Thurlow, M. L. (2003). *A national study on graduation requirements and diploma options for youth with disabilities* (Technical Report No. 36). Minneapolis, MN: University of Minnesota, National Center on Educational Outcomes.

Jones, E. D., & Krouse, J. P. (1988). The effectiveness of data-based instruction by student teachers in classrooms for pupils with mild handicaps. *Teacher Education and Special Education, 11*(1), 9–19.

Kahn, W. J. (1989). Teaching self-management to children. *Elementary School Guidance & Counseling, 24*(1), 37–46.

Kalechstein, A. D., & Nowicki, S., Jr. (1997). A meta-analytic examination of the relationship between control expectancies and academic achievement: An 11-yr follow-up to Findley and Cooper. *Genetic, Social, & General Psychology Monographs, 123*(1), 27–56.

Keith, T. Z., Pottebaum, S. M., & Eberhart, S. (1986). Effects of self-concept and locus of control on academic achievement: A large-sample path analysis. *Journal of Psychoeducational Assessment, 4*(1), 61–72.

Kennedy, C. (2005). *Constructing PADI measurement models for the BEAR scoring engine* (PADI Technical Report No. 7). Menlo Park, CA: SRI International, Center for Technology in Learning.

Kingsbury, G. G., & Hauser, C. (2004, April 13). *Computerized adaptive testing and No Child Left Behind.* Paper presented at the Annual Meeting of the American Educational Research Association, San Diego, CA.

Kluger, A. N., & DeNisi, A. (1996). The effects of feedback interventions on performance: A historical review, a meta-analysis, and a preliminary feedback intervention theory. *Psychological Bulletin, 119*(2), 254–284.

Koretz, D., Barron, S., Mitchell, K., & Stecher, B. (1996). *Perceived effects of the Kentucky Instructional Results Information System (KIRIS).* Institute on Education and Training, RAND. Santa Monica, CA: RAND.

Koretz, D., Stecher, B., Klein, S., & McCaffrey, D. (1994). The Vermont portfolio assessment program: Findings and implications. *Educational Measurement: Issues and Practice, 13*(3), 5–16.

Kornhaber, M. L. (2004). Appropriate and inappropriate forms of testing, assessment, and accountability. *Educational Policy, 18*(1), 45–70.

Kossan, P. (2004, October 25). Students' stress runs deep over AIMS test. *The Arizona Republic.* Retrieved April 4, 2006, from http://www.azcentral.com/families/education/articles/1025AIMSkids25.html#.

Kossan, P. (2005, May 13). State deems failing grades good enough to pass AIMS. *The Arizona Republic.* Retrieved April 4, 2006, from http://www.azcentral.com/families/education/articles/0513scores13.html

Krueger, A., & Zhu, P. (2003). Comment. *Journal of the American Statistical Association, 98,* 314–318.

Kuhs, T., Porter, A., Floden, R., Freeman, D., Schmidt, W., & Schwille, J. (1985). Differences among teachers in their use of curriculum-embedded tests. *The Elementary School Journal, 86*(2), 141–153.

Lajoie, S. P. (Ed.). (2000). *Computers as cognitive tools, volume two: No more walls.* Mahwah, NJ: Erlbaum.

Lazear, E. P. (1999, September 2). Smaller class size isn't a magic bullet. *Los Angeles Times,* p. B9.

Lehr, C., & Thurlow, M. (2003). *Putting it all together: Including students with disabilities in assessment and accountability systems* (NCEO Policy Directions No. 16). Minneapolis, MN: University of Minnesota, National Center on Educational Outcomes.

Lillard, D. R., & DeCicca, P. P. (2001). Higher standards, more dropouts? Evidence within and across time. *Economics of Education Review, 20*(5), 459-473.

Linn, R. L. (1990). Has item response theory increased the validity of achievement test scores? *Applied Measurement in Education, 3*(2), 115–141.

Linn, R. L. (2004). Accountability models. In S. H. Fuhrman & R. F. Elmore (Eds.), *Redesigning accountability systems for education* (pp. 73–95). New York: Teachers College Press.

Linn, R. L., Baker, E. L., & Betebenner, D. W. (2002). Accountability systems: Implications of requirements of the No Child Left Behind Act of 2001. *Educational Researcher, 31*(6), 3–16.

Lonetree, A. (2003). Minnesotans cool to new wave of testing. *Star Tribune*, p. 6B.

Loveless, T. (2002). *The 2002 Brown Center report on American education: How well are American students learning? With sections on arithmetic, high school culture, and charter schools*. Washington, DC: The Brookings Institution.

MacMillan, D. L., Balow, I. H., Widaman, K. F., & Hemsley, R. E. (1990). *A study of minimum competency tests and their impact: Final report* (Grant G008530208). Washington, DC: Office of Special Education and Rehabilitation Services, U.S. Department of Education.

Madelaine, A., & Wheldall, K. (1999). Curriculum-based measurement of reading: A critical review. *International Journal of Disability, Development and Education, 46*(1), 71–85.

Massell, D. (2001). The theory and practice of using data to build capacity: State and local strategies and their effects. In S. H. Fuhrman (Ed.), *From the Capitol to the classroom: Standards-based reform in the states. One hundredth Yearbook of the National Society for the Study of Education* (pp. 148–169). New York: The University of Chicago Press.

Mayer, D. P., Peterson, P. E., Myers, D. E., Tuttle, C. C., & Howell, W. G. (2002, February 19). *School choice in New York City after three years: An evaluation of the School Choice Scholarships program*. Retrieved April 4, 2006, from http://www.mathematica.org/publications/PDFs/nycfull.pdf

McLaughlin, T. F. (1992). Effects of written feedback in reading on behaviorally disordered students. *Journal of Educational Research, 85*(5), 312–316.

McNeil, L. M. (2000). *Contradictions of school reform: Educational costs of standardized testing*. New York: Routledge.

McNeil, L. M., & Valenzuela, A. (2000). *The harmful impact of the TAAS system of testing in Texas: Beneath the accountability rhetoric*. Houston, TX: Department of Education and Center for Education, Rice University.

Mehrens, W. A. (1998). Consequences of assessment: What is the evidence? *Education Policy Analysis Archives, 6*(13). Retrieved October 26, 2005, from http://epaa.asu.edu/epaa/v6n13

Mehrens, W. A., & Clarizio, H. F. (1993). Curriculum-based measurement: Conceptual and psychometric considerations. *Psychology in the Schools, 30*(3), 241–254.

Miles, M. B., & Huberman, A. M. (1994). *Qualitative data analysis: An expanded sourcebook* (2nd ed.). Thousand Oaks, CA: Sage Publications.

Mislevy, R. J., Hamel, L., Fried, R., Gaffney, T., Haertel, G., Hafter, A., et al. (2003). *Design patterns for assessing science inquiry* (PADI Technical Report No. 1). Menlo Park, CA: SRI International, Center for Technology in Learning.

Muller, C. (1998). The minimum competency exam requirement, teachers' and students' expectations and academic performance. *Social Psychology of Education, 2*, 199–216.

Muller, C., & Schiller, K. S. (2000). Leveling the playing field? Students' educational attainment and states' performance testing. *Sociology of Education, 73*, 196–218.

Murnane, R. J., Willett, J. B., & Tyler, J. H. (2000). Who benefits from obtaining a GED? Evidence from High School and Beyond. *Review of Economics and Statistics, 82*(1), 23-37.

Murphy, J. (1990). Principal instructional leadership. In P. Thurston & L. Lotto (Eds.), *Advances in educational leadership* (pp. 163–200). Greenwich, CT: JAI Press.

Musher-Eizenman, D. R., Nesselroade, J. R., & Schmitz, B. (2002). Perceived control and academic performance: A comparison of high- and low-performing children on within-person change patterns. *International Journal of Behavioral Development, 26*(6), 540–547.

Myers, D. E., & Mayer, D. P. (2003). *Comments on "Another look at the New York City voucher experiment."* Washington, DC: Mathematica Policy Research. Retrieved April 4, 2006, from http://www.mathematica-mpr.com/publications/PDFs/anotherlook.pdf.

Myers, D., Pfleiderer, J., & Peterson, P. (2002). *After three years, school choice scholarships program in New York City shows positive impacts on test scores for African Americans, but no impacts on test scores for Latinos.* Retrieved December 29, 2005, from http://www.mathematica-mpr.com/press%20releases/past%20releases/nycchoicerel.asp.

National Center for Education Statistics. (2004). *Digest of education statistics, 2004. Chapter 2: Elementary and Secondary Education, Table 163 (total expenditure per pupil in average daily attendance in public elementary and secondary schools, in constant 2001–02 dollars),* from http://nces.ed.gov/programs/digest/d04/tables/dt04_163.asp.

Nelson, F. H., Rosenberg, B., & Van Meter, N. (2004). *Charter school achievement on the 2003 National Assessment of Educational Progress.* Washington, DC: American Federation of Teachers, AFL-CIO.

Ninness, H. A. C., Ninness, S. K., Sherman, S., & Schotta, C. (1998). Augmenting computer-interactive self-assessment with and without feedback. *Psychological Record, 48*(4), 601–616.

No Child Left Behind Act of 2001, Pub. L. No. 107-110. (2002). Available from http://www.ed.gov/policy/elsec/leg/esea02/107-110.pdf.

Nunnery, J. A., Ross, S. M., & Goldfeder, E. (2003). *The effect of School Renaissance on TAAS scores in the McKinney ISD.* Memphis, TN: Center for Research in Educational Policy, The University of Memphis.

Nye, B., Konstantopoulos, S., & Hedges, L. V. (2004). How large are teacher effects? *Educational Evaluation and Policy Analysis, 26*(3), 237–257.

O'Day, J. A. (2004). Complexity, accountability, and school improvement. In S. H. Fuhrman & R. F. Elmore (Eds.), *Redesigning accountability systems for education* (pp. 15–43). New York: Teachers College Press.

Olson, L. (2002, February 6). Ed. dept. hints Idaho's novel testing plan unacceptable. *Education Week,* pp. 18, 21.

Pedulla, J. J., Abrams, L. M., Madaus, G. F., Russell, M. K., Ramos, M. A., & Miao, J. (2003). *Perceived effects of state-mandated testing programs on teaching and learning: Findings from a national survey of teachers.* Chestnut Hill, MA: National Board on Educational Testing and Public Policy, Lynch School of Education, Boston College.

Perie, M., Moran, R., Lutkus, A. D., & Tirre, W. (2005). *NAEP 2004 trends in academic progress: Three decades of student performance in reading and mathematics.* Retrieved March 24, 2006, from http://nces.ed.gov/nationsreportcard/pdf/main2005/2005464.pdf

Peterson, P. E., & Howell, W. G. (2004). Voucher research controversy. *Education Next, 4*(2), 73–78.

Pomplun, M. (1997). State assessment and instructional change: A path model analysis. *Applied Measurement in Education, 10*(3), 217–234.

Porter, A. C. (2002). Measuring the content of instruction: Uses in research and practice. *Educational Researcher, 31*(7), 3–14.

Porter, A. C., Chester, M. D., & Schlesinger, M. D. (2004). Framework for an effective assessment and accountability program: The Philadelphia example. *Teachers College Record, 106*(6), 1358–1400.

Porter, A. C., Floden, R. E., Freeman, D. J., Schmidt, W. H., & Schwille, J. P. (1986). *Content determinants* (Research Series No. 179). East Lansing, MI: Michigan State University, Institute for Research on Teaching.

Porter, A. C., & Smithson, J. L. (2001). Are content standards being implemented in the classroom? A methodology and some tentative answers. In S. H. Fuhrman (Ed.), *From the Capitol to the classroom: Standards-based reform in the states. One hundreth yearbook of the National Society for the Study of Education* (pp. 60–80). Chicago, IL: The University of Chicago Press.

Powell, A. G. (1996). Motivating students to learn: An American dilemma. In S. Fuhrman & J. O'Day, (Eds.), *Rewards and reform: Creating educational incentives that work* (pp. 19–59). San Francisco: Jossey-Bass.

Qiu, L. (2005). *A web-based architecture and incremental authoring model for interactive learning environments for diagnostic reasoning.* Evanston, IL: Northwestern University.

Qiu, L., Riesbeck, C. K., & Parsek, M. (2003). *The design and implementation of an engine and authoring tool for web-based learn-by-doing environments.* Paper presented at the ED-MEDIA 2003—World Conference on Educational Multimedia, Hypermedia & Telecommunications, Honolulu, HI.

Reardon, S. (1996). *Eighth grade minimum competency testing and early high school dropout patterns.* Paper presented at the Annual Meeting of the American Educational Research Association, New York.

Reardon, S. F., & Galindo, C. (2002, April). *Do high-stakes tests affect students' decisions to drop out of school? Evidence from NELS.* Paper presented at the annual meeting of the American Educational Research Association, New Orleans, LA.

Renaissance Learning. (2002). *Results from a three-year state-wide implementation of Reading Renaissance in Idaho.* Madison, WI: Author.

Renaissance Learning. (no date-a). *STAR Math: Understanding reliability and validity.* Wisconsin Rapids, WI: Author.

Renaissance Learning. (no date-b). *STAR Reading: Understanding reliability and validity.* Wisconsin Rapids, WI: Author.

Richardson, V. (2001). *Handbook of research on teaching* (4th ed.). Washington, DC: American Educational Research Association.

Robinson, S. L., DePascale, C., & Roberts, F. C. (1989). Computer-delivered feedback in group-based instruction: Effects for learning disabled students in mathematics. *Learning Disabilities Focus, 5*(1), 28–35.

Roderick, M., & Engel, M. (2001). The grasshopper and the ant: Motivational responses of low-achieving students to high-stakes testing. *Educational Evaluation and Policy Analysis, 23*(3), 197–227.

Roderick, M., Jacob, B. A., & Bryk, A. S. (2002). The impact of high-stakes testing in Chicago on student achievement in promotional gate grades. *Educational Evaluation and Policy Analysis, 24*(4), 333–357.

Roderick, M., & Nagaoka, J. (2005). Retention under Chicago's high-stakes testing program: Helpful, harmful, or harmless? *Educational Evaluation and Policy Analysis, 27*(4), 309–340.

Rosenshine, B. (2003). High-stakes testing: Another analysis. *Education Policy Analysis Archives, 11*(24). Retrieved April 13, 2006, from http://epaa.asu.edu/epaa/v11n24/

Ross, C. E., & Broh, B. A. (2000). The role of self-esteem and the sense of personal control in the academic achievement process. *Sociology of Education, 73*(4), 270–284.

Rothman, R. (1995). *Measuring up: Standards, assessment, and school reform.* San Francisco: Jossey-Bass.

Rothman, R. (2004). Benchmarking and alignment of state standards and assessments. In S. H. Fuhrman & R. F. Elmore (Eds.), *Redesigning accountability systems for education* (pp. 96–114). New York: Teachers College Press.

Rothman, R., Slattery, J. B., Vranek, J. L., & Resnick, L. B. (2002). *Benchmarking and alignment of standards and testing* (CSE Technical Report). Los Angeles, CA: National Center for Research on Evaluation, Standards, and Student Testing, University of California, Los Angeles.

Rouse, C. E. (1998). Private school vouchers and student achievement: An evaluation of the Milwaukee Parental Choice Program. *The Quarterly Journal of Economics, 113*(2), 553–602.

Saulny, S. (2006, February 12). Tutor program offered by law is going unused: Free for failing schools. *The New York Times,* pp. A1, A27.

Scheurich, J. J., Skrla, L., & Johnson, J. F. (2000). Thinking carefully about equity and accountability. *Phi Delta Kappan, 82*(4), 293–299.

Schinoff, R. B., & Steed, L. (1988). The CAT program at Miami-Dade Community College. In D. Doucette (Ed.), *Computerized adaptive testing: The state of the art in assessment at three community colleges* (pp. 25–36). Laguna Hills, CA: League for Innovation in the Community College.

Scutari, C. (2005, January 3). Senator leads fight to dismantle AIMS. *The Arizona Republic.* Retrieved April 13, 2006, from http://www.azcentral.com/families/education/articles/0103highstakes03.html.

Shepard, L. A., & Smith, M. L. (1989). *Flunking grades: Research and policies on retention.* London: Falmer Press.

Shim, M. K., Felner, R. D., Shim, E., & Noonan, N. (2001, April 10–14). *Multidimensional assessment of classroom instructional practice: A validity study of the Classroom Instructional Practice Scale (CIPS).* Paper presented at the Annual Meeting of the American Educational Research Association, Seattle, WA.

Simon, S. (2001, May 30). Schools a $2 billion study in failure. *Chicago Tribune,* p. 8.

Skinner, E. A., Wellborn, J. G., & Connell, J. P. (1990). What it takes to do well in school and whether I've got it: A process model of perceived control and children's engagement and achievement in school. *Journal of Educational Psychology, 82*(1), 22–32.

Skrla, L., Scheurich, J. J., & Johnson, J. F. (2000). *Equity-driven, achievement-focused school districts: A report on systemic school success in four Texas school districts serving diverse student populations.* Austin, TX: Charles A. Dana Center.

Skrla, L., Scheurich, J., Johnson, J., & Koschoreck, J. (2001). Accountability for equity: Can state policy leverage social justice? *International Journal of Leadership in Education, 4*(3), 237–260.

Smith, D. E. P., Brethower, D., & Cabot, R. (1969). Increasing task behavior in a language arts program by providing reinforcement. *Journal of Experimental Child Psychology, 8*(1), 45–62.

Smith, E. G., & Clark, C. (2001). *School Renaissance comprehensive model evaluation.* Austin: Texas Center for Educational Research.

Smith, M., & O'Day, J. A. (1991). Systemic school reform. In S. Fuhrman & B. Malen (Eds.), *The politics of curriculum and testing* (pp. 233–267). Philadelphia: Falmer.

Smith, M. L. (1991). Put to the test: The effects of external testing on teachers. *Educational Researcher, 20*(5), 8–11.

Smith, M. L., Heinecke, W., & Noble, A. J. (1999). Assessment policy and political spectacle. *Teachers College Record, 101*(2), 157–191.

Smith, M. L., Noble, A., Heinecke, W., Seck, M., Parish, C., Cabay, M., et al. (1997). *Reforming schools by reforming assessment: Consequences of the Arizona student assessment program (ASAP): Equity and teacher capacity building [CSE Technical Report 425].* Los Angeles: University of California, Los Angeles, National Center for Research on Evaluation, Standards, and Student Testing.

Smith, M. L., & Rottenberg, C. (1991). Unintended consequences of external testing in elementary schools. *Educational Measurement: Issues and Practice, 10*(4), 7–11.

Spicuzza, R., & Ysseldyke, J. (1999). *Using Accelerated Math to enhance instruction in a mandated summer school program.* Minneapolis, MN: University of Minnesota, National Center on Educational Outcomes,.

Spicuzza, R., Ysseldyke, J., Lemkuil, A., Kosciolek, S., Boys, C., & Teelucksingh, E. (2001). Effects of curriculum-based monitoring on classroom instruction and math achievement. *Journal of School Psychology, 39*(6), 521–542.

Stecher, B., & Bohrnstedt, G. W. (2000). *Class size reduction in California: The 1998-99 evaluation findings, executive summary.* Sacramento, CA: California Department of Education.

Steinberg, L. (2001). Comment by Laurence Steinberg. In D. Ravitch (Ed.), *Brookings papers on education policy: 2001* (pp. 334–339). Washington, DC: Brookings Institution Press.

Steinberg, L., Brown, B., & Sanford, M. D. (1996). *Beyond the classroom: Why school reform has failed and what parents need to do.* New York: Simon & Schuster.

Stevenson, H. W., & Stigler, J. W. (1992). *The learning gap: Why our schools are failing and what we can learn from Japanese and Chinese education.* New York: Simon & Schuster.

Strauss, A. L. (1987). *Qualitative analysis for social scientists.* New York: Cambridge University Press.

Sullivan, P., Yeager, M., Chudowsky, N., Kober, N., O'Brien, E., & Gayler, K. (2005). *States try harder, but gaps persist: High school exit exams 2005*. Washington, DC: Center on Education Policy.

Teddlie, C., & Stringfield, S. (1993). *Schools do make a difference: Lessons learned from a 10-year study of school effects*. New York: Teachers College Press.

Teelucksingh, E., Ysseldyke, J., Spicuzza, R., & Ginsburg-Block, M. (2001). *Enhancing the learning of English language learners: Consultation and a curriculum based monitoring system*. Minneapolis, MN: University of Minnesota, National Center on Educational Outcomes.

Thernstrom, A., & Thernstrom, S. (2004). *No excuses: Closing the racial gap in learning*. New York: Simon & Schuster.

Title I—Improving the Academic Achievement of the Disadvantaged, Final Rule, 34 C.F.R. § 200. (2002). Available from http://www.ed.gov/legislation/FedRegister/finrule/2002–3/070502a.pdf

Tomlinson, T., & Cross, C. (1991). Student effort: The key to higher standards. *Education Leadership, 49*(1), 69–73.

Toulmin, S. E. (1958). *The uses of argument*. London: Cambridge University Press.

Toulmin, S. E. (1988). *The uses of argument* (9th ed.). Cambridge, England: Cambridge University Press.

Traub, R. E., & Wolfe, R. G. (1981). Latent trait theories and the assessment of educational achievement. In D. C. Berliner (Ed.), *Review of research in education* (Vol. 9, pp. 377–435). Washington, DC: American Educational Research Association.

Trotter, A. (2003). A question of direction. *Education Week, 22*, 17–18, 20–21.

University of the State of New York. (2005). *What Regents exams are required for graduation? (General education students)*. Retrieved June 17, 2005, from http://www.emsc.nysed.gov/parents/gradreqtsfs.shtml

U.S. Department of Education. (2000a). *National Assessment of Educational Progress Mathematics Assessment*. Washington, DC: National Center for Education Statistics, Institute of Education Sciences.

U.S. Department of Education. (2000b). *National Assessment of Educational Progress Science Assessment*. Washington, DC: National Center for Education Statistics, Institute of Education Sciences.

U.S. Department of Education. (2001). *National Assessment of Educational Progress History Assessment*. Washington, DC: National Center for Education Statistics, Institute of Education Sciences.

U.S. Department of Education. (2002a). *National Assessment of Educational Progress Reading Assessment*. Washington, DC: National Center for Education Statistics, Institute of Education Sciences.

U.S. Department of Education. (2002b). *National Assessment of Educational Progress Writing Assessment*. Washington, DC: National Center for Education Statistics, Institute of Education Sciences.

Vygotsky, L. S. (1978). *Mind in society: The development of higher psychological processes*. Cambridge, MA: Harvard University Press.

Wainer, H. (1993). Some practical considerations when converting a linearly administered test to an adaptive format. *Educational Measurement: Issues and Practice, 12*(1), 15–20.

Warren, J. R., & Edwards, M. R. (2005). High school exit examinations and high school completion: Evidence from the early 1990s. *Educational Evaluation and Policy Analysis, 27*(1), 53–74.

Webb, N. (1999). *Alignment of science and mathematics standards and assessments in four states* (Research Monograph No. 18). Madison, WI: National Institute for Science Education.

Weiss, D. J. (2004). Computerized adaptive testing for effective and efficient measurement in counseling and education. *Measurement and Evaluation in Counseling and Development, 37*(2), 70–84.

Wenglinsky, H. (2000). *How teaching matters: Bringing the classroom back into discussions of teacher quality* (Policy Information Center Report). Princeton, NJ: Educational Testing Service.

Wesson, C. L. (1991). Curriculum-based measurement and two models of follow-up consultation. *Exceptional Children, 57,* 246–257.

Wesson, C. L., King, R. P., & Deno, S. L. (1984). Direct and frequent measurement of student performance: If it's good for us, why don't we do it? *Learning Disabilities Quarterly, 7,* 45–48.

Wilson, S. M., & Floden, R. E. (2003). *Creating effective teachers: Concise answers for hard questions. An addendum to the report* Teacher preparation research: Current knowledge, gaps and recommendations. Denver, CO: Education Commission of the States; American Association of Colleges for Teacher Education.

Wolf, S. A., Borko, H., Elliott, R. L., & McIver, M. C. (2000). "That dog won't hunt!": Exemplary school change efforts within the Kentucky reform. *American Educational Research Journal, 37*(2), 349–393.

Yeh, S. S. (2001). Tests worth teaching to: Constructing state-mandated tests that emphasize critical thinking. *Educational Researcher, 30*(9), 12–17.

Yell, M. L., Deno, S. L., & Marsten, D. B. (1992). Barriers to implementing curriculum-based measurement. *Diagnostique, 18,* 99–112.

Ysseldyke, J., Spicuzza, R., & McGill, S. (2000). *Changes in mathematics achievement and instructional ecology resulting from implementation of a learning information system.* Minneapolis, MN: University of Minnesota, National Center on Educational Outcomes.

Ysseldyke, J., & Tardrew, S. P. (2002). *Differentiating math instruction: A large-scale study of Accelerated Math: First report.* Madison, WS: Renaissance Learning.

Index

About the Author

Stuart S. Yeh is Assistant Professor of Evaluation Studies in the Department of Educational Policy and Administration at the University of Minnesota. His current research focuses on the relation of assessment and accountability policies to student engagement and achievement. Previously, Dr. Yeh was Senior Research Associate at the Center for the Study of Testing, Evaluation, and Educational Policy at Boston College, where he worked on a national study of educational testing. He has also coordinated education and work experience programs in San Francisco. He has evaluated critical thinking and analytical writing programs for underprivileged students in East Palo Alto and San Jose, California, as well as Head Start preliteracy programs in the Dorchester, Jamaica Plain, and Allston-Brighton communities in Boston. His scholarly publications cover testing policy, critical thinking and analytical writing, literacy, early childhood development, evaluation theory, and student engagement and achievement. In 1998, Dr. Yeh was awarded a postdoctoral fellowship at Harvard University. He received his B.A. in Economics in 1982 and Master of Public Policy degree in 1984, both from the University of Michigan, and his Ph.D. in Educational Evaluation in 1998 from Stanford University.